No Half-Way House

HARRI WEBB:

Selected Political Journalism

compiled and edited by

MEIC STEPHENS

First impression: May 1997

© Meic Stephens and Y Lolfa Cyf., 1997

This book is subject to copyright and may not be
reproduced by any means or for any purpose
except for review without the prior, written consent
of the publishers.

Cover design: Robat Gruffudd

ISBN: 0 86243 407 6

Published in Wales by Y Lolfa Cyf.,
and printed on acid-free and partly recycled paper
by Y Lolfa Cyf., Talybont, Ceredigion SY24 5HE
e-mail ylolfa@netwales.co.uk
internet http://www.ylolfa.wales.com/
tel (01970) 832 304
fax 832 782

Harri Webb
No Half-Way House

'I'll ha'e nae hauf-way hoose, but aye be whaur
Extremes meet – it's the only way I ken
To dodge the curst conceit o' bein' richt
That damns the vast majority o' men.'

Hugh MacDiarmid, *A Drunk Man Looks at the Thistle*

CONTENTS

Harri Webb in naval uniform

Introduction

Harri Webb had a reputation as a political journalist long before he became known as a poet. Waiting to be demobilized from the Navy in 1946, after five years' active service in the Mediterranean, he discovered the work of Hugh MacDiarmid while on shore-leave in Scotland, and this experience proved decisive in shaping his political views. MacDiarmid, a Communist and Scottish Nationalist (who was often in bad odour with both camps), had also as a young man been a journalist, contributing to Keir Hardie's newspaper, *The Merthyr Pioneer*, while living in Ebbw Vale. Hitherto, during his time at Oxford and in the Navy, Harri had been not much interested in politics. It was MacDiarmid who made Harri politically aware and conscious of the claims of Wales upon him. The Scot's verse and prose, particularly his autobiography, *Lucky Poet* (1943), in which his combative and often anti-English views were brilliantly set forth, planted in the Welshman's mind the idea of an independent Wales, a Welsh Republic no less, an ideal to which he was to devote the rest of his life as writer and political activist.

Two years later, in 1948, Harri joined Plaid Cymru.

It was not long, however, before he was chafing at the bit. Dissatisfied with what he saw as the Party's 'milk-and- water' stance and craving more of 'the hard stuff' he had learned from MacDiarmid, in the year following he decided to throw in his lot with the Welsh Republican Movement, which had just been founded, largely as a consequence of Plaid Cymru's refusal to take a more Republican line. The Welsh Republicans were a small group of militants, mostly ex-servicemen and intellectuals, who enlivened the political scene in Wales during the 1950s in a coalition of left-wingers whose natural homes should otherwise have been in the ranks of the Labour Party or Plaid Cymru. Prominent among them were Ithel Davies, Gwyndaf Evans, Huw Davies, Gwilym Prys Davies, Cliff Bere, John Legonna, Pedr (Peter) Lewis, and Ivor Wilks. The Movement – it was not a party though it put up a candidate at Ogmore in the General Election of 1950 – was hostile towards the Labour Party because of its broken promises on self-government for Wales, critical of Plaid Cymru on account of its pacifism and recognition of the English Crown, and utterly opposed to the Tories on just about every other count.

Besides heckling speakers from the main parties, at which they were adept, the Republicans went in for painting slogans and burning the Union Jack in public places, and holding open-air meetings up and down the industrial valleys of South Wales. Another of their initiatives was a bookshop which they opened at Bargoed in 1951, though this venture failed within the year. What they excelled at was invective and sometimes scurrilous attacks on prominent politicians of the day. One of their many *bwci-bos* was James Griffiths, the Labour MP for Llanelli, who in 1964 was to become the first Secretary of State for Wales. They reviled him for what they thought were his sanctimonious manner and ambivalence to the claims of Wales within the context of 'the country as a whole'. Another of their targets was Thomas Jones, the civil servant and anti-Nationalist propagandist who in their eyes was the very epitome of *'Y Cymro Da'* ('The Good Welshman'); they also had a bone to pick with Aneurin Bevan, whom they considered to be a lost leader of his class and people. Nor were the Republicans loth to make fun at Plaid Cymru's expense for its lack of a credible economic programme for industrial Wales: to Harri Webb is attributed the remark that the Party's policy consisted of 'three acres and a Welsh-speaking cow'. The Movement was also involved in several campaigns, helping to secure the release of André Geoffroy, a Breton patriot gaoled on charges of collaboration with the Germans, and in 1953 some of its members, notably Pedr (Peter) Lewis and Gwyndaf Evans, were implicated in the explosion at the Fron Viaduct, in Radnorshire, which carried water out of Wales to Birmingham. A consistent strand in Republican thinking seems to have been that English law could be broken with impunity in the cause of Wales, and they often found the police at their doors.

This selection of Harri Webb's political journalism opens with a personal account of the Welsh

13

Republican Movement's first two years. Although not strictly journalistic, since it was originally a private document not meant for publication, this frank memoir is included here not only for the light it throws on Harri's own commitment to Republicanism but also because, in its comments on some of the other personalities involved, it supplements the valuable accounts given by Ithel Davies in *Bwrlwm Byw* (1984), Gwilym Prys Davies in *Llafur y Blynyddoedd* (1991) and Cliff Bere in *The Young Republicans* (1996).

The Movement's main activity, particularly after 1954, was the publication and distribution of a bi-monthly newspaper, *The Welsh Republican*; although it was also known as *Y Gweriniaethwr*, most of the paper's contents were in English. It had a small circulation of a few hundred copies but was remarkable for its coverage of Welsh affairs, especially matters relating to the economy of South Wales such as the future of the coal and steel industries and the plight of the Cardiff docks. It also provided a running commentary on the Labour Party's attitude towards the question of self-government for Wales, and this at a time when no such critique existed; see, for example, the long article by Harri Webb entitled 'Labour's Next Step' which appeared in 1955-56. The paper was sceptical towards the Parliament for Wales Campaign (1951-55), which had the support of Labour MPs such as Goronwy Roberts and S.O.Davies, and of Megan Lloyd George, at the time Liberal MP for Anglesey, because its aim fell short of the Republic on which the Movement had set its sights; in 1952 it deplored the appointment of David Maxwell-Fyfe ('Dai Bananas') as part-time Minister of State for Welsh Affairs. It also spoke out against military conscription in Wales (though it argued in favour of a Welsh army), and prior to the Coronation in 1953 it expressed staunchly anti-royalist views.

The newspaper's style was, on the whole, abrasive and iconoclastic and sometimes bitter in its denunciation of prominent people in Welsh public life, notably in the column 'Guilty Men', to which Harri Webb contributed. It also ran a series about figures from the Welsh past, such as Owain Glyn Dŵr and Dic Penderyn, which was more polemic than straight history. But unfortunately, it has proved impossible to identify which of these short pieces were in fact written by Harri, and so they are not represented here. On the other hand, it is known for certain that as Caradog (one of Harri's many *noms de guerre)* he contributed a regular column to the paper entitled 'A Letter to Mr.Jones' in which he used his considerable gifts as a writer in the demotic style to set out some of the basic arguments in the case for a Welsh Republic. The full-blooded, two-fisted, campaigning style of *The Welsh Republican* – the like of which had not been seen in Wales since the Radical news-sheets of the 19th century – was set by its first two editors, namely Huw Davies and Ivor Wilks, but it was under Harri Webb's editorship that the paper was to be at its liveliest.

Harri made his debut as a contributor in 1950. In the year following he left Wales temporarily to find work as a bookseller and librarian, first at Malvern and then in Cheltenham, but continued to write for the Republican paper. Although still a member of the Movement – he spoke at a rally in Trafalgar Square in 1952 – it was in Cheltenham, a Conservative stronghold, that he joined the Labour Party. Also at this time he devised the White Eagle of Eryri, a symbol later adopted by the Free Wales Army as part of its insignia. He took up his unpaid post as editor of *The Welsh Republican* in April 1953, about a year before his return to Wales as Branch Librarian at Dowlais in Merthyr Tydfil. For the next five years he remained an active member of the Labour Party, flinging himself into work for the local branch and enjoying a growing reputation as a speaker at the Party's conferences. He took a leading part in founding the Merthyr Eisteddfod, learned the distinctive Dowlais form of Welsh (which he spoke with some panache), and became a friend of S.O.Davies, the town's MP. So prominent a member of the Labour Party did Harri become that there is some evidence in his diaries to suggest that he began to entertain hopes of inheriting the latter's mantle. But it was not to be. Impatient with the Labour Party's failure to introduce any measure of self-government for Wales, and dis-illusioned by the brutishly anti-Welsh attitudes of some of its members in Merthyr, he left the Party. He remained for the rest of his life implacably hostile to the Labour Party, reserving some of his most vitriolic wit for its policies and leaders.

Some measure of the animus of Harri's views will be found in this selection of his political journalism. It includes not only some of the substantial editorials which he wrote for *The Welsh Republican* but also a number of articles on a variety of subjects which he contributed to its pages between 1950 and 1957, when both paper and Movement were wound up. Although some of these pieces were unsigned, it is usually easy to recognize the stamp of Harri's journalistic style and political preoccupations in almost every paragraph. In a few cases where it has proved difficult, forty years on, I have relied on the advice of Cliff Bere and Ivor Wilks in detecting Harri's hand in the writing; if the work of some other contributor has been inadvertently attributed to Harri, the responsibility must rest with me.

With the demise of the Welsh Republican Movement in 1957, some of its members went back into the Labour Party. Gwilym Prys Davies, for instance, stood as Labour candidate in the Carmarthen By-Election of July 1966 at which Gwynfor Evans won the seat for Plaid Cymru; he was given a life peerage in 1982 and was later appointed Opposition Spokesman on Northern Ireland. The mutual respect between him and Harri Webb was unaffected by their party political allegiances, even after Gwilym's going to the House of Lords, though the divergence in their views continued to animate their friendship, as the letter published here (with the recipient's kind permission) clearly shows; the more public aspect of their dialectic is to be found in Harri's article entitled 'Compromise or Appeasement?' which was published in the *Welsh Nation* in January 1968. Other Republicans, such as Cliff Bere, joined Plaid Cymru, while some, such as Huw Davies, seem to have withdrawn from active politics, and one or two, including Ivor Wilks, left Wales altogether to pursue distinguished careers overseas.

As for Harri Webb, after a year or so in the political wilderness (during which he too contemplated leaving Wales for good), he rejoined Plaid Cymru at its Summer School in 1960. His speech at the Party's annual conference of 1961 was published in its newspaper, the *Welsh Nation*, under the headline 'We Stand for the Integrity of Wales' in November 1961. What drew him back to his old Party was the failure on the part of Welsh MPs, though supported by the unanimity of public opinion in Wales, to prevent the passing of the Bill which allowed Liverpool Corporation to build a reservoir in the Tryweryn Valley in Merioneth and, after the drowning of the village of Capel Celyn, to take the water for its own needs. Harri was one of the many thousands who flocked to Plaid Cymru after this brazen demonstration of the English majority's power at Westminster over the fate of Welsh communities. He felt the shame and outrage of Tryweryn as keenly as most. One of his last editorials in *The Welsh Republican* (December 1956-January 1957) had dealt with Liverpool Corporation's scheme, in which he had called on the country's MPs to form a united front against it and tried to introduce some practical considerations into the controversy over the use of Welsh water resources. He was to return to the subject as newly appointed editor of the *Welsh Nation* in 1962, with an editorial entitled 'The Breed of the Sparrowhawk', published after the first acts of sabotage had been carried out on the site of the reservoir, and again in 1963 after Emyr Llewelyn Jones had been imprisoned for his part in causing damage at the site, and yet again in 1965 after the official opening of the dam at which Nationalist anger had boiled over and the ceremony was interrupted. The ex-combatant Harri could not find it in himself to disapprove of what was euphemistically known in Nationalist circles as 'direct action' and, as a consequence, he once again found himself at odds with his Party's leaders and policies. It would be unkind to suggest that he derived a vicarious thrill from the sabotage at Tryweryn but he lent it as much support from his editorial chair as he thought the Party would tolerate. His disappointment at Plaid Cymru's refusal to condone more militant methods found expression in 1964 through his association with the New Nation/Cilmeri Group, a band of disaffected Nationalists (led by Emrys Roberts and the old Republican, John Legonna) whose aim was to reform the organization of the Party, reinvigorate its policies and tactics, and remove some of its leaders, the President Gwynfor Evans among them, from office. He also supported the campaigns of *Cymdeithas yr Iaith Gymraeg* [The Welsh Language Society], which he had joined shortly after its inception in 1962. The society's challenge to the law in a bid to win a measure of official status for the language was welcomed by Harri as the sort of tactics he expected from a movement of national liberation. From 1960 to 1972 he lived in the house known as Garth Newydd in Merthyr Tydfil and it became a centre for Nationalist activity of all kinds. It was not only Plaid Cymru's headquarters in the constituency: Radio Free Wales, the pirate radio launched in an attempt to thwart the BBC's ban on the Party, often broadcast from its attic, with some of its transmissions introduced by Harri. In 1964 he was appointed to the post of Librarian at Mountain Ash in the Cynon Valley and from 1972 until shortly before his death he lived in the village of Cwm-bach, where he again found a role to play in the affairs of Plaid Cymru.

During the three and a half years of his editorship of the *Welsh Nation* (from June 1962 to December 1965) Harri wrote a monthly editorial and contributed many articles to the paper. Quite a few of these pieces dealt with local issues such as Welsh-medium education in Merthyr Tydfil, the by-election in Montgomeryshire in 1962, and the victory of Gwynfor S.Evans of Betws, near Ammanford, Plaid Cymru's candidate at a county election, in securing the right to use Welsh on his nomination forms. Although Harri always thought in national (and international) terms, trying 'to see Wales whole' (as in, for example, his editorial about broadcasting in Wales), he was always prepared to act locally, and as a journalist he drew great satisfaction from the fact that his paper was often bought and read for its coverage of local affairs. He may not have been a practical politician in the usual sense (though he served on Plaid Cymru's Executive Council and stood as the Party's candidate in Pontypool at the General Election of 1970), but he was genuinely interested in doorstep issues and had a firm grasp of grassroots politics, especially when canvassing in the industrial Valleys. If, however, there is sometimes a lofty, even portentous note to what he wrote, it must be remembered that Harri was also a poet who saw his role in the national movement as essentially inspirational and that, for him, there was only a thin line between politics and poetry. Those who remember the rhetoric of his speeches, or who are familiar with his *Collected Poems* (1995), will understand what is meant.

Having given up the editorship of the *Welsh Nation* at the end of 1965, Harri still continued to write for it, often with some of his usual wit and erudition. That his anti-royalist fervour showed no sign of waning is borne out by the memorandum on the Investiture of Charles Windsor as Prince of Wales in July 1969, which is published here for the first time. But some of the sparkle had gone out of Harri's political journalism. By now his health was beginning to give cause for concern. A man of prodigious appetite for both food and drink, he made innumerable attempts to lose weight, mostly without any visible effect, and even gave up alcohol, one of the sternest sacrifices of which he was capable. He was, too, it must be remembered, now putting more of his energies into his career as a poet and performer, and turning more to his literary journalism, a selection of which will be found in his book *A Militant Muse* (1997). Despite his retirement from the library service in 1974, his contributions to the *Welsh Nation* began to grow more intermittent and lightweight, although his columns 'One Man's Wales' and 'Land of Pong', the latter about the fictitious, Labour-dominated Valleys town of Cwmgrafft, continued to make many readers chuckle. Some will recall the Great Laverbread Rebellion, the effusions of the municipal bard Catullus Clinker, the heroic exploits of Mr.Glyndwr Goodman's Free Cymrutarian Party and the goings-on in the Regency Lounge of The Navvy's Boot where CASH (Corruptly Appointed Socialist Headmasters) and AWFUL (Anti-Welsh Federation of Unionist Loyalists) used to meet.

In 1975 Harri fell out with certain members of Plaid Cymru over several thousand pounds he had invested in Triban, a trading company which he had helped to start, and the acrimony of it troubled him greatly. During the 1970s only the prospect of a Welsh Assembly, which was being mooted by the Labour Party in response to the electoral progress of Plaid Cymru, seemed to elicit any enthusiasm in him, and that was lukewarm, for Harri had nothing but scorn for the feeble measure of administrative autonomy that was on offer. His view is summed up here in the two articles 'Cheers for the Coal Exchange' and 'Labour and Devolution'. Nevertheless, his disappointment at the outcome of the referendum on the Government's proposals held on 1 March 1979, when a clear majority of the Welsh electorate rejected the idea of an elected Assembly, was keenly felt. This was a dark hour for Harri, as his diaries show: he raged against what he saw as the treachery of the Labour Party in Wales which had failed to implement its own policy. He soon rallied, however, regaining his old conviction – perhaps flying in the face of all evidence to the contrary – that Wales was moving inexorably towards the Independence that had always been his goal. But there was no more journalism, political or literary. Harri's last contribution to the press was a letter to the editor of *Y Faner* (28 October 1983) in which he warned against 'pseudo-Socialists' like Neil Kinnock, one of those who had caused the fiasco over Welsh Devolution in 1979. In 1985 he suffered his first stroke. Although he was to live for another ten years, his health continued to deteriorate and he was confined to his flat in Cwm-bach. His last years were sad and lonely: he saw few of his old comrades and showed little interest in political affairs, not even reading the newspapers. He died in a nursing home in his home town of Swansea on 31 December 1994 at the age of seventy-four.

The selection of Harri Webb's political journalism reprinted here (about a third of his total output) has been chosen not only for its intrinsic interest, reflecting as it does the course of Welsh politics over nearly three decades, but also on account of its relevance to Wales today. After all, some of the major issues that Harri raised and expounded with such passion and eloquence have not yet been resolved. It remains to be seen whether the Labour Government elected yesterday – despite its huge majority at Westminster and the fact that the Conservatives no longer have any seats in Wales – will be able to deliver the feeble measure of devolution that it has promised to put to a referendum later this year, or whether it will wriggle out of its commitment as it did in 1979. Perhaps it will decide, from a position of strength, to bring in a Welsh Parliament with sufficient powers to ensure the economic revival of Wales and the democratization of its political life that are so urgently required. I am pretty sure what Harri's view would have been on these scores. He believed that the sorry plight of his country would not last indefinitely and that the time would eventually come when the Welsh people would have to make more strenuous efforts to ensure their survival as a national community with control over its own affairs. In this he thought his writing, both prose and verse, would have some part to play. 'I've had my say,' he used to tell me whenever we met during his last years, 'my stuff will be there when it's wanted'; to which I always replied, *'Brysied y dydd'*.

Meic Stephens
Whitchurch, Cardiff
2 May 1997

Up the Republic!

The Early Days of the Welsh Republican Movement

AT A POINT where my personal history merges at last with the history of my country, some memorial must be raised. My entry into Welsh politics, as a Republican, demands a backward look in two directions, one, my own private path, and the other, the tortuous and rough road that has been trodden out by the idea of Independence.

When I went to work with Keidrych Rhys in Carmarthen in 1948 there was a pamphlet lying about the office entitled *The Welsh Republic* by Cliff Bere. But there was so much lying about that office, the accumulated visions of every visionary who had ever envisaged a new Wales – a Wales run by Christianity, electricity, or British Israel – Waleses of all shapes and colours, all sent to Keidrych, all accumulated from the years of the locust to the years of the broken promises. Among this great choir, which was visible at first glance only as a drift of untidy papers, the sensible and unsensational voice of the Welsh Republic seemed too calm, too academic, to attract much notice. The author, I felt, was probably right in his analysis, but it didn't look as if anything would ever be done on those lines, unless it became the official policy of Plaid Cymru, which didn't seem likely.

I was a member of the Blaid at the time, and had been

since early in 1948. But it had been more of a gesture on my part than anything else. Oddly enough, I can't remember the exact circumstances which led me to the decision. I can only write briefly about my growing consciousness of nationality. I have already documented its betrayal by the English educational system which led to an adolescent rejection of my Welsh heritage, and the sudden revulsion precipitated by actual experience of the English in all their sniggering horror. At Oxford, after declaring myself a Nationalist, I did nothing about it. If there was a branch of Plaid Cymru there I didn't bother to go looking for it; I sought no Welsh connections, pursued no Celtic Studies. I did buy a Welsh Bible and a Mabinogion, and would declaim passages from the former, mostly ones with which I was already familiar in English, and I do seem to have remembered a good deal more Welsh from my two years at the feet of E. Glyn Lewis than either of us deserved. But it was all window-dressing. My friendship with the other Welshman of the College, Tony Snelling, was not due to our common nationality so much as to our common tastes; but it is surprising how much it meant to both of us, and it reinforced our friendship. I think an inferiority complex about the language was my chief barrier to absorption in Welsh affairs at Oxford. I remember referring to Anglo-Welsh writers as 'pestilential'. I liked Rhys Davies's stories, and through David Jones I discovered John Cowper Powys. But I never read Keidrych's magazine *Wales*, the early avant-garde numbers; there seemed to me then to be so much more of Bloomsbury than of Wales about them, a criticism I never dared to make to Keidrych. In 1938 I couldn't bear Dylan's stuff. Two years later I took *The*

Map of Love on holiday with me and by 1941 *Portrait of the Artist as a Young Dog* had quite converted me. But the chief factor was that people kept on asking me about Dylan and whether the Wales depicted in his writing was really like that, and so on. I *had* to take an interest, and so, to return from a slight literary digression, I slowly came to realize what it was to be a Welshman.

Then I went into the Navy, but whether I thought of Wales at that time, I can't remember clearly; I had so many purely personal problems to grapple with. Abroad, England was as pleasant a place to be nostalgic about as Wales; Scotland came into it, too. My feelings, I suppose, were very 'British'. But I was well and truly a Welshman, on board ship and later ashore – in the desert, in Malta, Algiers, Chatham, and Largs. The unselfconscious non-Englishness of the Scots certainly helped, and so did the work of Hugh MacDiarmid. Demobbed in 1946, I wanted to work abroad, or in Scotland, but in the black months that followed I would have gone and worked anywhere. Wales was still not a compulsive element in my being, though war had made me, as it makes everyone, more conscious of my roots than ever before: it was the local patriotism of Gower that I felt most keenly. Then came the remote possibility of a job in Cardiff, with Welsh essential.

At the beginning of 1947 I started learning the language again. A few interviews with nice old Professor Ernest Hughes, some evening classes with the Rev.R.S.Rogers, and private lessons with Myrddin Harris who started me off on Williams Parry, Saunders Lewis, and *Y Cymro*, a number with the pilgrimage to Llyn y Fan in it. I now made an investment which was to prove decisive. In three

Separatism.

If there's a sword-like sang
That can cut Scotland clear
O'a' the warld beside
Rax me the hilt o't here,

For there's nae jewel till
Frae the rest o' earth its free,
Wi' the starry separateness
I'd fain to Scotland gi'e.

Hugh MacDiarmid.

Hugh MacDiarmid © Crossland Process and Print Ltd

months of hard work I learned Welsh. I had made other and more expensive investments in the past which could, and should, have taken me out of Wales, but this was the scruple thrown in the balance. It was still a year before I was to join the Blaid, but by then the gesture was more in the nature of a confirmation than a baptism. Most of my surplus energy was taken up in Cardiff, in 1948, with the Unity Theatre, after I had fully recovered from the attack of impotence which war and the feeling of being unwanted had laid upon me. My plan for the Unity was to make it the basis of a Welsh Natio0nal Popular Theatre; God knows how. I wrote to Keidrych Rhys about it, he printed my letter in *Wales*, and that was me launched on the printed page and the public stage at last. The letter brought Keidrych to my door at the beginning of last year, and so began my career as *something* in the life of Wales, ten years too late perhaps but never mind that now.

Then in the *News Chronicle*, a telegram from Ithel Davies in the name of the Welsh Republican Movement. I had forgotten the pamphlet by Cliff Bere, having read so much. But I wrote to Ithel Davies at once; this was what I had been waiting for. I got a nice letter back offering to send me a manifesto, which never arrived. I mentioned this to Keidrych, who wasn't impressed. I found another copy of the pamphlet in Mr.Thomas's shop in Nott Square and noticed, for the first time, that it was published in Cwmoernant. I spent a couple of evenings trying to find Cwmoernant, pleasant Carmarthen evenings, going up the wrong lanes and over strange hills. There was no Bere at Glaslwyn. I did find a cousin, Wyn Jones, who was not a Republican, to whom I gave my address, but there was no attempt by this Bere to contact me. It appears that he was baffled by the removal of both the Druid Press and myself to a new office and new digs. But by now the idea of the Republic was well and truly under my skin.

In my letter to Ithel Davies I had voiced a criticism of the Blaid which, I said, needed a more cogent, urgent, and radical approach to the national problem. The dismal quality of the *Welsh Nation* and *Y Ddraig Goch* was uppermost in my mind, as were the endless, futile protests and motions, and that trip to Caerffili Castle with Roy Lewis and his harem of flat-footed schoolmarms, which was my sole activity during my membership of the Blaid in Cardiff. There were good things, though, such as the ragging of Shinwell at Aberystwyth, the hauling down of the Union Jack at Dolgellau, the barracking of Jim Griffiths at Garnant, and the leaflet raid during 'Welsh Day' in England's parliament. About Garnant I wrote a poem which was published in the *Welsh Nation*, which gave great pleasure to the Republican faction who were, of course, responsible for all these things except the Dolgellau episode, which was spoilt by Gwynfor Evans's disclaimer at Swansea to the Chamber of Commerce, in which he also repudiated Republicanism, later in the year. Then I read of the Republican motion being rejected at the Blaid Summer School in Ardudwy. *"Maen nhw wedi taflu'r Repwblic ma's,"* [They've thrown the Republic out] said Eirian Davies to Keidrych and me one wet day soon afterwards.

The first and last thing I did for the Blaid was to organize the press coverage for the Machynlleth Rally which initiated the Parliament for Wales Campaign. They tried to get Keidrych to do it but he was fed up with the way they had behaved over the Llyn y Fan pilgrimage, so he passed it on to me. At Aberystwyth, where we stopped for lunch, on a day that will be memorable for many things, I was sold a copy of the Manifesto by a cheerful little man with a long jaw and a big voice called Haydn Jones from Clydach, who seemed a refreshing change from the usual moronic Plaid member. Then, in rapid sequence, the confusion and collapse of my personal life and my move, before the month was out, to Cardiff, and the months of darkness and despair that followed.

On January 3rd of this year, when one set of complications was at last removed for a long time, but the atmosphere of my life was still bleak, I was downstairs in the shop when a pleasant chap introduced himself to me as Huw Davies, Secretary of the Welsh Republican Movement. He had been given my name by Ithel Davies, whom I had met in connection with Keidrych's legal bother. The General Election was in the air and I got down to work with the Movement straightaway. On January 16th I enrolled as an associate member and on April 17th I received an invitation to become a member of the Council, as well as a member of the periodicals committee.

Now what is it I have joined? It would, I think, be useful if I gave an account of these early days of Republicanism while the atmosphere and the facts and the impressions are still fresh. I came upon the scene too late (by two years, say) to be able to give a first-hand account of the very earliest post-war stirrings of Republicanism within Plaid Cymru and, in any case, I don't want to write history just yet. For that I would have to draw at length on the detailed situation of Wales, the set-up within the

Nationalist Movement and inside that again, the intrigues and cross-currents that have shaken the Blaid in recent years. I will stick to people. I wouldn't under-rate the influence that certain personalities have had on the present position – on the one hand, the antipathetic personalities of people like Roy Lewis and Davies Aberpennar, and others I hardly know who continue to impose their dead ideas on Plaid Cymru, and on the other, the group of live intelligences which constitutes the core of Republicanism. These are the personalities through which the appropriate ideas filter and are diffused; people are all-important.

First of all, Ithel Davies. First because he has come to be regarded as the leader of the Movement, and also because I can never really remember a time when I didn't know his name. I suppose he must have been an *enfant terrible* in Swansea, ever since his imprisonment as a member of the ILP during the First World War, and all the time I was growing up there, alas, regardless. His name, mispronounced as Eye-thel, comes to me from my later school-days, associated with sweeping and outrageous pronouncements, presumably on ultra-left-wing lines. But it is all so vague in my memory. I remember, however, a review of T.I.Ellis's life of his father Tom Ellis in *Wales* ––not respectful, but not outrageous either. Ithel is short, broad, deep-eyed, square-jawed, with iron-grey hair; obviously a public man, a barrister; an incisive speaker but not very convincing, and mono-tonously loud; his voice occasionally squeaks on the top notes. As a character he is difficult to describe: highly egocentric, that's for sure, which accounts for his sometimes imperious manner, and his insensitivity towards his audience, which makes for long-windedness. But does it account for his long years in the wilderness? 'I didn't leave the Labour Party,' he is fond of saying. 'They left me.' I can't imagine him rising to great heights in a Labour administration, and he is not particularly successful as barristers go, but he could have found some niche there, from which he could have boomed to his heart's content and stuck his jaw out. He would have been much more at home, at fifty plus, in an established party than with us. Egocentricity alone doesn't make a Welsh Republican. I find Ithel difficult to account for or analyse, which is perhaps all for the best. The rest of us are young enough to learn. Ithel is best accepted as he is; I think we all like him.

Associated quite fortuitously with Ithel are Tom Williams and his wife Joyce. The three form the Swansea Branch of the Movement, though none of them is from Swansea. Joyce is from the Rhondda and Tom from Pwllheli, I believe. But oddly enough, they hold an attitude in common which distinguishes the Swansea Branch from the Cardiff. There is no doubt about Tom: his sincerity and forthrightness are there for all to see. Called up just after the war, he could have been exempted on health grounds, because his heart is bad, or as a technician, for he is a brilliant engineer. But he chose to object as a Welsh Nationalist: he appeared before the Socialist judge, Walter Samuel, and was sent to jail. During his sentence he was awarded his MSc degree. He is only twenty-five now. I first came across him when answering an advert in the *Welsh Nationalist* (as it then was) for the Breton paper, *Le Peuple Breton*. It was very bad, very federalist, and run by a horrible careerist called

Joseph Martray, who is loathed by the Breton militants but praised by old Llygad Llwchwr as 'dapper and dynamic'. Tom was an agent for this unlikely organ and was living then at Burry Port. When he moved to Swansea I tried to get in touch with him, but he was always out when I called, which is a pity because I might have been in touch with the Republican Movement a good deal sooner. I learned of his record from Keidrych, who didn't know him but who respected him as one of the few Blaid people untainted by pacifism, which in the opinion of everyone I have any respect for is a filthy and pharasaical doctrine as far as it is comprehensible at all. Republicanism really started hotting up its attack on orthodox Nationalism in the pages of *Y Faner* after the Dyffryn Ardudwy conference, which according to some observers secured the crushing defeat of Republicanism by methods typical of the milk-and-water moderates. One of the most horrible letters was from Tom, telling Saunders Lewis to go to Timbuctoo.

The Movement's manifesto is not a notable piece of work: it sounds no trumpet note, it is involved, laboured, legalistic, and dry. In short, it was written by Ithel and a committee and soon, I hope, it will be superseded. The *Welsh Republic* pamphlet is hardly a literary masterpiece either: it belongs to a very early stage of Cliff Bere's political evolution. Judging the Republic from these productions, its showing was not very impressive last winter. Furthermore, this letter of Tom's, which was no more than guttersnipe invective against one of the most distinguished minds Wales has produced, one of the few genuinely heroic characters in her later history, nearly put the tin hat on the idea as far as I was concerned. This mood of revulsion lasted until the Republicans made personal contact with me and much superficial misunderstanding was cleared up, largely in conversation with Huw Davies. But the Timbuctoo letter certainly throws a bleak light on the less attractive necessities of politics. It is to Tom's credit that he faces them. He is tough, rather rugged: a long North Wales face and a fierce moustache. He has been ejected from various enemy meetings, which isn't strictly necessary in his state of health.

With Tom must be considered his wife Joyce, for man and wife are one flesh and, in this case, one mind also. Joyce is a very refreshing personality to the point of being too much so – almost a caricature of the South Wales virtues. It's odd that I get on so well with her because we are two of a kind – subjective, romantic, loquacious, artistic, over-personal, with a talent for mimicry, a creative urge, and a too-ready tongue. She has been described as a blaggard, a fishwife, and a disgrace, in her public appearances at least. She writes as she talks and has no finesse; neither of her feet is on the ground, which is part of her impact, I suppose, or if you like, her charm. I knew her poetry before I met her in the flesh at Bridgend during the General Election. It was mostly good poetry, in a highly personal sort of way. [Joyce Williams writes under the name Joyce Herbert.] The letters she used to write to Keidrych were even more fun; perhaps she's altogether too much fun. But a movement like ours needs some effervescence and with Joyce we shall get plenty. Also, for an intellectual, a poetess, a Pasionara, she is an excellent housekeeper and a divine cook. Her recent conversion to Popery is probably the result of a too conscientiously agnostic upbringing, combined with a romantic infatuation with Ireland, which I find a bit boring. I hope it doesn't last, though I wouldn't like to prophesy. She can't relax, there's a very rough edge to her tongue, but she's not really a shrew. She's a woman and therefore not easy to describe.

So much for the Swansea Branch of the Movement. As I have already said, none of them has any roots in Swansea: I am the only Republican who holds that distinction. As representative of our second city, it gives me very little pleasure to record that it has, in our circle at any rate, become the centre of reactionary deviationism. Or has it? Since I started writing these notes the first annual Congress of the Movement has been held and the point aired, though a motion condemning the attitude of mind in question was withdrawn. The author of this resolution was Huw Davies, in collaboration with Cliff Bere and supported by myself in debate. I believe we either convinced or silenced the Swansea lot. Huw is editor of *The Welsh Republican* and is likely to continue as such for some time; the opposition is not likely to get much hearing, and the Cardiff view is the one that's going to be put over. Huw's unkind words for the Swansea heresy were 'socialist irrealism', by which he sums up Ithel's constant invocation of Keir Hardie and Robert Owen, Joyce's Rhondda bloody-mindedness and vehemence, and Tom's blind belief in violence, to name only a few tendencies with very little relevance to the real world. Ithel has been described as an old-fashioned ILP man and he is certainly an old-fashioned Radical, preoccupied with the abolition of hereditary titles and other legalistic shibboleths. His attitude to the redistribution of wealth and land is also confusing, a mixture of Utopianism and laissez-faire that takes my breath away. Joyce's obsession with Ireland and the emotional atmosphere of the Rhondda of her youth also makes her a liability. Tom, too, though he is by far the soundest of them, has been equally extravagant. During the special circumstances of the General Election last spring, we all called ourselves Welsh Socialists, except Huw, but the Swansea contingent seem to have believed it.

Also in the Swansea area is Haydn Jones, a represent-ative of Cwm Tawe, the little man with the big jaw, big voice and pipe whom I met in Aberystwyth. He is a traveller for Bristow Wadley, the paint people, and a man of moods which sometimes remove him from active circulation. His ancient car and endless goodwill were most providential during the Election, but after that he sank into solitary apathy and has only just re-emerged. He doesn't seem to have much capacity for original thought: action is his line, selling, heckling, driving, shouting through the loudspeaker; I have many mental pictures of him from that time. When he came up for the Congress he was full of the Workers' Forum, a greasy Popish effort which had obviously been getting at him; he didn't really know whether it was a good thing or not until he was told by Huw and myself in the bar of the Westgate Hotel.

The mention of that dubious organization makes this the place to record casualties and defections from the Republican Movement in Cwm Tawe, those people who came so far with us but would not face a break with the Blaid: Timothy Lewis of Tŷ'r Wern, Ystalyfera, whom I don't know at all, and Llewelyn Davies of the same place who spoke for us at Bridgend but who has now gone back to the Blaid and the Forum. From Swansea, working my way west and north, I come to John Legonna at Llanarth, running three farms, doing a thesis for Idris Foster on the status of women in medieval Welsh law, brooding and meditating an unconscionable magazine, and not answering any letters. John Legonna, the Celtic synthesis of Cardigan and Cornwall, whose odd, challenging name (he was born Brooks, disappointingly) I have known since Oxford, where he was a firebrand, a protégé of A.L.Rowse, a Cornish Nationalist, and a name whose writings I have found as stimulating as they are rebarbative, usually in University magazines where they stuck out like Celtic rock among the decadent rococo of elegant Oxonianism, in *Wales*, and recently in the pages of the *Republican Bulletin*, one number of which we completely unbalanced in order to get in his review of Gwynfor Evans's book about Plaid Cymru. Scant thanks we got from our readers for performing this service for them. Legonna, it seems, is strong meat, and Huw and I, the editors of the *Bulletin*, were in a minority of two. Since Legonna's mysterious and uncooperative behaviour over the forthcoming magazine, and my withdrawal of some of my more extravagant remarks about him, Huw feels himself to be in a minority of one. But however uncomfortably enlightened I may be about Legonna as a man to work with, my admiration for his intellect remains. Whether he can gear this intellect to the practical problems of creating a Republican frame of mind at the highest level is a matter very much open to doubt. We shall see. Meeting him was one of the important things about the Election for me, and we talked fruitfully. I seem to have missed the unpleasant side to his character on which Tom and Joyce dilate so endlessly. I think Legonna must be an acquired taste.

It strikes me that none of the people I have discussed so far can in any sense be considered the constructive mind of the Movement. However valuable their contributions and whatever historical priority their writings possess, none of them have the attributes of 'movement-builders'. This is Huw Davies's judgement from a central position, and how true it is: Ithel, the political outcast, Legonna, the intellectual hermit, Tom and Joyce, the projectors of their own personalities – there's nothing cohesive about any of them. But the next group of people, though spread throughout the rest of Wales, seem to constitute another class, another section of the Movement almost, owing nothing to their remoteness from Cardiff. I don't know them well, or their activities, though the latter sound quite impressive.

First among this group is Gwilym Prys Davies at Aberystwyth. I first met him, and the rest of the militant Republicans, during the Election. The most impressive thing about Gwilym was the way other people talked about him, especially his fellow-students. Those who came down from Aberystwyth with him believed in him implicitly, referring to him in terms which are rare on the lips of undergraduates describing their contemporaries. Despite his adherence to the least popular belief in Wales today (if the Election results are anything to go by), he has been elected President of the Student Body at Aber by the largest majority ever. I have never heard him speak in public but I have Huw's word for it that he has done very well: once at Tregaron, at a Blaid protest meeting, he completely put Gwynfor Evans in the shade, which is quite something, for Gwynfor – whatever his deficiencies as a practical politician – is an excellent speaker; at other meetings in the Middle West, Gwilym has impressed or shocked his audience (according to their Welshness or otherwise) with his fire and eloquence. Added to this there is his solid ability, his constructive and fearless plans, constitutions, and other proposals: these I do know about and they seem to me the best sort of thing which we as a Movement could possibly have. The constitution of the Welsh Republican Movement is entirely his work, as amended by Congress. It stands out as a remarkable one-man achievement, the more so as certain of the amendments proposed, notably by Ithel, displayed a complete lack of the qualities of clarity, single-mindedness and incisiveness which characterized the original. Gwilym is in very delicate health and seems doomed to a Thomas Davis-like fate, to die young in the cause of Wales. His whole future career is a question mark; he may not even be resuming his leadership of the Republicans at Aber this year. He has sufficiently impressed Sean MacBride to be given an invitation to recuperate at his expense in the Irish sanitoria. He came down to the Election at Bridgend in a very bad state indeed, and to subsequent Council meetings at obvious risk. He is perhaps the most fierce Republican of us all.

So far all the people I have mentioned are officially in positions of leadership in the Movement. But at Aberystwyth there is a Branch as well, with ordinary members who are, or who do, nothing special, but are just Welsh Republicans. A lot of them turned up at Bridgend and, I'm afraid, being students, they all resembled one another so much that I couldn't tell Royden John from Cyril Huws, though of course I can never forget Gwyn Huws who turned up to Congress and is for ever associated in my mind with one of the most amazing and surrealist evenings of drunken inconsequence that I can recall in long experience of such matters. Gwyn Huws is off to the English colonies, a victim of our imbalanced economy, but I am sure he will turn up again one day with his bland smile. Then there's Gareth Evans who must hold the distinction of being the only pacifist in the Movement who can make it sound convincing by sheer patient sincerity; he looks after the money at Aberystwyth and, I'm sure, works hard. Cyril Huws, the Secretary, is a more flighty type, and Royden John, who was had up for painting slogans all over Bridgend, is even more unstable, having written a disastrously apologetic letter to the court. I wish I could tell these two apart.

There are Republicans at Aber whom I don't know. In fact the Branch has historical importance in the formation of the Movement. It was there that Huw Davies, John Legonna, Gwilym Prys Davies and Cliff Bere met just after the war. I believe Cliff's attendance at the University was of short duration and Huw did not stay on to do a full Honours course, and Legonna was of course farming. But they were all there long enough to turn the local branch of the Blaid into a Republican Movement, and with Eirian Davies, refounding that useful periodical *Y Wawr* and initiating such spectacular moves as the Shinwell reception and painting the walls of Carmarthen for Elizabeth Windsor's visit to the Royal Welsh Show, for the last of which Keidrych Rhys got the blame. Eirian's Republicanism is unknown to me; I knew him before I knew of the Movement, through Keidrych

Rhys; he is now married to a fierce Blaid woman. All this is part of the prehistory of the Movement, like the painting of Republican slogans at Cardiff Arms Park just before a Wales-France match in 1948. The Movement at Aberystwyth was part of an attempt by ex-servicemen to turn orthodox Nationalism into more effective channels. It has served its purpose by the foundation of the Movement, but it has also left a useful tradition for the different type of student now coming up.

I must now get back to the builders of the Movement, which means moving on to Bangor. I suppose this is the most numerous Branch of the Movement and it's largely the creation of two dissimilar but complementary characters – Ifor Huws Wilks and Pedr Lewis. Wilks is the perfect ex-officer type: safe, middle-class, North Welsh, studying Philosophy, creating an atmosphere of perfect normality and confidence around the outrageous propositions of Republicanism. Pedr, on the other hand, is almost odd: gauche, tongue-tied, aggressive, proletarian, a runaway to sea, then Coleg Harlech, sent down from Bangor and now chopping at trees. Between them they are a perfect team with complete mastery of the ball. Both are re-immigrants, the one from Liverpool and the other from Wolverhampton, though Pedr's roots are in the Rhondda; he is very hot on the subject of trade unionism and the 'fish-and-chips' attitude to politics. I don't think he could ever have been a member of the Blaid: he seems to have come in straight from the Labour Party. With Wilks this attitude works out more academic and not quite so soundly perhaps: for a brief period during the Election he wanted people to vote Labour in constituencies where there was no Nationalist or

Republican candidate, but this was watered down to 'vote progressive and in the best interests of Wales'. Pedr confesses to being influenced by Wilks, but doesn't see an obvious reciprocal influence which must happen when people work closely together. They seem to have more energy and organizing ability than the residual legatees of proto-Republicanism at Aberystwyth. They take more than their share in the selling of *The Welsh Republican* and are always pressing for more pamphlets. Wilks, I believe, was responsible for putting out the first organ of Republicanism, a cyclostyled sheet called *Llais y Gogledd*, which was meant to buck things up and get the South moving. Among some very keen members in Bangor there's Desmond Huws from Flintshire who is defiantly 'Anglo-Welsh'. I should have mentioned earlier that one of Wilks's first and most characteristic activities was to found an Anglo-Welsh Society at Bangor; whether this was a front organization for the Movement is difficult to say, but that's what it became. I took to Desmond Huws, even after he had written to Huw a letter which was a distressing mixture of Herbert Read, Eric Gill and Lewis Mumford; Pedr asked me to correct some of the poor lad's more horrid heresies. I feel that we've got someone in Desmond Huws, even if founding an Anglo-Welsh renaissance in Flintshire is a bit beyond anybody's strength at present.

And so south again, to consider perhaps the most anomalous member of our Movement, namely Dr.Ceinwen Thomas. She lives with Dr.D.J.Davies at Gilwern. I feel that her conduct has been so uniformly unsatisfactory as to outweigh any prestige that accrues to us through her defection from the Blaid, of which she was such a model, and in some ways such a typical member, or the advantage we get from her contact with Dr.D.J.Davies. In this respect she is more a source of leakage than of information. She has just blown the gaff in *Y Faner* about the Committee of Celtic Action which we've been discussing for some time; it may mean that the Blaid will muscle in on an idea which needs the stern counsels of Republicanism. This is only the latest (as it is by far the most serious) of her actions that must inspire distrust and sheer exasperation. Her article in the first number of *The Welsh Republican* was very good, but she completely neutralized the good of it by writing what was to all effects the same article on the same subject for the number of the *Welsh Nation* that came out at the same time. This has annoyed me beyond measure and it colours my view. Her opposition to the Republican tricolour also seems to have been out of place in the context of early Republicanism, and I for one was very surprised to hear that she was a Republican at all, after reading the typically schoolmarmish stuff she'd done for the Blaid papers.

I have left the Cardiff Branch till last because I know it best and can appreciate all sorts of significances, and also because it is in a way the most powerful and active Branch in the whole Movement – powerful in the sense that it has more seats on the Supreme Council than any other, includes the whole Secretariat and the editors of the Movement's paper, and is in the most favourable position for activity in the most densely populated part of Wales. It is in fact, though certainly not by any prescription, an HQ Branch, the sort of branch appropriate to our capital city. It is also a conscious creation in large part, by which I mean that people like Cliff Bere and Huw Davies have deliberately chosen to live in Cardiff with a view to establishing Republicanism here. This is perhaps the most significant and courageous action any young man could perform in Wales today: deliberately to choose to stay in his own country, to forgo the advancement and preferment that await the person of average ability in England and which do not exist in Wales, to turn one's back on the amenities of London, the promiscuous, irresponsible cosmopolitanism that at times makes life here seem so bleak and stern in contrast, to dig one's heels in and choose to stay in Wales and serve Wales at all costs and against whatever strong currents of economic and social attraction seek to uproot and whirl her away. In this category of pioneers Huw Davies and Cliff Bere must honourably be placed. Huw has told me (and from him I have had much of the Movement's history) that a very early decision was taken at Aberystwyth by the people I have already mentioned 'to try to keep together', to be in constant everyday contact, so that a Welsh Republican atmosphere would be created, a common climate of opinion in which it would be difficult to claim any new ideas as personal property. As far as Aberystwyth was concerned, this plan fell through, but Cliff, with that tenacity and iron will of his, came south and went underground, and Huw, resisting the blandishments of the Appointments in England Board, found a job in the docks with Cory Brothers. These two are as responsible as anybody for the persistence of the Welsh Republican idea and the survival of the Movement as a separate force.

For after the Summer School at Dyffryn Ardudwy,

when Republicanism was put to the vote and arrested, the idea, which had been making headway within Plaid Cymru, became officially discredited. Even the Swansea group, for all their fervour and idealism, didn't see the clear necessity for making an issue of the Republic and making a stand for it. The majority of the Movement, in fact, acquiesced in their not unexpected defeat by the chapel-pacifist element in the Blaid, and were prepared to carry on as a pressure-group minority inside the party. Not so Cliff Bere. 'At one time,' said Huw Davies to me once, 'it looked as if the Movement would consist of two men selling Cliff's pamphlet up and down the valleys'. That must have been a bad period indeed, before the logic of the situation became apparent and it was Cliff Bere's sense of purpose that kept the way clear for events to take their course. It's going to be very difficult for me to describe these men with whom I have worked at close quarters for the best part of a year, Cliff in particular.

There are so many elements here which are contradictory. With the most intransigent Republicanism Cliff combines an equally obstinate belief in social theories whose only true home is in the *perchentyaeth* of the Blaid – back to the land, de-industrialization for the sake of moral well-being, and so forth. It takes my breath away sometimes, this tremendous contradiction between ideas the Movement aims to sweep away and the most single-minded Republicanism of any of us. His record, read out accusingly by the officers of the English law in their courts of injustice, sounded like an accolade. His was the brilliant idea of burning the Union Jack in our public meetings. Early in the summer we twice went to Caerffili to carry out this 'simple ceremony', as Cliff insists on calling it. Twice we came away, unable to attract a crowd in the deserted streets. But Cliff was insatiable: he wanted to burn the flag audience or no audience. As we caught the bus with the flag still unburnt, Cliff exclaimed, *'Wel, rhaid imi ddweud hyn – mae'r faner 'ma yn llosgi yn fy mhoced!'* [Well, I have to say this – this flag's burning in my pocket!].

After that the flag burned well and truly, first at Neath on a very successful Saturday afternoon, and then all over South Wales until we got to Aberdâr, when police action resulted and, as a grand climax, at the Caerffili Eisteddfod; the law is taking its course as I write these notes. At Coed-duon, where we held one of our most effective open-air meetings, I watched Cliff as he held out the flag at arm's length after I had put a match to it. He strode well out into the middle of the road so that everybody in the mile-long main street should have a chance of seeing what we thought of England. His eyes were almost glazed with rapture, his face tense with fulfilment. If a car had come along I don't think he would have got out of the way; I don't think he'd have noticed if he had been knocked down. From that evening on I have put up with all the wet Liberal heresy I have heard from Cliff because fundamentally I know he is tougher and more fanatical than any of us. How he contrives to be a better door-to-door seller of papers than either Huw or myself I just don't know, but it is invariably the case when we go out together. It's the Liberal approach perhaps, the invariable raising of the hat, the mild conciliatory voice, and before the householder knows it, he has forked out for two penn'orth of the most seditious stuff since the old *Daily Herald*. It is an ambition of Cliff's to go to prison and refuse to wear uniform, as a political prisoner. Confronted with the possibility of distraint on his scanty goods for non-payment of police costs, he exclaims, 'Think of the effect it will have – taking away a man's sticks. Excellent!' It will take more than the English Empire to pull down Cliff Bere. On his visit to Cardiff last summer, Keidrych was impressed by the improvement he noted in Cliff since their discussion over a year previously. I have noticed too that Cliff is not a natural speaker. He has to force himself cruelly to make a speech in public. It has been almost embarrassing at some of our open-air meetings to hear him cut his sentences, begin to say 'Ladies and…' and then remember, and switch convulsively to 'Welsh men and women'. Neither is he a fluent writer. Yet he forces himself unsparingly in these activities. I must not go on writing much more about Cliff Bere. I must just take my hat off to him.

These notes were written by HW in 1949 and 1950; they were found among his papers and are published here in a slightly edited form.

Letters to Mr.Jones

Dear Mr.Jones,

I am writing to you because I have heard you say that there is no sense in Welsh Republicanism and that under the present system Wales has full equality with England. Well, Mr.Jones, I know that you are a fair man who believes in 'Wara Teg' for both sides of a question, so I am sure that you will listen to a reasonable case reasonably argued. Even if you think that some sort of Home Rule for Wales is a good idea, you don't consider it to be as important as other matters and accordingly you give your vote to the Labour Party or the Liberals or the Conservatives.

But you may have noticed that practically every candidate for your vote in 1945 and 1950 made special promises about what he or she would do for Wales. The Labour Party, in fact, made Five Promises which received much publicity at the time. I will write to you again about this Famous Five but in the mean while I will just ask: *why* were all these special promises thought necessary? Politicians at election time don't waste breath on matters that are not really important, so I suppose we must conclude that Wales really and truly is a special case, a *Special Area* as it is sometimes called.

Now why is this so? What makes the problems of Wales different from the problems of England? Let us take a look at some of these problems and perhaps we shall find some sort of answer. I suppose the problem that most of us would name as the most urgent in society today is unemployment. I don't want to baffle you with a lot of figures but the figures about unemployment are very important and you can easily check up on whether I am telling you the truth or not. And I don't suppose you'll be really surprised if I tell you that for the last five years there have been four Welshmen on the dole to every one Englishman, in proportion to the populations of the two countries. I think this fact deserves greater prominence than the papers like to give it, and I am sure it is one which touches you deeply. The last few years have been prosperous compared with the period between the two wars, but that is no excuse for shrugging your shoulders. You are a fair man, Mr.Jones, and even if you feel that you are better off now than you ever were, I am not going to think much of you if you say that all this unemployment in Wales is no concern of yours as long as you have got a job yourself. If that is your attitude, then you can stop reading this letter now, because it is no use appealing to you. But I know that you don't really take such a selfish and narrow view of matters. You don't really like to think of anybody being up against it through no fault of their own, and little children, maybe, having to go without. Yes, it is still happening, Mr.Jones, and there is proportionately four times as much of it in Wales as in England. And with such a bad start isn't it likely that if there is even the very mildest depression ahead, then things in Wales are going to be four times worse again than in England? And it might be your turn next time, never forget that.

It's no good saying that when things are bad in Wales they are bad in England as well, as if that were an answer. Of course there were black spots in England. But Wales was one big Black Spot, otherwise we would not have lost 500,000 of our people by emigration. And that figure is not challenged by anybody. It's a lot of people, a lot of people to have educated and reared and then to lose them, and their wages and their muscle and their brains. And where did all these people emigrate *to*? You know as well as I do: Slough, West Bromwich, Aston, Cowley, Coventry, Wembley, Harrow, Ealing, Redditch – I could go on, and I am prepared to bet that you have relatives in at least one of these English towns I have mentioned. And I am prepared to bet that they didn't particularly want to go. They went 'because there was nothing for them in Wales'. But there was something for them in England, wasn't there? So it doesn't look as if England was in too bad a way, does it?

Ah well, you are going to say, Wales is a poor little country, and England is rich and full of opportunity. Shame on you, Mr.Jones. Whatever your MPs tell you, you are not going to believe that, I hope. I don't ask you to take my word that it is not so. I will refer you to a practical scientist, Dr.F.J.North, President of the South Wales Institute of Engineers in 1944, who said, 'Europe and Asia are most favoured among the continents in regard to concentration of coal reserves, Great Britain has the greatest concentration in Europe, and South Wales the greatest in Britain'. In other words, Mr.Jones, *South Wales has the greatest capacity of any coalfield in the world.*

I think that is an encouraging note on which to end

this letter. It gives you food for thought, doesn't it? Especially when you think of the half a million people we lost 'because there was nothing for them in Wales', and the 30,000 Welshmen on the dole when the rest of the United Kingdom boasts of 'full employment'. And coal is only part of our wealth, after all. This is only the beginning of the story. Oh, Mr.Jones, you and I have got a lot to talk about, more than you thought perhaps.

Well, I will be writing to you again soon, so look out for another letter.

Yours truly,
CARADOG.

The Welsh Republican (August 1950)

Dear Mr.Jones,

How did you enjoy the Eisteddfod this year? I don't think the 'All-Welsh Rule' that there was so much fuss about hindered your enjoyment of the singing and the brass bands or the Arts and Crafts, but I expect you were very sorry to see that the *Western Mail* lost such a lot of sleep over it. Every day there was some attack by this 'national newspaper' on the use of our national language. And the letters in the *Echo* on the subject are rubbish.

We all know by now that the purpose of the Eisteddfod is to safeguard the Welsh language and culture. And 'culture' in Wales is not something highbrow and exclusive and expensive like it is in England, but something you and I and all the rest of us take an interest in, if it's only raising our voices in the *Gymanfa*, or cheering the winning bard. Maybe you don't think that there's anything wonderful in all this, but that's only because we're so used to it. In England the bard either starves or hires himself out as a sort of clown. In Wales he is honoured, and that is something which does honour to our people and the high standards of Welsh life.

To call all this sort of thing 'regrettable', 'disastrous', 'narrow', and 'rude', like that stupid paper the *Western Mail*, is not only bad manners, we are used to that in the Tory Press, but sheer ignorance. The real cause for this display is that they are afraid of the Welsh language and everything it stands for. It is still the language of one Welshman in three, and it belongs to us all even if a lot of us have been deprived of the opportunity of enjoying it. That doesn't mean to say that you are not a 'good Welshman' if you can't speak Welsh. The *Western Mail* will try to tell you that we Welsh Republicans believe that everybody who can't speak Welsh should be victimized. On the contrary, we see all the people of Wales as one people, the Welsh people!

Our Ness Edwards did his best with his talk about 'Iron Curtains' and 'Sudetenlands' to divide the Welsh people, but he was booed for his pains, and the Lord Mayor of Cardiff got his answer, too. Remember the headlines in the *Echo*? *'The Union Jack must not be burnt,'* said he. Then before the week was out, *'Union Jack Burnt'*. And all this goes to show that the real division in Wales today is not between Welsh-speaking and English-speaking, but between self-satisfied politicians who have an attachment to English Rule and the ordinary people whose hearts are with Wales. Ness Edwards said, 'Now there are more smiles in Wales than for half a century'. Were they smiling, Mr.Jones, at Cilely, Treorchy, Trawsfynydd, Blaenafon or Rhandir-mwyn?

It's the same old story, Mr.Jones, in the mouth of a Labour MP or a Tory Lord Mayor. You are going to hear a different story from us, the Welsh Republicans. We're going to tell you that a Welshman should listen to nobody who tells him that he has no right to run his own country or be loyal to his own Welsh flag and who stuffs him up with a lot of rubbish about the Union Jack which is an insult to Wales. And if the courts come down on us and make us out to be criminals, remember that they are English Courts, that they take their orders from over the border and their laws come from English Statute Books. Is that Justice, Mr.Jones? Just think it over.

Yours truly,
CARADOG

The Welsh Republican (October-November 1950)

Dear Mr.Jones,

I expect you have heard people who believe in Welsh Independence saying that Wales is a Colony of England's, and I expect you have wondered what they were on about. You know what a colony is and you are pretty sure that Wales isn't anything of the sort.

But think again, Mr. Jones, think again. And ask yourself, 'What exactly is a Colony?'.

A Colony, surely, is a country that, in the first place, has no Government of its own, or only an inferior Government with not much more power than, say, a County Council. And as a consequence of not having a proper Government, a Colony is an exploited country, that is to say, its economy is run for the benefit of the country that 'owns' the Colony, not for the welfare of the inhabitants themselves. Wales is a Colony by both these tests, Mr. Jones, and I shall prove it!

Take the Government side of it first. We elect our 36 MPs to the Parliament in London, and that is supposed to put us on a level with England and safeguard our interests. Oh, Mr. Jones, use your loaf! How can it? When England imposes conscription in readiness for her next war, a majority of Welsh MPs voted against it. But what were their twenty-odd voices among the uproar of the hysterical English in full cry? The fate of your own flesh and blood will answer you soon enough, as the youth of Wales is sacrificed on some far-flung futile battlefield for England's fading Empire. Do you have to wait until that happens before you will be convinced that Wales is a Colony? Or are you so doped with English press propaganda that you are quite happy for the same senseless old slaughter of the last two generations to happen all over again, then kid yourself it's all in aid of some noble cause? Come off it, Mr. Jones, it's later than you think.

And if you like to go on thinking that Wales is

getting a square deal, well go on thinking it, but don't blame me when you find there's no job nearer than Birmingham, and 'No Welsh need apply'. Because it's the same thing with industries as with armies. You are there to do the dirty work. When I say the words 'Colonial Economy' I suppose you think of the poor blacks sweating in the sun to grow groundnuts or some other raw material which is then sent to England to be processed and re-exported, and all the profits going to the guzzling parasites who live in luxury in London. Yes, Mr.Jones, but think of the raw materials we produce in Wales: the tinplate that is exported to the English Midlands, the coal that could command its own price in the world markets, but is sent to England at 'Special Industrial Prices', the bulk electricity, the wool, bought up in bulk by Bradford – do I have to go on? Your job is to lie on your guts in the hard heading, roast in front of the furnace, or stagger through the frost and snow of the lambing season, and the stuff you produce is whisked off before you can look around and cushy processing jobs are carried out for twice and three times your money in the thriving towns of England.

The 'poor blacks' are beginning to think things out for themselves, Mr.Jones. What are you doing about it?

Yours truly,
CARADOG

The Welsh Republican (December 1950-January 1951)

Dear Mr.Jones,

I believe you are gradually coming to see that our country, though small, is very wealthy, and that the black times we have seen, and will see again if we don't stick up for ourselves, are not due to poverty but to scandalous mismanagement. Have you ever asked the question, 'Who runs Wales'? And have you ever had a satisfactory answer? The odds are No! The answer has usually been supplied for you. 'The Owners' it used to be, didn't it? Well, there aren't any owners any more, are there? Or are there? It's a question that it isn't polite to ask these days. But the Welsh Republicans are good at asking awkward questions. And good at finding out the answers, too. There is a proverb: 'Where there's muck there's brass', and in a rich country like Wales, where there's brass there's muck... English muck, or just as bad, Welsh muck clinging to England's boots.

Nobody really believes now that nationalization really got at the root of the evil in Wales. One set of owners took over from another set, and very often it was a case of 'the same old faces in the same old places'. Men who had been denounced as enemies of the workers turned up smiling on the boards of nationalized industries. And well they might smile. Absurdly over-compensated, their subsidiary activities untouched – their brickfields, their breweries, their export companies and their shipping lines. Look in the phone book, Mr.Jones. The old black names are still there, with hosts of companies still belonging to them. Hard hit? Tell me another!

Yes, you'll say, and all these so-and-sos were Welshmen like you and me. And you'll give that as an excuse for pooh-poohing Welsh independence. But exactly how Welsh were those characters with proud Welsh names, Lord Merthyr, Lord Rhondda, Lord knows who? They fawned on England as zealously as our 'Welsh' MPs today. They were all for the English Empire and coal-wharves wherever the Union Jack waved. The bigger the Fleet the bigger the bunkering contracts, then bang! – oil replaced coal. And who suffered? Who starved? Who marched with empty bellies and draughty boots, begging for bread and justice? You know, Mr.Jones, you know!

You can no more blame Wales for the actions of these traitors than you can vilify the English Labour Party for producing heroes like Jim Thomas and Ramsay Mac. What you can blame is the exploitation of a whole community in the interests of a foreign Empire – that used Welsh resources to enrich England and Welsh blood to defend England, and then left the Welshman to rot when he wasn't wanted. And it is still going on. Under all the glib talk and glossy camouflage – the Trading Estates, the Remploy schemes that aren't employing, the flopping Grenfell factories, there are the same old faces: the London capitalists and bankers, the London-controlled Tory Press, the big landlords and their leaseholds and their hangers-on – all waiting, Mr.Jones, to do you down once again. And if you think you can stop that happening under the present set-up, with a handful of MPs in London, and them pledged to support an English Party – well think again. The answer to the question 'Who runs Wales?' is this: everybody except the People of Wales. Everybody who is willing to take his orders from the London money-men and the Whitehall office-wallahs; English spivs and Welsh bootlickers. Everybody except

YOU, Mr.Jones.

Best wishes and happy dreams (you'll need them),
from CARADOG

The Welsh Republican (February-March 1951)

Dear Mr.Jones,

You can make as many funny jokes as you like about
Dai Maxwell-Fyfe, the Scotch-English Minister for Wales.
It's going to be no joke for any of us before very long, you
can take that from me, if you don't realize it already. Here
have I been on at you all the time about Welsh
Independence, and here are you still going stubbornly
on in the old way of our fathers before us, and this is
what we get! Makes you think, doesn't it? Think back a
bit then, Mr.Jones. No, not to the days when the Labour
Party was in favour of Welsh Home Rule, though that's
not very long ago either, nor to the 1945 Election when
there was no end to their promises of big things for Wales,
but just to the last couple of years.

Maybe you've heard of the Council for Wales. Maybe
you even think that it's one of the 'Things Labour Did for
Wales' before the English gave them the push. If so,
Heaven help you!

What's the Council for Wales got to do with Dai Fyfe?
Plenty!

What have any of them got to do with the welfare of
the Welsh People? Dam' all!

You see, Mr.Jones, the boys who get on the Westminster

Bandwagon, Labour or Tory, all say the same thing, that Wales doesn't really exist except as a place to sing sentimental songs about; that there are no special problems in Wales that the almighty London Government can't handle. Our derelict countryside? Our lopsided, all-the-eggs-in-one-basket industrial set-up? Housing? Employment of the disabled? Silicosis? Shsh! Oh please don't mention these distressing topics. There's a White Paper about them, isn't there? Or is it a Blue Book? I forget.

And if the questions you ask get a bit too near the bone, well, they distract your attention by pulling a rabbit out of a hat; the Labour Party dreamed up the Council for Wales (they must have had Welsh Rarebit for supper before dreaming it up, too); the jolly old Tories have given us Dai Fyfe (we'd rather have had Will Fyfe any day)! Happy now, are you Mr.Jones?

If not, go on asking questions. You'll get the right answer one day, and then Heaven help the lot of them. Listen to the Welsh Republicans whispering it in your ear, will you? All these sideshows wouldn't be necessary if we had good government. The only way to get good government is to govern ourselves. Now go and shout it out: not Dai Fyfe but Dai Jones! It's up to you.

Yours truly,
CARADOG

The Welsh Republican (December 1951-January 1952)

Dear Mr.Jones,

Let's see how things are panning out, shall we? There's a
lot happening in Wales today that wouldn't have been
thought possible before the war. The independence of our
country is the main issue now, despite all the claptrap about
side issues that darkens the air at election times.

Yes, Mr.Jones, *'Hen Wlad fy Nhadau'* is the tune today,
not 'God Save the King', and all the English Parties are trying
to dance to it. Nobody was more surprised than Yours Truly
when the Tories appointed Half a Minister for Wales. It's
the only election promise they even half-kept. So that proves
he won't be much good, otherwise we wouldn't have got
him. But you're in a minority in Wales if you're a Tory,
Mr.Jones. The Welsh People have always stood up for Fair
Play, Equality of Opportunity and all the rest of it. And that's
meant one thing so far – the Labour Movement.

And fair play to them too, the Labour Party has done a
bit of good in Wales. But where are they now? That's the
question, and that's the answer too. We want fair play,
equality, etc. all the time, not just when our friends in
England feel like it. And the rank and file of our People are
beginning to see just what went wrong. Some of the big-
shots are seeing it too. Half a dozen Labour MPs have come
out for a Parliament for Wales. Even the clever Dicks and
fence-sitters are realizing that they've got to face up to it.

Some do say that the enemies of Welsh Independence
have got the upper hand in the Labour Party in Wales at
the moment. But let me tell you, if you need any telling,
they won't have it for long even if they have got it now.
Nobody can have it both ways. Either you are for Wales
and her People and faithful to the Welsh Labour

Movement or you are an Imperialist, no better than the Tories. Nothing stands still in this world, and we must move with the times and kick out the 'internationalist' goons. It's up to you, Mr.Jones, to see to it that the ones who are coming round come quicker and that the enemies of Wales get it in the neck.

Yours truly,
CARADOG

The Welsh Republican (February-March 1952)

Dear Mr.Jones,

Perhaps you've got this paper propped up in front of a pint pot of a Saturday night when the lads have been round selling in the pubs, or you're reading it in front of the fire at home with a nice supper waiting. Just think, Mr.Jones, you weren't always so comfortable, were you? Perhaps you're one of the old veterans who left your mates in Mametz Wood, pint-sized colliers who tore the heart out of the Prussian Guard. You know what thanks somebody else's King and Country gave you for that. Some of the men who went over the top in 1916 singing 'Cwm Rhondda' were singing it in the gutter ten years later.

Or perhaps you fought for freedom under the well-known democrat, Mr.Winston Spencer Churchill. In that case you needn't think he's finished with you. There's always the Z Reserve. There's always a spot of trouble wherever the map's painted red. And you know what that means. Even the English gutter press had to protest against War Office inefficiency in equipping Korean Troops. All England's wars are fought on the cheap (except for the officers and gentlemen) and the cheapest cannon fodder is the Welsh Worker who wants to get away from the pit or the farm and there's nothing for it but the Army. Then he goes to Egypt with England's trigger-happy thugs, or freezes in Korea, or stews in places like Malaya.

It's going on now and it'll go on all the time until we stop it. The English military machine has still got us by the throat just as in World War I when Churchill, finding he couldn't down the Welsh by bayoneting them in the streets, sent them to Gallipoli and let the Turks finish his dirty work for him. And you needn't think that it'll all blow over and you'll still be sitting with your pint in front of you and your supper in the stove. English capitalist rule has only two alternatives to offer the Welsh worker. Unemployment or War. Already the Labour Exchanges are more crowded than they were. And it's no good thinking that getting the Labour Party back will do the trick. Who was a bigger Blimp than ex-conshie Shinwell?

No, Mr. Jones, we've got to smash the treadmill of blood and barbarism. When we stand up for ourselves in industrial disputes we put up a good show. It's time to settle the dispute once and for all, and decide: England, War and Want, or Wales, Peace and Prosperity. I think I know which it will be.

Yours truly,
CARADOG

The Welsh Republican (April-May 1952)

We Believe in the Welsh People

THE WELSH REPUBLICAN Movement stands alone in Wales today in affirming, as the basis of our belief and action, the inevitable soundness of the instincts of the Welsh people. The common people *are* Wales; that is why, in 'The Century of the Common Man', Wales is coming to the forefront and may well play a part that will redeem all the humiliations of her past.

Practical difficulty is likely to arise for this reason: Wales has defended her identity with such perfection of technique in the past that our people have often been reluctant to abandon the old techniques when circumstances have made them more a hindrance than a help. This has been the case with Welsh Nonconformity. In the days when the parson and the squire represented the whole machinery of English Government, the chapel was a fine and fitting symbol of Welsh independence. Our people paid the price in victimization and eviction, but they fought the alien system – and they won.

When industrial problems had to be faced, a new and independent technique was evolved, with great obligations to the older, but supporting a new and hostile set of vested interests. Again the Welsh people fought. They fought Lord Penrhyn and Powell Duffryn. And again they won. Today, their support, and their support alone, keeps a Labour Government in power in England. But the Labour Government is no longer truly representative of the Welsh people. As His Majesty's Government it has no choice but to shoulder the White Man's Burden. Its responsibility is not to Wales but to England: a bitter, and to many, an unexpected paradox, a Through-the-Looking-Glass situation in which sincere Socialists who believe in Wales will have to run very hard to keep in the same place.

And just as our country districts go on voting Liberal because thirty years ago Lloyd George disestablished the English Church, so our industrial districts go on voting Labour because twenty years ago Aneurin Bevan threw the mace at the Speaker of the English Parliament. Our fellow-nationalists who identify themselves with Liberal techniques are two laps behind. Socialism has replaced Liberalism and now Welsh Republicanism must succeed Socialism.

The common people have not 'let Wales down'. They were historically justified in their Liberalism and later in their Socialism. They were justified in rejecting bourgeois nationalism and they were even justified in rejecting Welsh Republicanism, when at the polls a year ago it was an untried force. But if the Welsh people are slow to convince, they can be sudden to convert and history moves fast.

The common people will not let Wales down in the future either, but they will rally to the cause of the Republic only if that cause has been truly sustained, only if our actions have been hallowed by sincerity and sacrifice.

We must never make the mistakes of approaching our task in a spirit of middle-class superiority and exclusiveness, of indulging in Welsh-language snobbery, or of reproaching our fellow countrymen for their 'lack of patriotism'. It is rather for them to reproach us if our leadership is not dynamic and effective. Our attitude must be one of keenly felt humility. We have to be worthy of Wales and the Welsh people. No higher standard could possibly exist.

The Welsh Republican (February-March 1951)

Who's Living in the Past?

THE CHORUS OF Village Maidens of the English Labour Party in Wales, from Company Director Cliff Protheroe upwards, have one stock answer to the claims of Welsh Independence: 'It would be a return to the past'.

They have played this record so often that it is pretty cracked by now. But so are they, so they don't notice. This is the only charitable thing to say about Huw T.Edwards's latest outburst* against even the very moderate ideas put forward at the Llandrindod Home Rule Conference. Huw has given birth to a pamphlet, all written by hand, with a whole page of real statistics in tonic sol-fa and old notation, and a Draig Goch on the cover keeping goal for Transport House United. If you thought the Welsh Republicans were Radical, think again. Here's the real stuff! While we are messing about with old-fashioned ideas like democratic control of industry and social responsibility, Huw has taken a running jump into the clouds. Capital Cities, National Homes, Lord Mayors, Parliamentary Secretaries, Culture and Committees all shower from his horn of plenty. The only thing missing is Sunday Opening.

A serious analysis of this attempt to sidetrack Welsh demands is out of the question. But the Welsh Republicans have the distinction of being the only political body in Wales whom the Chairman of the Welsh Advisory Council chooses to ignore. Huw once asked, in 1943, for 'a reawakening of that fiery Welsh spirit, ready to dare all and risk all' for the Land of Our Fathers. It's a pity he has not the generosity to recognize that so much at least of his 1943 programme is being implemented by Welsh Republican Movement.

But this is 1951 and we mustn't live in the past, must we? Unless, of course, you are faced with the task of maintaining English supremacy and pretending to be a Good Welshman at the same time. Then you may dish up the cold leftovers of Cymru Fydd – cultural county-council nationalism that went stale with Lloyd George – smother it with internationalist slush that went out with George Lansbury, justify your desertion of Wales with a CHANGE OF HEART in big print, of the Evan Roberts Revival vintage, and serve with appropriate sauce!

Nevertheless, from one aspect at least, Mr.Huw T.Edwards has performed a valuable service. The ideas of the English Labour Party can now be accurately dated at 1910. As such they will form an interesting addition to the collection of antiquities in the new Welsh Folk Museum. When next you visit St.Fagans, do not touch the waxwork figures in Ye Olde Welsh Committee Room. They may really be an Advisory Council.

* Review of Huw T.Edwards: *They Went to Llandrindod.*

The Welsh Republican (April-May 1951)

Compromise Be Damned!

Wales wants Independence

THESE ARE DAYS when the very words 'Welsh' and 'National', however harmlessly or neutrally used, are invariably given a political significance. No mistake about it, the Welsh National Front, long dormant, is waking up.

The mass of our countrymen are still kept in ignorance of the vast issues that are looming ahead, by the English propaganda smoke-screen, but to those even on the fringes of public life, the signs are unmistakable. All must choose and that soon, whether they will be true to what is best in them and serve Wales, or be renegades, candidates for that lowest circle of Hell in which Dante places the traitors.

It is a desire among some of these gentry to make the best of both worlds and shirk ultimate responsibilities that has spawned the monstrous and futile Petition to England's Parliament which, it is fondly hoped by such people as 'Lady' Megan Lloyd George and 'Sir' Ifan ab Owen Edwards, will save at least one of their faces. The morass of contradictions and cross-purposes into which the unlikely success of this Petition would plunge our people is obvious to any sane person at first glance. The confusion with which the issue is regarded by the English parties in Wales, the differing voices with which they speak, are a sign first, that no English-style politics have any real relevance to Welsh conditions, next, that they aren't taking the business very seriously, and last, that when the tidal wave of national awakening sweeps up the foul water-courses of careerism and compromise, these big-mouthed gentry, on both sides of the Petition, will have no idea of what has hit them.

So much for these accidental and temporary loyalties. The pages of *The Welsh Republican* have been filled from the very beginning with cogent and realistic arguments against any tie-up with England's comic-opera monarchy, its seedy and discredited Empire, its cannibalistic financial system, its utter spiritual and moral bankruptcy. We have also advocated, as the only sane and logical course for the Welsh People to choose, the path towards an autonomous Republic. It is not an easy path, but neither is it the broad road paved with good intentions and woolly thinking. For we have taken what has been noblest in the traditions of all loyalties which in their day have served Wales well and proclaimed their dedication to the one enduring loyalty. The shabby gold-digging, muck-raking, and back-scratching, which are the chief pursuits of public men in Wales today, are a disgrace to the ideals which they profess. But 'this corruptible shall put on incorruptible' for Wales has never been without an answer yet.

At this crucial moment in the history of Wales the Welsh Republican Movement believes itself fully justified in rejecting the Parliament Petition with contempt. Indeed, we believe that the Petition and moderate activities and programmes associated with its sponsors would in themselves possess no significance at all were it not for the existence of a body of opinion which resolutely stands by complete independence and nothing else!

It is the proud privilege of the Welsh Republicans to proclaim in the teeth of the compromisers the one doctrine which has been the core of Welsh Resistance and survival since before 'European Civilization' emerged: the Faith of Wales Invincible, Wales Eternal, Wales the Altar of Liberty and Shrine of her People's Abiding Hope.

The Welsh Republican (October-November 1951)

Against Military Conscription

SO LONG AS THE Welsh Nation is deprived by English Government of its rightful sovereignty, military exploitation of the people and resources of Wales is inevitable. All can see the injustice of Military Conscription, imposed on Wales by the Government of England in defiance of Welsh opinion and of the votes of the Welsh representatives at Westminster. So Welsh Youth has been used indiscriminately for the protection of English imperial interests for generations. Today the annexation of Welsh land for the training and development of English Armed Forces is a further injury to Welsh honour and interest. Again, persecution of individuals and social inconvenience are caused by the call of England on Welshmen who have formerly served in the Forces of the Crown. Deepest of all her indignities, Wales is forced to be without those necessary institutions of present-day Statehood – National Forces, maintained for the defence and integrity of the Motherland.

There are those in Wales who desire a Welsh State without armed forces at its disposal. This unrealistic ambition is not shared by the Welsh Republican Movement. We have to acknowledge not only the necessity of Armed Defence in the modern world, but also the social and psychological value of the Military Departments of State. A nation without its own

Government, without its own Defence Forces, cannot hope to survive, even in a cultural backwater. Nor can we in Wales afford to ignore the very real dignity and valour of National Armed Forces, trained in self-sacrifice, honour and vigilance for the People's security.

The rich plunder available to the imperialist invader of Wales will, at least until the lasting Peace of all sane men's hopes is achieved, require the establishment of strong, well-equipped and effective Welsh Defence Forces. Whatever the circumstances, our people must be assured of resolute opposition on their behalf to any attempt to violate the territorial integrity of our country. The Free Wales would, necessarily, be prepared to come to defensive alliances with neighbouring countries, and to contribute to any genuine International Force for the preservation of World Order. We should also consider, despite our abhorrence of military conscription under English Rule, the possible advantages of national service for Welsh Youth in accordance with legislation approved by a majority of the representatives of the Welsh People in a Free Parliament of Wales.

But today, subject Wales has neither the comfort of her own Armed Forces, nor defence against use of Welsh Land to the destruction of Welsh life, nor protection against the militaristic demands of English Imperialism on Welsh conscript and reservist alike. Repeated appeals for the establishment of integral Welsh Armed Services, even under the present constitutional arrangement, have been steadfastly ignored by the English authorities. No less determined has been the resistance of successive English Governments to any suggestion of Welsh political autonomy. We are not unaware of the economic and strategic reasons underlying the English Imperialist's attitude. These enemies of the free life of the People of Wales need not, therefore, affect surprise if Welsh Armed Forces grow ultimately from military units, founded, ordered and mobilized for the defence of Welsh Territory, and the establishment of Welsh Freedom. For our Nation will not for ever tolerate its present subordination to the will of England's warmakers.

Editorial, *The Welsh Republican* (April-May 1952)

Wales Will Not Be Tricked!

Concessions Mean Nothing

THE APPOINTMENT OF Sir David Maxwell-Fyfe as half-time Minister for Welsh Affairs marks a change of tactics in London policy towards Wales. The War Office has been checked in Llŷn and the Forestry Commission in the Tywi Valley. There is reorganization in Education and Agriculture. There is talk of even greater concessions to come.

We hesitate to pour cold water on any enthusiasm these moves may have aroused. We are loth to interrupt the mutual congratulations of MPs, journalists and moderate political bodies who see themselves as successful defenders of Wales. We would be hardhearted indeed to be unmoved by the spectacle of Socialist personalities like Huw T.Edwards and Ness Edwards falling on the neck of the wicked Tory Sir David, or the touching scene of homage when the Welsh local authorities licked his boots at Shrewsbury.

Our duty, nevertheless, is clear. It is to point out that these concessions add up to precisely nothing. It is to remind all who fight for Wales that an experienced campaigner is never more dangerous than when he gives ground.

There is, of course, a feeling of relief in the threatened communities. But the English Army may yet move into Llŷn and it was no love for the Welsh farmer that lifted the threat to Tywi. Capital expenditure cuts were the official excuse. And in both areas one suspects a Tory plot to woo the agricultural vote. Even the Cardiff gutter press came out against the Llŷn seizure, thereby provoking a doubt that this monstrous scheme was really intended to go through in one piece. This would be in complete accordance with Tory deceit and hypocrisy at its most accomplished.

The English Tory crimes against the people can never be forgiven because of this squirming and scheming. We are not going to be fooled by Sir David Maxwell-Fyfe.

One clear lesson emerges from these events. We will get nothing we are not prepared to fight for. If the Civil Service juggles with a few offices and appointments at Cardiff and Aberystwyth, there is still no responsibility in Wales.

As for our land and prosperity, the miners have already begun to show fight. And what did the trick in Tywi? Pretty speeches? Or the crudely-daubed slogans on the walls of Llandovery calling on Rebecca to ride again, as she did a century ago, to rid the land of oppression?

What has saved the Llŷn smallholders for a space? Greasy Tory benevolence? Or the memory of Saunders Lewis's act of incendiary defiance in 1936 and the knowledge that any aggression there would be a challenge that the manhood of re-arising Wales would meet in no uncertain manner?

English concessions and Welsh compromise are all part of a movement to prolong English exploitation of Wales. But it comes too late.

The Welsh Republican (April-May 1952)

The English Monarchy

Symbol of Welsh Subjection

WHY ARE WELSH Republicans so Republican? What have they got against the English crown as such? All true patriots will know the answer. Those who can remember the days (not long ago) when news reels showing English royalty were booed off the screens of cinemas up and down the Valleys will know too. But a lot of filth has poured from the sewers of Fleet Street since then, and arguments in favour of this alien monarchy have found favour with some people in Wales.

First there is the Political Argument: the Crown as the symbol of 'Empire Unity'. In other words, the symbol of exploitation of defenceless races, military heroism of the Ismaili brand, and, underlying all, the financial ramifications of the City of London. Wales can have no part in this 'Unity' of flies in a cobweb. A clean break must be made.

Then there is the Social Argument: the Crown as the symbol of 'National Stability'. First question: Whose Nation? And wouldn't it be truer to say that the Crown is the fount of flunkeyism, snobbery, debutantism, 'honours', and all other such highly coloured sauces as disguise the stinking fish of England's social decadence? What has Wales, the People's Nation, to do with all this mummery?

More recently there has been the Psychological Argument. We are asked to swallow the political and social implications of the Crown for its 'deeper values in these days of insecurity' and so forth. This newest argument is least relevant of all to Wales, quite apart from the way Royalist mysticism sometimes verges on the blasphemous. Wales has no need of reassurance from a set of jewelled baubles and newsreel puppets. She stands firm on the rock of National Popular Accomplishment. We are not the servile Cockneys who blazon 'Poor but Loyal' across their slums for a royal occasion. Wales was a proud nation before the Saxon and his kings had shambled up from the slime of their swamps. And the Republic that is to come will stand secure on the achievements of the Welsh People when history has swept the tinsel trappings of English Monarchy into the gutter.

The Welsh Republican (August-September 1952)

The Saga of Welsh Resistance

To say that Wales has long ceased to offer any effective resistance to English oppression is a lie against which the very earth and stones of Wales cry out! 'Effective resistance' has only one meaning – armed resistance, and despite the academic quislings and prostituted pedagogues who are always eager to distort or ignore the truth, the history of Wales may be written as the saga of one long struggle of the Welsh people against English oppression and exploitation – the longest continuous struggle of any nation against an aggressor.

In this struggle there have been many changes of fortune between the dateless, unrecorded beginning and the present mustering of new forces but, throughout, the spirit of Wales remained unconquerable. When, in 1282, Prince Llywelyn lay dead, it seemed that the first long battle was over. But no one who has stood within the massive walls of Caerffili or any other Welsh castle can fail to respond to the atmosphere of hemmed-in oppression that must have been the daily lot of the conquerors' garrisons. Nor were these 'conquerors' English; they were an international, French-speaking aristocracy with whom our own princes were soon on equal terms. The English crept in their wake, carpet-baggers and hucksters, a race of shopkeepers then as ever.

But the tragedy of 1282 was, in any case, temporary; the early years of the fifteenth century witnessed the triumphant re-establishment of the Welsh State under King Owain Glyn Dŵr. And, later in the century, the grandsons of Glyn Dŵr's soldiers marched with the Welshman Henry Tudor to Bosworth Field, where they sought, by setting their leader on the throne of England, to reassert the independence of their nation.

Like all Welsh careerists, however, ancient and modern, with their eyes on London, Henry Tudor forgot Wales, and his renegade dynasty lured first the Welsh aristocracy, and then, with the so-called Act of Union, the Welsh middle classes, from their loyalty to Wales.

There remained the common people, the Rock upon which the modern Welsh Nation is built. Without leaders, without allies, the people patiently reorganized over the centuries; some took to the hills as brigands, some to the seas as pirates, preying on the fat English merchants and the renegade Welsh aristocrats. Others fought against the English alongside their fellow-Celts in Ireland. But the main effort consisted in perfecting a self-contained national community with its own language and discipline under the very eyes of the English. This community in time came to be centred on the chapel, the focus of resistance to landlord and squire, parson and bishop. The might of the English Church, 'the Tory Party on its knees', and the English State were effectively set at nought, the Welsh people learned democracy and self-respect, decency and discipline, so that when the Industrial Revolution came, the Welsh proletariat were already well-trained and thoughtful, able to resist from the first the new form of English exploitation.

A series of small localized risings against the new exploitation culminated, in 1831, in a larger rebellion in the Merthyr area which gave to Wales one of her great heroes and martyrs, Dic Penderyn. Following the suppression of this rebellion by English troops, the Welsh workers re-formed and re-armed underground in a movement known as the 'Scotch Cattle' because it scotched all blacklegging and treachery to the Welsh workers' cause. In 1839 the Welshmen again rebelled, this time throughout the whole industrial area of the South, and scarcely had this insurrection been put down by English troops than the whole of West Wales rose in guerrilla warfare against English 'justice', led by the mysterious 'Rebecca' who was never caught and remains one of the great unknowns of Welsh history.

And now we are within living memory. Old people still survive from the Tithe Wars, when Queen Victoria's Redcoats poured into North Wales to defend the landlord and parson against the rage of the Welsh country-dwellers. In the South, the long series of strikes and riots are too well remembered to need mention. In two world wars the colliers struck in defiance of the might of England, and in some Welsh districts conscription was enforced only after pitched battles with the police. Conscientious objection even became a weapon in the struggle.

But conscientious action was soon to follow. Saunders Lewis and his comrades struck at the English Air Force in 1936, and their burning of the aerodrome marked a new phase in the struggle. In the 1930s England made Wales a Belsen of TB, dust disease, starvation and the Means Test. But in 1939 many Welshmen volunteered and fought fiercely against what was a still greater tyranny. But they returned to a Wales still denied her freedom, and in 1952 the new restlessness led to an angry gesture of protest when the eve of the English Queen's visit to mid-Wales was marked by a bomb explosion under the Elan Pipeline.

Wales has seen the darkest hours before the dawn. To the struggles of the future, Welshmen look forward in the light of a glorious past, and in the full confidence of victory.

The Welsh Republican (February-March 1953)

We Speak in the Name of Wales

IN WHOSE NAME do we Welsh Republicans speak? Who are the 'great men', the leading figures who inspire our policies? These are some of the most frequent questions we are asked on the street corners, in the pubs, on the seaside proms in summer, wherever we take the message of Welsh freedom. The answer is simple: we speak in the name of Wales and her people.

For the time is coming when the people of Wales will arise and demand their rights. And take them. This is not wishful thinking. It is based on facts as unchallenge-able as Snowdon and as hard as anthracite. We do not deal in decayed and discredited doctrines.

And because it is on these facts we stand, we face the future of Wales with confidence. Because it is the unconquerable soul of the Welsh people that we trust we do not need to tout for the favours of the great. What better off is Wales for the energy and eloquence of Lloyd George or the brilliance and bounce of Aneurin Bevan?

No, it is to the plain people we speak, and from whom we take inspiration: the plain people who marched with John Frost to Newport or rode out with Rebecca against oppression, the country folk who for a generation fought the Tithe Wars against Queen Victoria's redcoats, the collier who faced Churchill's bloody bayonets and the women who kept house and family, yes and nation, together while the Christian gentlemen of England garrotted them with the Means Test.

Under the uneasy swell of this moment of calm and the surface currents of compromise, the deep tides of history are flowing fast. In the coming onset there is no place for the cynic or the doubter.

The Welsh people is one. One nation, one achievement, one corporate act of faith in the dignity of man, one voice that will never be silenced, testifying to the eternal values of Justice and Freedom.

Once there was a Labour Party with fair promises for a nation that trusted them. But they no longer see Wales. They see the 'Industrial Proletariat' whom they think they can keep sweet indefinitely with a few crumbs of concession; they see 'the backward Welsh-speaking peasantry' who must be brought to sense by sharp measures. The reality they do not see.

Once there was a Liberal Party that won the support of all Wales, and sold it in the markets of Mammon.

The others, the Tories, have never seen Wales at all. Dimly they discern 'a problem', and tinker with it like a monkey trying to mend a machine.

Even many who call for Home Rule do not see Wales as one. To them the language is everything, the people nothing.

As Welsh Republicans we take none of these easy ways out, these broad roads to destruction. We speak across all false divisions within the nation. Whether the Welshman spends his Sunday in the chapel or the club, the land of Wales is his and his alone.

There is one inheritance, and one duty. That is the message, that is the task of the Welsh Republican Movement.

Editorial, *The Welsh Republican* (April-May 1953)

Queen Elizabeth II of England

THE APPEARANCE of this number of *The Welsh Republican* coincides with the crowning of Queen Elizabeth II of England. This is not an event of any great historical importance, and has no relevance at all to Wales, but as it is receiving a certain amount of attention in the Press, we would be failing in our duty if we offered no comment.

The whole ceremonial sums up to perfection the main tendencies in English society. Royalty is the ritual expression of Toryism at home and Imperialism abroad. Wales, on the other hand, has always upheld Socialism as opposed to Toryism, and Nationalism as opposed to Imperialism. We uphold the right of the individual to a decent life and of the nation (any and every nation) to an independent existence. For unless the nation is free to order its own affairs, the individual's chance of a decent life is a thin one, as we in Wales know to our cost.

Here today then stand two nations, neighbours who could and should be good friends, but completely divorced in sentiment, for the one has followed evil courses and is rapidly harvesting the dire consequences. The other, our own, has never coveted an inch of any other people's land or a penny of other people's money. It may be that we too are soon to harvest the consequences.

When one nation cherishes what another despises, it is useless to think of them as one unit. It would be folly to persist in a 'Union' which was imposed unilaterally by force and fraud, and which has never had any reality even on the football field. It would be criminal to acquiesce in the disastrous economic consequences of this 'Union' which have left such scars on our land. And this Coronation, at which the Standard of Wales will be carried in Westminster Abbey by the chairman of the Midland Bank will, we hope, be the last opportunity which anyone will have of hailing an English Monarch as sovereign of Wales.

Editorial, *The Welsh Republican* (June-July 1953)

'An Old and Haughty Nation Proud in Arms'

Our Duty – Defiance, Our Destiny – Deliverance

MANY SHADOWS have drifted across the hills of Wales and the people that holds them – the eagles of Rome, the ravens of the North, the vultures of London. But always we have stood firm. The Welsh people are, and the Welsh people shall be. Two thousand years of history cannot be shaken off like a dream, or analysed away as a meaningless fable. Much of that history is dim and distant now, many of its great figures mere names. But what names! Rhodri and Cadwaladr, Hywel and Llywelyn, Owain Glyn Dŵr and Owain of the Red Hand. Such names as we are proud to give our sons, and with a right instinct, for these were our fathers who fought to preserve the inheritance which we in turn must pass on to our children.

That inheritance is the land of Wales in all her stern beauty, with all the wealth of opportunity that the riches of her soil provide, her fish-crammed seas and sheep-crowded mountains, valleys flowing with milk, rocks bursting with coal, ports teeming with trade. All this at our feet, ours by right of birth. And all this in pawn, the cranes rusting over the empty quays, the waters gathering in sealed-off seams, the drip of rain in silent quarries.

But never the despair gathering in the heart or the rust

in the brain. The great furnaces may be drawn, the proud chimneys fallen, the viaducts sold for scrap. Dowlais and Landore are deserts of sulphur and slag, but there is one fire that has never been slaked, one aspiration that has never been brought low, one crop that has never been blighted. That fire is the Welsh passion for a just society. That aspiration is the Welsh demand for a free people, that harvest must be the prosperity and security of our children, for which the Welsh people have fought since before the dawn of written history.

For it was the Welsh people who took up the sword of their fallen princes, it was the Welsh people who kept in their hearts the wisdom of the old, abolished laws, it was the Welsh people who kept warm and living the songs that have inspired the longest resistance that history knows.

If all this were mere mist and memory, there would be no Welsh Republican Movement today, you would not be reading these words. But it is so, and we ask you to think it over. If you think that the history of which we speak ended too long ago to matter, consider the words of the scholar who told the Welsh Church Congress this year that the reason why Wales deserted the Church in the past two centuries 'was because the Church's official policy had become orientated to England'.

If you think that Industrialism and Socialism fall like an Iron Curtain between the past of which we speak and the problems of the present, remember that history knows no Iron Curtains, that a century and a half of militant resistance to English capitalism by the Welsh Worker in mine, quarry, farm, railway, dock and mill is a tale of endurance and achievement worthy of any nation and any age, a chronicle of courage and sacrifice which could not but be a continuation of what had gone before.

The Welsh Republican Movement reminds you, the citizen of Wales, the heir to great things, that the final stage of that struggle has yet to be faced, that there is no refuge in pious hopes, compromise politics or ostrich complacency. Our duty is to resist English aggression by any and every means. Our reward will be to enter into our inheritance.

The Welsh Republican (June-July 1953)

No More Blood for England

IT IS TAKEN for granted by many Welsh people that to pursue a policy of national independence by any and every means, as advocated by the Welsh Republican Movement, will inevitably end in bloodshed. This is not necessarily the case, but obviously the people who question display a profound mistrust of England's ability to yield to reason or acknowledge anybody's rights but her own. England's record is not encouraging in this respect, as Ireland and other countries know only too well. We need not contest this point. What we have to decide is whether we are morally justified in advocating policies which may lead to open English aggression against Welsh citizens and the resultant retaliation – the whole situation which the hostile questioner refers to as 'a river of blood'.

Obviously, a question put in these terms is not asked in cold blood. It is an emotional reaction pure and simple, an attempt to take refuge from facts in fine phrases. The Welsh connection with England has been one continuous blood tribute, and this is not an emotional phrase, it is a fact which can be supported by statistics and indeed, illustrated from the common knowledge of every one of us who lives and works in Wales.

Between the wars, who did not watch the Armistice Day Parades, the handful of survivors from some great offensive standing before a memorial inscribed with hundreds of names? Wales had more casualties than the

USA in the First World War. Figures for the Second World War are hard to come by. The English authorities know better this time. Sometimes the questioner who doesn't want a 'river of blood' is a survivor of one of these picnics. Here is a bitter irony which can only be explained when we understand that the facts are suppressed and distorted by the English press and the 'educational' propaganda racket in Wales.

There are other ways in which England levies her tribute of Welsh blood. Wales is a country of heavy industry, deliberately starved of all but a few of the safer and more secure types of work. In the mines the capitalist owners were notorious for their lack of consideration for the workers.

Senghennydd, Morfa, Cwm, Gresford, Garn Goch, Aber-carn – these are names at least as bloody as Arras or Mametz Wood. And who can forget the picture that appeared in a magazine a few years back, captioned 'The Beaten Team'? Here were eleven tough-looking young colliers who had won a football cup, and beneath the picture was printed what became of them: dead, diseased or crippled every one before he was 30. And in those days there was no pension for 'dust' victims.

And perhaps the questioner who doesn't want 'a river of blood' is himself a miner or at least lives in a mining community. Perhaps he has voted Socialist for 30 years and got a Labour Government off and on for five of them. It has never struck him that an independent Wales would not have waited for the ruin of a whole generation before taking over the pits, enforcing decent conditions and generous compensation. It doesn't strike him that an independent Wales would be a Socialist Wales, and that he'd get the government he wanted and not the government that Bournemouth wants. He's blathering about a 'river of blood' while all the time Welsh boys are getting killed keeping up the English Empire in parts of the world that have decided they don't want it.

The Welsh Republican Movement was formed largely by returned ex-servicemen whose knowledge of war is not academic. They do not want bloodshed between England and Wales, but if it comes, and with it national independence, then it will be a small price to pay to end the iniquitous tribute of subjection which has gone on too long.

The Welsh Republican (June-July 1953)

Welsh Patriot Pays the Price

PETER LEWIS, ex-merchant seaman, undergraduate and factory worker, and a well-known member of the Welsh Republican Movement in the Bangor area, was sentenced by Judge Oliver on May 14, 1953 at Caernarfon, to 18 months imprisonment, for having in his possession a number of detonators, in circumstances claimed to be 'suspicious'. According to reports in the English Press, the case for the prosecution rested to a large extent on references to the explosion at the Fron Aqueduct in October 1952, and to comments on the incident in *The Welsh Republican*. As a Welsh Republican, Lewis was treated as having been 'connected' with that action, although it was admitted that there was no evidence to show that he had taken part in it. He maintained throughout that he was not guilty.

Peter Lewis was convicted according to English Law, under an act specifically aimed at the maintenance of English state authority over Ireland, Scotland and Wales. The term of imprisonment was twice as severe as that previously meted out to Welsh Patriots who had burned the notorious Bombing School in Llŷn in 1936. It will also be remembered that the judge himself, at the time of this trial of Peter Lewis, was already the subject of criticism by Welsh MPs, and by a resolution of the Assembly of the Baptists' Union of Wales, for his attitude to the Welsh Language at the Merioneth Assizes.

The severity of the sentence brought immediate public comment. The President of the Welsh Party, Mr.Gwynfor Evans, widely respected as a Patriot and a convinced Pacifist, and leader of Welsh Nonconformity, speaking in a conference at Bangor, protested against the 'savage sentence' imposed on Lewis which was 'out of all proportion to the offence'. The speaker referred to a similar case in Cardiff when the accused was set free without sentence, although he had stated an intention of using explosives to attack the Birmingham Pipeline. The Welsh Party must express its indignation at the sentence, and should petition the English Home Secretary for Lewis's immediate release. Addressing a meeting in South Wales the previous day, Welsh Republican speakers condemned the sentence as being an attempt to intimidate Welsh opinion. Mr.Huw Davies emphasized that increasing English persecution of Welshmen for their political beliefs would not prevent the growth of nationalist discontent in Wales any more than similar policies had killed the Irish national movement, or the growth of Socialism in Wales. At the time of going to press it is understood that Peter Lewis has lodged an appeal against the sentence.

The Welsh Republican (June-July 1953)

A Free and Independent People

WITH THIS NUMBER of *The Welsh Republican* we begin our fourth volume. During the last three years we have had the satisfaction of seeing a gradual transformation in the Welsh scene, and a retrospective glance may help us to understand the nature of this change and to appreciate the pattern of the future.

The Welsh Republican Movement took official shape in the immediate post-war period, when two outstanding facts forced themselves on the consciousness of all who were ready to work for Wales. The most important of these facts was the abandonment by the Labour Party of a Welsh Home Rule Policy. This represented a betrayal of one of the fundamental doctrines of Socialism by an organization which since 1945 has been dazzled by the prospect of becoming the second party in the English state. Gradually there has developed in the party a difference of opinion which in the course of time will amount to an open schism: the difference between the purblind careerists who wish to maintain the exploitation of Welsh resources and labour by English Imperialism and on the other hand the genuine Socialists and patriots who believe in a Free Wales.

The other dominating feature of the Welsh scene was the hesitancy and general middle-class inadequacy of the established Nationalist organization, Plaid Cymru.

Many Welshmen who had returned from a World War

or had grown up in the harsh realities of the new age could align themselves neither with the musty mixture of doctrinaire Marxism and Imperialist apologetics that characterized the Labour Party, nor with the pacifism of the Blaid. They chose instead the Welsh Republican Movement, proclaiming the interdependence of National Self-Government and Social Justice, and the advisability, to say the least, of not limiting policies in pursuit of these fundamental ends to measures suited to the convenience of the English State.

We have had our reward. The tempo has quickened. Under the stimulus of competition both Plaid Cymru and the Welsh Labour Movement have improved out of all recognition while the renegades have been driven to hysterical excesses of self-justification that only further reveal their unfathomable baseness.

Meanwhile the Welsh Republicans drive forward. There is no need to remind our readers of the numerous occasions on which a hostile press has been reluctantly compelled to devote its headlines to the activities of the forces working for Welsh Independence. Welsh Republican literature has permeated the whole community. Our public meetings have been notable and our speakers everywhere favourably received. Not concerned with grinding any axe but the one that will be laid to the roots of English Rule, the Movement gains in strength and influence. The future beckons the Free and Independent Welsh people.

Editorial, *The Welsh Republican* (August-September 1953)

Against Imperialism

THOSE WHO SEEK to influence opinion and so control events must justify themselves by cogent social diagnosis and accurate historical analysis. The Welsh Republican Movement alone can claim an all-inclusive appraisal of the Welsh scene today, unrestricted by doctrinaire pedantry or post-sectarian hangovers. We now give detailed attention to a spectacular failure of analysis by an outstanding Welshman. Aneurin Bevan, addressing the National Committee of the Chinese People's Consultative Conference, said: 'The struggle takes various forms because it is fought under different historical conditions. These conditions do not determine the ultimate objectives of socialism, but they do influence the ways in which they are achieved and also the pace of the change. There is no universal recipe for social progress. If there were, our task would be easy. There are two elements always present in every political situation: the character of the goals we set ourselves, and the framework of tradition in which they must be pursued. If we fight for our objectives without regard to the national and traditional inheritance then we are in danger of cutting ourselves off from the attitude of the masses whose representatives we are'.

With this realistic appraisal of the world picture we fully agree. It explains, for instance, why Communism may be the right thing for China, but the wrong thing for

Wales. Within limits he has justified his analysis, as his whole career has proved. But the limits are sharp and fatal. For he goes on: 'The second respect in which we differ from you is that the struggles which you have waged are at the same time a struggle for national independence against imperialism. This has the effect of supercharging the social struggle with the emotions derived from national self-consciousness and the yearning for liberation. You are therefore possessed of an emotional dynamic which is not present with us'.

Mr.Bevan comes from the Tops of the Valleys. It is hard to believe that even in China he can have forgotten the difference between the exploitation of the English worker and the wholesale rape and ruin of that region where the epic desolation of Dowlais, the generation of despair that engulfed Blaina and Bryn-mawr, seal the utter damnation before God and man of the Gentlemen of England.

No national struggle against foreign imperialism indeed! No emotional dynamic! Mr.Bevan has not only strayed into the very dead-end described in the first quotation above, he has undermined the whole 'raison d'être', the 'pace' and power of 'Bevanite' socialism. He has in effect disproved his own existence.

This is not good enough. He, and the whole Labour Movement, must learn (the hard way if necessary) that only by fusing the ancient national aspirations of the Welsh people with their equally deep-rooted passion for social justice will any progress out of the present stagnation be possible.

Mr.Bevan may be content with the limits he has set himself, content 'to end up an elderly burlesque of an agitator living in Chelsea'. We who do not live in Chelsea can set no limits to the efforts and sacrifices necessary to redeem Wales from the filthy clutches of foreign imperialism.

Editorial, *The Welsh Republican* (October-November 1954)

The Better Government of Wales

Labour MP's Patriotic Stand

A bill for the better government of Wales: this is the title of a measure presented to the English Parliament by Mr.S.O.Davies. It is a sign of the times.

Never since before the First World War has such a Bill been promoted at Westminster.

Then it was the work of an undaunted representative of the old Welsh Radicalism, E.T.John, who refused to follow the devious paths of Lloyd George. Today, after two wars and a depression (and that was the real war which England waged on our country), it is that gallant veteran, the Labour and Home Rule MP for Merthyr Tydfil, the successor of Keir Hardie in more senses than one, who takes up the cause of Wales.

His measure is supported by five other Welsh Socialists and a similar number of Scottish Socialists. This support is significant and encouraging. The Welsh members between them represent no less than four out of our thirteen counties; and in Mr.Peter Freeman and Mr.Davies himself, our third and fifth most populous urban authorities.

The adherence of Mr.Freeman of Newport is particularly welcome. For Newport houses a nasty knot of snobs and renegades to whom the very existence of Wales is anathema. How they must be gibbering and gnashing their

S.O.Davies, Western Mail and Echo Ltd, 1970

gums at the fine independent stand of their MP.

Some might demur at the support of Scottish members being sought for the Bill. We do not. The two countries united in the strength of their Celtic and Socialist tradition will have to pull together to win the freedom of which they have been deprived, and this is a promising and imaginative start.

Mr.Davies has not gone outside the ranks of Labour for his parliamentary backing, and in this he has shown a sound instinct, for the liberation of Wales is the concern of her working people. Nevertheless, now is the time for Welsh Liberals also to remember their promises. We shall watch them with interest.

Indeed, we look forward to being pleasantly surprised by what many of our representatives will have to say. Even those who have not been prominently identified with the Home Rule wing of Labour, and perhaps too those even further to the right, will emerge with their reputations enhanced and a clearer conception of their duty.

But there are also those from whom we can expect nothing but the worst. Already we can sniff the malodorous cauldrons of lies and sneers brewing in the thieves' kitchens of apostasy and careerism.

We warn these perjured wretches that their 'arguments' against their country will be carefully noted.

The time will come when the Welsh people will stuff these misbegotten sophistries down the throats of those who have cheated them of their birthright.

For in the last resort, it is on the organized will of her people that Wales will establish her independence. The Bill for the Better Government of Wales is only one manifestation of our renewed strength and awareness. We urge every Welsh citizen, every Trade Union Branch, Miners' Lodge, and Co-operative Society to instruct their representatives to vote for this Bill, and to continue the struggle in Parliament and in the country by means of the massive economic strength and high degree of political awareness which are the irresistible weapons of the Welsh people.

Mr.S.O.Davies is a true Socialist who can neither be bullied nor bought. He alone of the Welsh MPs voted against German rearmament. In doing so he fulfilled his mandate as a miners' representative. The other Welsh miners' MPs pocketed the Union's money and ignored the Union's precise instructions. He alone of the Welsh MPs refused to be a party to the sickening Tory propaganda demonstration which marked Churchill's birthday, when even Aneurin Bevan went soft. Churchill's bloody record in Wales makes it a matter of humiliation to us that any Welsh MP whatever was involved in this Jamboree. The MPs of Tonypandy and Llanelli, where the worst outrages occurred, had no qualms about signing Churchill's birthday book. It is no accident that 'representatives' of this calibre are also among the loudest assailants of Welsh Independence. They signed their manhood away a long time ago. But Mr.S.O.Davies's example is a promise of regeneration for Welsh Labour.

The Welsh Republican (February-March 1955)

Welsh Wizards Who Went Wrong

A FEW MILES apart along the coast of Llŷn are the stone memorials that mark the birthplace of T.E.Lawrence and the grave of Lloyd George. A strange parallelism is at once apparent in the lives of these two commanding figures, who both turned their backs on Wales to seek distinction in 'wider fields' and who both paid a terrible price for their apostasy.

Yet neither was an ordinary shop-soiled careerist, on sale to the highest bidder, like so many Welsh public figures of our own day. Their personalities and achievements have still the power to arouse passionate controversy, as the widespread interest in the latest books about them has amply shown.*

Lawrence's Welsh origins and background have been ignored and belittled by his family and his biographers in a rather dated Imperialist manner. Lawrence, we were once told, took advantage of 'the accident of his having been born in Wales' to qualify for a scholarship at Jesus College, Oxford, which was the basis of his career. Lawrence himself does not seem to have been anxious to recall that his family came from Talsarnau and that his grandfather, 'Lawrence bach', was a leading figure in the typically Welsh cultural life of a Snowdonian village. Yet he managed to transcend the pathetic semi-detached snobbery which usually inspires such an attitude.

After visiting the Middle East as an archaeologist he

was caught up in that addiction to the Arabs which is one of the odder traits of the English character – a mixture of bogus romanticism and cynical imperialist intrigue typical of the sludgy Teutonic mind. (It eventually fitted in with the slum anti-semitism of the monumentally witless Bevin to harass the triumphant nationalism of Israel – with little effect.)

Lawrence, who while still an undergraduate had totally disproved certain archaeological theories expounded by the most senior professors, had just the sort of brilliance to be captivated by the Arab cause. Yet it was to their nationalist feeling that he appealed, quite against the grain of their strongly cosmopolitan religion. And he fought in the desert a guerrilla campaign that would not have disgraced his forebears who must have struck and dodged with Owain Glyn Dŵr in the wet woods of Gwynedd.

And then England, having empowered him to make certain promises to the Arabs, ratted on them as usual. The delusions of a decadent culture had seduced Lawrence's intellect, but could not corrupt the stubbornness and integrity expressed in his craggy North Welsh features. He withdrew into his pride, into the solace of word-spinning, into a twisted enigmatic private life of disguise and solitude. His death was a drab statistic – the end of any lout with a big motor-bike.

We turn now to Lloyd George: here, too, the brilliant, precocious genius, 'the boy alderman', the genuine idealism expressed in the achievements of the young Radical Chancellor. Here, too, the tragic choice of the wrong allegiance. Both men achieved honour and glory in the First World War, and as soon as it was over, both were disowned, chucked on the scrap-heap together, their talents never made use of for the rest of their lives. Both, like the tragic victims of Greek Drama, retained to the end a dimension of greatness in the midst of humiliation. They desired to atone for the consequences of their actions but the unrelenting facts withheld the means. In characters of such stature and such supreme gifts the doom of those who choose to desert Wales is writ large for the warning and edification – and maybe the purification – of which our country stands in need.

*A review of *Tempestuous Journey: Life of Lloyd George* by Frank Owen and *T.E.Lawrence* by Richard Aldington.

The Welsh Republican (February-March 1955)

The Transfer of Sovereignty

THE PRESENTATION by Mr.S.O.Davies MP of a Home Rule Bill in the English Parliament has completely changed the situation in Wales. The voting on the Bill is irrelevant (and in many cases, as shameful) as the speeches of its assailants.

What matters is that the first rounds have been fired in a close encounter with the enemy. In naval gunnery a straddle counts as a hit and those effective ranging shots, discharged with great skill by Mr.Davies and his supporters, must herald salvo after salvo, dead on the target until the English flag is finally hauled down in Wales.

It may seem we have gained nothing more than the half-promise of a Royal Commission. But even these monstrous creations have their uses. Were there not once certain Blue Books? A Royal Commission may well make great advances in the way of executive and even judicial devolution. These we would regard not as hard-won concessions, or gracious gifts, but as instalments in the transfer of sovereignty. They must not only be demanded, but once obtained, made the basis for further enlargements of Welsh power. We recollect how even the Council for Wales must have seriously embarrassed its creators by certain of its recommendations.

Central to our whole case is the belief that responsibility, however limited, is an 'appetite that grows with what it feeds on'. 'Concessions' will be seized and used. Intransigence on the other hand will only lead to 'extremism' taking the initiative in Wales. The forces of Welsh freedom, long hindered, deceived and scattered, are on the march, and so deployed that victory is inevitable.

The Welsh Republican (April-May, 1955)

Wales Defies the Tories

When Will We Ever Learn?

ONCE AGAIN a general election to the Parliament of Westminster has brought its urgent lesson to the people of Wales.

Wales has returned 27 Labour representatives out of 36. Seventy-five per cent is an overwhelming proportion for one party to secure in any country. Yet Wales is doomed to all the evils of Tory rule.

Our people have shown that their minds are made up and that they stand firmly by the choice which has been theirs throughout the years. There is not the slightest change in the pattern of Welsh representation since 1951 and indeed, where the advance of Labour has been most recent and most contested, Socialist candidates were returned with increased majorities.

The Welsh people are to be congratulated on the high degree of responsibility and maturity they have once again shown. The seductions of 'Tory prosperity' and the lies of the London press have not prevailed against the determinations of our country to build a society based on social justice and equality of opportunity.

But there is a black side to the picture also. Wales is politically tied to a country which has time and again declared itself a victim of its bad history and unfortunate traditions. Against the reaction-sodden rural areas and snob-ridden suburbs of England, the handful of Welsh Labour men at Westminster will contend in vain. England has swung further and further to the right since 1945, and has by the fatal choice of 1955 opted for social snobbery, economic anarchy and political extinction – as a puppet state of the Hydrogen Maniacs of America.

We refuse to believe that the Welsh people will acquiesce much longer in this dismal state of affairs. In fact we could claim that Wales by continuing to keep the Red Flag of Socialism flying when it is being hauled down everywhere else has already, in effect, declared her independence – and is even now assuming some of the historic and world-wide responsibilities which will one day be hers.

Wales can only assume this proud position, however, can only do justice to her citizens and her ideals, if to her lively social conscience she adds a stiffening of stern national self-respect. The Welsh Republican Movement has proclaimed that only by uniting these two great streams of energy can the dams of reaction and imperialism be broken. And that time is soon to be. There are signs of it on every hand. Plaid Cymru's intervention on a wider scale than ever before has on the whole paid off, and in the Labour Party itself a new attitude to Welsh affairs is emerging and must ultimately triumph.

But these turbulent floods must be negotiated with skill if the boat is not to be capsized. And while Plaid Cymru is to be congratulated on its considerable advance in electoral favour, and on such crusaders in its ranks as Chris Rees, fighting an election from jail, its record on the whole suggests that its appeal is to the right rather than to the left. There is nothing particularly sinister in this but it suggests that the Blaid will never become a force in the populous industrial districts of Wales, and more seriously, that many on the left will turn their back on cultural and linguistic traditions, which although dear to us all, may well come to be associated with political reaction. (The empty chapels show that this has already happened to some extent.)

Despite a statesmanlike appeal by the Editor of *Y Faner* before the election, Plaid Cymru opposed not only enemies of Home Rule, which was their obvious job, but also its supporters. One unfortunate result of this seems to be that a Home Ruler was deprived of the seat in Carmarthen which continues to be occupied by the meaningless figure of Sir Rhys Hopkin Morris. While certain unspeakable enemies of Wales went unopposed by Plaid Cymru in the South, Labour in Gwynedd was subject to an out-and-out assault. One of the more absurd reactionary candidates in that province was reported as saying, 'If you can't vote for me, vote for the nationalist'. And a Labour spokesman seems to have been near the mark when he said, 'The Blaid hates Labour more than they love Wales'.

The inter-party agreement which was the sole support of Plaid Cymru's pup, the Parliament for Wales Campaign, has now been liquidated by the Blaid, and as if to prove that Socialism has come to stay in Gwynedd as in the rest of Wales as the expression of our national radical tradition, Lady Megan Lloyd George has made the realistic move of joining the Labour Party.

There is no room for complacency anywhere. There never is, least of all in Wales, where it is a sort of endemic disease. Under the apathy and decreased polling figures of the 1955 election, mighty currents of history are moving. Wales must be ready to catch the tide 'which taken at the flood leads on to fortune'.

The Welsh Republican (June-July 1955)

Labour's Next Step

'THE MARVELLOUS GROWTH of the Socialist movement in Wales is a phenomenon which has not yet been satisfactorily explained.'

These words remain almost as true today as when Keir Hardie first wrote them in 1907. The special relation of Socialism to the national requirements of Wales, the special status of the Labour Movement as the contemporary expression of the historically evolved attitudes of the Welsh in politics, economics and social philosophy generally – these are matters which remain inadequately covered by research, and imperfectly apprehended by unbending nationalists and doctrinaire socialists alike.

Its overwhelming electoral predominance places Welsh Labour in a different category not only from its rivals in Wales, but from Labour in the other countries of these islands, and perhaps in most other countries as well. We are, in fact, confronted by a situation where quantitative predominance has led to qualitative change. To the nationalist, the present state of affairs is a monstrous and largely inexplicable aberration, and it is to be feared that the attitude of many Socialists to the application of Socialism to the problems of Wales is equally devoid of understanding. As we have said, much research will be necessary to uncover the processes whereby, as Labour came to represent more and more of Wales, it found itself with less and less of a Welsh policy, and finally, by the early 1950s, with 75% of the Welsh parliamentary representation, and no Welsh policy at all.

In this marshy territory, eschewed by Swyddfa'r Blaid and Transport House alike, we must endeavour to trace the lines of our national political development. For if the Labour Movement is indeed the expression of our national attitudes in contemporary terms, the weaknesses of Labour's various Welsh policies are in effect the weaknesses of the nation. We opened this survey with a quotation from an article written by Keir Hardie in 1907. In that article he relates the rapid growth of Socialism in Wales to the historically evolved economic and social patterns of Welsh life, and the 'primitive communism' of Welsh custom until a comparatively late period.

'Socialism,' he wrote, 'is spreading like a prairie fire in Wales today because it touches a familiar chord in the heart of the people and awakens a dormant strain in their lives. The true Celt longs for fraternity and beauty, and in Socialism he sees both.'

This interpretation of our history, as we may imagine, conflicted with the vested interests of many who then, as now, tried to claim a monopoly of the 'Welsh way of life' for various sectarian and reactionary ends. Under fire from such 'Nationalists' as D.A.Thomas and Sir Alfred Mond, Hardie uttered this historic declaration:

'Men and women of Dowlais!... The Nationalist Party I have in mind is this: the people of Wales fighting to recover possession of the land of Wales, the working class of Wales acquiring possession of the mines, of the furnaces, and the railways, of the great public works generally, and working these as comrades, not for the benefit of shareholders, but for the benefit of every man, woman and child within your borders. That is the kind of Nationalism I want to see brought about. And when that day comes, the Red Dragon will be emblazoned on the Red Flag of Socialism, the international emblem of the working class of the world.'

This magnificent statement, uttered on a spot made sacred by the blood of Dic Penderyn, at a time when Churchill's thugs were running amuck from Llanelli to Tonypandy, laid down once and for all the synthesis of national and international effort, of social and political independence, against which Labour's subsequent achievements and failures must be judged. The vicissitudes of war and depression through which Wales was to be dragged at the heels of the rulers of London and Birmingham, so soon after these lofty aims were laid before Welsh Labour, is a familiar story, and the ineffectual, academic nature of the Party's resolutions on Welsh Home Rule during that period is an accurate index of the demoralization which was then our lot. Towards the end of the late war, the publication of the first Interim Report of the Advisory Committee on Post-War Reconstruction in Wales, another landmark, gave an impressive basis for a constructive national policy. But, as the story of the first Labour Government was to show, it was now possible for many leading Socialists to deny that separate Welsh legislation was desirable or even permissible, and for others, with as much sincerity, to advocate a Five Point Policy for Wales, which has been the subject of polemic and recrimination ever since – and from which the present official Labour policy seems largely to derive. This policy we shall examine in detail in our next article.

The Welsh Republican (June-July 1955)

Here is a summary of the matter of 'Labour's Policy for Wales'. Then follows our comment, 'Labour's Achievement 1945-51'.

- 'The Labour Party claims to have shown a far more practical devotion to Welsh needs and a keener appreciation of Welsh needs than any other political party.' New industries were brought in, old ones modernized, the disabled looked after.
- The Agricultural Act of 1947, the Hill Farming Act of 1946, the Livestock Rearing Act and Marginal Land Production schemes helped farmers. Rural housing and amenities were improved. Rate equalization benefitted local authorities. National Insurance, the Health Service, the Industrial Injuries Act, Maternity and Child Welfare Services were established.
- Education was stimulated and the WJEC set up.
- Devolution took place in the Social Services, Education and Agriculture.
- Wales had its own White Paper on Government Action, Parliamentary time, and an Advisory Council.
- The Parliament for Wales Campaign proposes that outstanding problems be solved by the establishment of a Welsh Parliament with wide powers on the lines of Northern Ireland.
- This solution is 'a serious error in political thinking'.
- The prosperity of Wales is bound up with the prosperity of the United Kingdom as a whole.
- 'A Welsh parliament would be unable to resolve Welsh economic and social problems for these cannot be isolated from those of the UK as a whole.'

The overall policy of the Labour Party, simply by implementing a small measure of Socialism, helped Wales to recover from the dislocation of war and pre-war depression. This achievement, though welcome, is only impressive compared with the preceding squalor. The claims of Wales as a nation were laughed to scorn at Scarborough and the Labour Party conspired against separate political broadcasts for Wales in the 1955 Election. For Labour to claim sole credit for full employment is excessive. Wales is a rich country and prosperity should be our normal lot. Even so, migration continues, noticeably among technical and professional workers, who can be least spared, as also from the land. Rural Wales does not present the rosy picture claimed, as the reports of the Council for Wales in matters of housing amenities confirm. Anti-Welsh policies of War Office and Forestry Commission (cf. the 'Battle of Rhandir-mwyn'!) were unabated under Labour rule, and in some cases actively supported by Trade Unions.

No one questions the value of the Insurance and Health Services, but as the Labour Party admitted in the 1955 Election propaganda, there was much more need for these services in Wales (they do not attempt to think why!) and it is important to remember that these measures were sponsored and directed by Welshmen. Educational reform, too, was largely overdue and inevitable.

As for administrative devolution, this begs a great many questions, and its recognition really involves the anti-Welsh apologists in many deep contradictions. Neither White Paper, Council for Wales, nor Welsh Debate involves a single executive change. And yet it is claimed that they are 'significant'.

'It is easy to understand why Welshmen should seek to control their own affairs' (there is a damaging admission here, isn't there?) but the 'error in political thinking' surely is with those who consider the 'United Kingdom' as sacrosanct. We claim that the tie-up with England was indeed mainly responsible for the pre-war misery of Wales. Wales first returned a Socialist majority in the 1920s. Even if we had had only a subsidiary government in those years, is the faith of the policy-makers in Socialism so limited that they would deny that this would have effected some alleviation in our lot?

Here we face a conditioning limitation in official Labour thinking. These limitations have occurred before and it was the glory of people like Keir Hardie that they transcended them and proclaimed the duty of Socialists not to accept but to challenge and to admit no limits to their power to change circumstances.

We claim that there is a better status for Wales than that of a permanent minority at Westminster. The Parliament for Wales Campaign is open to serious criticism but it would not exist if Welsh Labour had done its duty. It is merely 'passing the buck' to blame the Tories. 'Where there is no vision, the people perish.'

To the complacent and parochial-English attitude which denies Wales any independent contacts with the rest of the world our policy-makers add a supine acquiescence in an economic status for Wales which is really one of ruthless exploitation by London and Birmingham. Wales is tied largely to primary production in electricity, coal, timber, steel and water. These are exported to English centres where the processing industries yield congenial jobs, fat pay packets, profits and rates. A flashy veneer of light industries on the Trading Estates will not disguise these brutal facts which Labour's Welsh Policy does not so much as mention.

While it may be true that a subsidiary parliament would have insufficient power to attract industry, the answer is not to reject the idea but to work through it to achieve as much control as possible over our own affairs. The duty of the Welsh Labour Movement is to work for the Welsh Socialist State.

The Welsh Republican (August-September 1955)

Distribution of Industry: A Welsh Parliament would not be able to exert any statutory powers over 'British' industry. The advantages of a single economy are illustrated by the connection between the Southern Ports and the English Midlands. Welsh control over national-ized industries is 'unrealistic'. Welsh Aviation doesn't pay. Welsh Railways would be impracticable. North Welsh electricity serves Merseyside. The Welsh coalfield is run at a loss. Separation would restrict capital expenditure and disrupt the Unions.

It seems more than probable that the tax yield from Wales is lower than the 'national' average.

Welsh local authorities are poorer than English. Therefore Wales could not afford separate social services.

Separation would involve duplication of legislation. Wales would gain no sense of unity. Industrial Wales would 'dominate' rural Wales, and 'weighting' of representation to avoid this would be undemocratic and lead to friction.

The arguments adduced by our Labour policy-makers

in favour of an integrated 'British' economy are uniformly unfortunate. The 'natural connection' between our Southern Ports and the English Midlands does not seem to be a paying proposition. As the Council for Wales Report makes clear, the Southern Ports are penalized by discriminating traffic rates. Welsh raw materials are sent by rail to English centres and the finished products exported from London and Liverpool – as indeed are the products manufactured in Wales by Development firms which are branches of concerns with Head Offices and export facilities in England. The 'natural relationship' of the Southern Ports is with the Southern Coalfield.

As for the 'realism of Welsh control of nationalized industries' it should not be beyond the ability of the movement which carried out the vast programmes of overall nationalization in the first place and is committed to more.

Welsh Aviation stands at least as good a chance of flourishing as Aer Lingus and Cambrian Airways, both of which are doing well.

The arguments against the separation of Welsh railways are vitiated from the outset by the very existence of the present set-up by which the whole of Wales is included in the Western Region except the important North Coast Line. Welsh Railways are separated, but not for the convenience of Wales. The example of the Anglo-Scottish Joint Rail Assessment Committee proves that separation is perfectly workable.

Our leaders appear to acquiesce in the state of affairs by which North Welsh Electricity 'serves' Merseyside. It should serve the quarries and kitchens of North Wales.

Coal, the foundation of our economy, can hardly be

dealt with in a summary manner, so we confine ourselves to making two points:

1. We fail to see how Wales could not attract capital to her rich coalfields, at least as easily as primitive Arab States can attract capital for their oil.
2. An independent marketing policy for Welsh coal would go far to transform the look of the unfavourable balance-sheet.

The suggestion that wages would go down and Unions be hampered in their work is pure fantasy, given the inevitable pressure of the miner's vote in a Welsh Parliament. We believe that the Unions would be able to look after themselves. The official leaders of Welsh Labour apparently do not!

The crux of the argument here appears to be the contention that Welsh tax yield is lower than the 'national' average. This is pure supposition and the fact that the Inland Revenue will not publish separate Welsh figures suggests quite the reverse. It is in any case quite impossible to drag fiscal arguments from the jungle of local government finances. If Welsh rate yield is low let us remember the vast concentration of derated industrial plant in Wales. 'Socialism', may we remind our leaders, 'is a matter of priorities' and the priority calls on revenue in Independent Socialist Wales will be very different from those of Imperialist England.

The 'separate social services' whose extra cost would fall on Wales exclusively, would of course be used exclusively in Wales and the costs would be in proportion, an elementary point which seems to have escaped notice.

'The range of activity of the proposed Welsh Parliament is so wide that membership of that body would have to become the main occupation at considerable cost of many leading people in Wales who might be more usefully employed in other ways than in the minutiae of detailed legislation.'

We quote this extraordinary sentence as an example of the sinister and undemocratic undertone which is apparent in many of these 'Socialist' arguments. As for the 'confusion' which would result from independent Welsh legislation, have our zealous 'internationalists' never heard of the wide range of reciprocal agreements on social services, labour regulations, taxes and customs which exist between so many European countries today?

With a final flourish we are confronted with the tattered *bwbach* of 'Welsh disunity'. This argument comes ill from those whose nationalization schemes furthered the splitting up of Wales. In any case in 1954 the Welsh local authorities voted overwhelmingly for Cardiff as the Capital of Wales. And in the last few years rural Wales has become almost as Socialist as industrial Wales. So where's the big split now?

The 'weighting' proposals of the Parliament for Wales campaign to obviate the 'domination of Glamorgan and Monmouth' may be rightly criticized as undemocratic, but Labour's own plan for Wales gives prominence to a non-elected body, as we shall see in our next article where we shall examine the five-point policy which has emerged from the arguments considered here.

The proposed five-point policy:

1. Economic Development

'Much more needs to be done to secure the prosperity of Wales.' Labour's programme includes measures to improve the efficiency of the fuel and power industries and to provide a balanced industrial structure, full employment and expanded factory buildings.

Investment programmes will be undertaken in coal, gas and electricity. Iron and steel will be re-nationalized. Grenfell and Remploy factories will receive special consideration.

2. Rural Wales

'Much remains to be done' – housing, water supply, sewerage, roads, gas and electricity. Labour will examine the recommendations of the Council for Wales in the light of 'Challenge to Britain'. Labour will ensure capital and credit facilities for farmers.

3. Cultural Life

Labour will assist in the preservation of the Welsh language and culture.

4. Administrative Devolution

Labour will 'consider the possibility' of further devolution in Agriculture and Education.

5. Parliamentary Arrangements

Labour proposes a Ministry for Welsh Affairs, extra time in Parliament for 'detailed and effective scrutiny' of legislation affecting Wales. 'A day might be set aside' for the discussion of the Council for Wales Report.

The Council for Wales will be made more representative and effective.

It will at once be apparent that Labour's proposed Five Point Programme for Wales consists largely of vague generalities and pious platitudes. In the first Point, for instance, there is nothing specifically Socialist apart from the re-nationalization of iron and steel. We reiterate the elementary point that an Independent Welsh Government would never have de-nationalized iron and steel in the first place, neither would the special factories for disabled workers be threatened.

While paying lip-service to the Council for Wales, the Labour Party refuses to endorse its recommendations outright, as they thoroughly merit. It will merely 'examine' them. As if the plight of rural Wales needed any further examination! As for the promise of further capital and facilities to farmers, Labour seems to be unaware of the criticisms, so widely publicized at the time of the 'Battle of Rhandir-mwyn', which the Agricultural Workers' Union made of the abuse of already existing facilities. It is no good promising financial help to the farmers without framing measures to make sure that the money actually goes into improving the land, not into the long stocking.

Labour can take credit for its sympathetic attitude to the *Ysgolion Cymraeg* [Welsh-medium schools] but certain Socialist-controlled Local Authorities earned themselves a bad name in the same matter. Here, Labour for the most part merely played the role of an onlooker. Not a hostile one, it is true, but if Labour had been true to its principles it would have been actively identified with this most important development. In any case, we hate to think what would have happened to Mesdames Wilkinson and Horsbrugh or anybody else who laid hostile hands on the *Ysgolion Cymraeg* once they started on their triumphal progress. This is not 1848.

Labour has not declared that it will reverse the unutterably stingy policy of the Tories towards helping the publication of Welsh books.

Neither has Labour declared that it will raise the Welsh language to a status of official parity with English. This is the one simple concrete act which in this day and age will do more than anything to help the language and culture of Wales. Instead we are fobbed off with patronizing generalities.

In admitting the principle of administrative devolution, even to the extent of a few fiddling changes of address, the Labour Party involves itself in a fundamental inconsistency. How defensible is it to organize the Ministries on national lines and leave the economic basis of the country on the non-national, ad-hoc, any-old-lines which are a legacy from the days of competitive chaos? We would go further. The Government departments which are, or are to be 'devolved', are 'spending' departments – Social Services, Education, Agricultural subsidies etc., in which Wales is the recipient of benefits. But the Board of Trade, Inland Revenue, Customs and Excise – not to speak of the nationalized industries – do not acknowledge Wales, for here Wales is the contributor! What Wales receives from the bounty of London is thus easily established. What Wales pays in for all this is not officially recognized or acknowledged and remains difficult to assess. This is as clever a stroke of psychological warfare as was ever devised. Our Labour policy-makers do not appear to have realized this point.

These consist of a Minister for Welsh Affairs with a seat in the Cabinet, something like a Welsh Grand

Committee on Scottish lines, more parliamentary time for Welsh Affairs and a revision of the Council of Wales to make it 'more representative and effective'. In other words a vague approximation to Scottish arrangements. Our internationally-minded leaders appear to be unaware of the uproar from Scotland that from time to time hits the headlines. Neither do they condescend to tell us whether the Minister will have a Welsh Secretariat.

As for the Council for Wales, its very existence must trouble our anti-Home Rule MPs considerably, for it is a concrete acknowledgement that Westminster is incapable of dealing with Welsh problems. When questioned about the reorganization of the Council, Jim Griffiths said that he did not visualize it as an elected body. It would be, in his own words, 'undemocratic'. But it also proposed to make the Council 'effective'. It is difficult to see how this can be done without giving it some executive authority. It is therefore open to exactly the same objections as Labour itself makes against the suggested 'Second Chamber' which was one of the tentative proposals of the Parliament for Wales Campaign.

The Welsh Policy of the Labour Party is meaningless and worthless. There is a call for Labour rethinking. Nowhere is it more urgently needed than in Wales. In our next article we shall try to indicate a real Socialist policy for our country, which will be worthy of Labour's honoured place in Welsh history.

The Welsh Republican (December 1955-January 1956)

As a supplementary to Labour's Five Point Policy for Wales (which as we have shown in previous articles, is

James Griffiths

not policy at all), Jim Griffiths has in the press and Parliament added a Sixth Point – Local Government Reform. Despite its obvious limitations, this is a much more promising springboard for further advance, and Mr.Ness Edwards, hitherto a resolute opponent of the claims of Wales, has recently suggested an elected body of fifty which would represent local authorities in an assembly which would be 'less than a Parliament and more than a County Council'. Labour has thus by a great effort at last caught up with proposals similar in spirit but not in detail, made by Lloyd George and Tom Ellis in the 1890s!

However, if Labour in Wales were alive to its responsibilities, if for instance the Welsh Regional Council of Labour would spend less time in nattering fruitlessly at Welsh Labour Home Rulers and used its organization in a constructive and dynamic spirit, much could be done with the powers already possessed. Socialist Glamorgan and Monmouth alone possess a population equivalent to many small nations and the organizations of publicly controlled production units on a federal basis should be top priority. School furniture, bus bodies, building materials readily spring to mind among many similar examples. The experience and help of the Co-operative Movement could well be sought.

But what do we find? Supplies and services contracts actually being handed back to private enterprise. Direct Labour being dispensed with, and the private enterprise builder called in. If disciplinary action is needed it is against local authorities, nominally Socialist, who use such practices.

Probably millions of pounds leave Wales from these

two counties alone, in disbursements to contractors and suppliers who could well be dispensed with. As it is, the 'Socialism' of certain councils is looked at with grave suspicion by the ordinary Welsh citizen.

Remploy and Grenfell factories should be given priority in the allocation of contracts, and wherever possible, Welsh money should be spent in Wales. The Monmouthshire police authority has already given a valuable lead in this respect, and should be widely imitated. All its clothing contracts go to Welsh firms.

Socialism made a great appeal outside Wales (for the first and only time) in 1945, when the 'near-socialism' of many wartime measures were seen to have made sense and borne fruit. People normally vote for the system that 'delivers the goods'. Socialism can be revived in Wales, and Welsh Socialism can give yet another lead to our friends and neighbours elsewhere, if measures such as those were efficiently undertaken. It will need expert technical and legal advice, for although the principle is simple, the practice will meet with all sorts of obstacles from anti-social elements. Nevertheless, here is a great opportunity, and if the Labour Movement in Wales fails to take it, then it will deserve to crumble.

A minor, even doctrinaire, point: let our Socialist Councillors strip themselves of the meaningless 'honours' bestowed by a disdainful and alien monarchy. They only lend aid and comfort to the enemy by parading their MBEs and BEMs and God knows what, and their renunciation would not go unnoticed.

Combined Socialist action therefore by our local authorities in the overwhelmingly Labour areas where most of our people live will produce surprising results.

The Welsh economy could be consolidated and prosperity fortified. Mr.Ness Edwards's idea too is not a bad one, and could be tried. But when all is said and done, local government authorities, however they combine, cannot be expected to possess the unity of purpose and breadth of vision which we expect from national government. In our next article we will lay before the Labour Movement the minimum requirements for a Welsh National policy without which the efforts of our local authorities will never achieve maximum effectiveness.

The Welsh Republican (April-May 1956)

In previous articles we have analyzed the shortcomings, and demonstrated the essential meaninglessness of the Labour Party's official 'Welsh Policy' conclusively and in some detail. It is, by contrast, a relatively short and simple matter to say what the Welsh policy of the Labour Party should and must be. It can be stated in one sentence: 'The policy of the Labour Party in Wales is to work for the establishment of the Socialist Republic of Wales'.

In our previous article we indicated that under present circumstances a valuable lead and a concrete contribution towards the consolidation of Welsh political and economic independence could be given by the Socialist local authorities who control the major centres of our population. We also pointed out the sharp limitations of any such activity. If, for instance, Mr.Ness Edwards's scheme were adopted (and there is no reason why it should not be), providing for a body which would be 'more than a County Council and less than a Parliament', such a scheme would only have value if it were regarded not as a final solution (there are no 'final solutions' in history) but as a step towards the achievement of maximum autonomy.

The Labour movement owes its success in Wales to the degree with which it identified itself with the immediate requirements, as well as with the innate historically-evolved attitudes of the Welsh people. It is not too much to say that Labour is losing much of that status. It is an ageing party. The young are for the most part indifferent, but a vigorous minority, who should be working for democratic socialism, are attracted instead to the unstable eclecticism of Plaid Cymru which has nevertheless the merit of being irradiated by a genuine sentiment of patriotism. Who can say what sentiment irradiates Welsh Labour today? Obviously we cannot have a change of programme without a change of heart. Those in high places who bitterly oppose the national claims of Wales have only themselves to thank for the wilderness that surrounds them. And yet it should be a relatively simple matter to organize political and TU conferences on Welsh lines, with Welsh speakers and informed, documented discussion of Welsh problems. From a series of such conferences we could hope to see the following policy points emerge:

- National boards for all the public utilities already nationalized, together with cement, quarries and water.
- An overall industrial plan for Wales with special reference to automation and allied techniques
- Special authorities and schemes for ports and foreign trade, internal communications, rural and forest

industries, housing (industrial and rural), technical education, and industries in a parlous condition, such as fisheries and slate

- A survey of all Welsh natural resources. In the opinion of foreign observers many of our mineral resources are still unaccountably neglected
- The Welsh language to be given official parity with English and the use of Welsh as the medium of instruction in all school subjects to be actively encouraged
- Devolution (to start with) of all ministries and the administration of Justice to Cardiff (with further arrangements of convenience at Bangor, Aberystwyth and wherever else desirable)
- Welsh finance to stand on its own footing through the Bank of Wales and allied institutions. Company laws controlling retail and wholesale business to ensure that profits made in Wales are taxed in Wales
- Genuine international co-operation (as opposed to bogus 'internationalism') to be fostered by visits of commissions to countries from whom we may learn (Italy for roads, Switzerland for rail electrification and tourism, Ireland for peat utilization, Denmark for agriculture, Holland for land reclamation, etc.).

Much of this programme can be achieved now (or as soon as a Labour government is formed) by ordinary legislation at Westminster. We may look forward to an intensive period of such intermediate legislation.

But the fundamental provisions can only be achieved by the agency of a Welsh Parliament at Cardiff. Proposals for such a Parliament were put forward by Mr.S.O.Davies

MP in a private bill which will be well remembered. The essence of those proposals was a further period of transition, during which certain powers were 'reserved' to Westminster, but at the end of which the Welsh people, through their Parliament, would exercise the option of taking up such powers. The most important of such powers are the Crown, peace and war, relations with foreign states. Of the first, little need be said. There is hardly any serious case for the Welsh people continuing to contribute to the Duke of Windsor's undisclosed civil list pension, the Duke of Edinburgh's polo ponies, or the unedifying antics of the Duke of Kent.

The involvement of Wales in foreign military adventures must also cease. Welsh armed forces are of course essential, allied with a scheme of national service (not necessarily military service) for young citizens. They would co-operate with friendly powers in any eventuality which threatened Welsh soil and in United Nations policing duties, but would equally serve as a guarantee of Welsh neutrality in imperialist aggression.

This is a programme to be carried out democratically and over a period of transition. If Labour fails in its duty then the initiative will obviously be taken in other ways, and orderly methods superseded by a pattern of events tragically familiar elsewhere.

The Welsh Republican (June-July 1956)

The Strength of Wales

THE MINER IS at last beginning to appreciate his own paramount value in the market of industrial civilization. It is a self-appreciation which has been strangely slow to mature. But the fact that it is at last happening is one of the most significant and welcome developments of our time.

There is more than superficial truth in the old saying that miners are a race apart. We are all of us to a great extent created by the circumstances which surround us, moulded by our environment. Miners are a race apart because they are moulded by an environment in their working lives so different from that surrounding other men. Every working day in their lives demands not merely its quota of their energy and health and skill, it faces them with the increasing battle for survival against the irresistible and unpredictable forces of the earth and the danger from machinery in dark and confined places.

It is an environment which fosters less selfishness and a deeper humanity – in a word, comradeship. At least we know that that is the indisputable attribute of the Welsh miner – a comradeship which is part inherent, and part forged, in the galleries underground. This quality of the Welsh miners is the most vital and valuable asset of the Welsh nation today, for it is largely in their hands that the destiny of Wales lies.

That is why every move of the miners in their fight to

put a proper price on themselves and their labours – new wage claims, each plea for improved conditions of work and retirement, for generous sickness and accident compensation – demands the encouragement and support of every patriotic Welsh man and woman.

There are still too many of us playing into the hands of the enemies of Wales because we make the cardinal mistake of taking our mining community for granted. They are the élite of the labour force of the Welsh nation, and it is the duty of us all to do our best to promote the circumstances which will bring them a hard-won heyday of power and prestige in the life of Wales. What we shall gain for them, we shall gain for Wales.

The real enemies of Wales are one and the same as the enemies of her mining community, which has already shown itself to be in advance of every other section of our industrial life in the measure of its support for Welsh self-government. The final lesson for us all is that just as self-respect and prosperity for the miners must go hand in hand with their strength and independence in the community, so the self-respect and the prosperity of Wales as a nation must go hand in hand with her freedom. When we have learnt that lesson the fires of Welsh national aspiration which have smouldered so long underground will once again flame triumphantly into the open.

The Welsh Republican (August-September 1955)

The Green Gold of Wales

The Future of our Forests

THE FORESTS OF WALES were once her chief glory and a guardian of her independence. Ruthlessly ravaged by English exploiters for industrial and naval purposes, they are now being replanted. Their contribution to the future of our national economy is one of the brightest prospects of the next few generations. The Forestry Commission waxes almost lyrical over the excellent quality of our woodlands. Yet the harsh fact remains: the Forestry Commission is on the whole unpopular in Wales and finds it hard to get labour. It has received unfortunate publicity for some of its grand schemes and is subject to criticism from many different interests.

One would expect the Welsh country man, used to hard work, to flock to the new forests. If he does not, the reason is not hard to seek: the pay and conditions do not appeal to him. Pay in the Welsh forests is lower than in the English forests. Piece-time rates are a continual source of friction and grievance. 'They try to get us to work for nothing,' wrote one forestry worker to the Editor of *The Welsh Republican* as soon as he knew that we intended turning our spotlight on the Welsh woodlands. The industrial worker, too, fights shy of the forests. He, or his Dad, remembers the bad old days when the unemployed of the Valleys were herded into bleak sheds at Brechfa, and worked hard for not much more than the dole.

The set-up of the Forestry Commission is almost military in structure. Foresters wear a khaki uniform with green lapels – not in itself a bad thing, but suggesting, perhaps, that the administrative pattern has been copied from the forests of Germany, which are admittedly efficient but adjusted to a rather cruder social norm. Work on a small upland farm may be hard, but Siôn Cefn Gwlad prefers the well-established, rough-and-ready social democracy which exists between the farmer and the *gwas* to the fantastic set-up which has produced characters such as the one known to his subordinates as the 'Commissar for Christmas Trees'. Faced with a shortage of Welsh labour, the Commission tried the English cities. One of the most shocking exposures which have appeared in the Welsh press for a long time, described how people from poor, even sordid homes in Birmingham and Manchester were brought to the forests of Wales, and were continually doing a moonlight flit, leaving the Commission with empty houses. As if we hadn't had enough experience of the evacuees and the key workers.

This is the reality behind the boast of the Forestry Commission that they are halting the tide of rural depopulation. Wales is a country that needs men, not the shiftless spawn of the 'great' cities of England. If the wages and conditions were adequate to attract the right kind of man, the problem would be less difficult.

The Professor of Forestry at Bangor has made similar criticisms. Houses in forest villages, he says, are like Army married quarters. Facilities like shops, pubs and places of worship are shown on the propaganda maps of the Commission but do not exist except on paper. The workers at Tair Onnen ('the biggest forest nursery in Britain' tootles the shiny hand-out) had to build a Village Hall at their own expense. In its handling of labour the Forestry Commission is damaging the prospects of an important sector of the Welsh economy.

Perhaps the Forestry Commission got its biggest publicity ever when it attempted to seize forty farms in Dyffryn Tywi and precipitated the rumpus known as 'The Battle of Rhandir-mwyn'. This surely speaks for itself. The Commission is a legitimate successor to many of the great landlords whom Lloyd George finally dished (even to carrying on some of their social attitudes, as we have seen), and it seems to be utterly out of sympathy with real Welsh rural life. Bad advice, bureaucratic stupidity, the brazen pushfulness of the London bosses, all contributed to this humiliating fracas which was only the worst of many such. Meanwhile there are communities in Wales which are crying out for forests on their doorstep, and for the ancillary industries based on forest products. There are many almost derelict industrial communities, grouped around old quarries and ironworks. Here facilities and communications and a social life already exist. Here is the ideal channel for bringing the industrial worker nearer to the land. Much has been done, we know. It is a pleasure to see the forests growing again in Ebbw Vale and the Rhondda Valley. But infinitely more effort is needed in districts like these. We have referred before now to the plight of dead-end Blaenafon. Why can it not become a coal-and-forest town as it was once a coal-and-iron town? Massive afforestation where it is needed, not barging in to well-farmed land – that is surely common sense. Many incidental problems would be solved: straying sheep a nuisance of the past, erosion checked and drainage made easier. The possibilities of forestry in industrial districts are endless.

We do not believe that sufficient attention is being paid to forest products. The main concern at the moment seems to be pitprops. This is right and proper, but if the forests are to be planned in the interests of Wales, then forest industries and wood derivatives must be systematically fostered. A Forestry Commission spokesman has said that it is 'too early' to think of joinery industries on a large scale in connection with the Welsh woodlands. The Forestry Commission was established in 1931. How long does it take soft-wood to grow? Montgomeryshire, a well-wooded county, has complained that timber is exported and finished products re-imported. From Breconshire come complaints that the Commission refuses to set up or entertain tenders for a factory dealing with 'thinnings' which are the waste products of tree-planting. It makes one suspect that their marketing policy is hand-in-glove with well-established vested interests in England. There are more genuine difficulties stemming from central government specifications which favour imported timber and make it difficult for our own to compete in certain markets. As with coal, iron and steel, Wales has the heavy work in primary production. The secondary industries are syphoned off to England.

Welsh independence of course would solve all these problems. We would have a labour policy more in accord with our social tradition, an understanding land acquisition policy, forceful action for forests in industrial Wales, an independent marketing policy, our own specifications and a systematic encouragement of the many derivatives of timber, hardboard, chemicals, furniture, paper and many others.

But in the mean time we press upon the Forestry Commission its duty to Wales now. It is perhaps vain to expect much while far-away London rules the roost. But many respected public men, many Welsh Socialists, are already associated with the Commission. We urge them to insist on a separate Forestry Commission for Wales. Let the Council for Wales look to it. Let our MPs bestir themselves. We acknowledge gladly the good work that has already been done. The thrill of pride that comes from a drive through Coed Morgannwg, through Crychan or Tarenig in all their beauty and promise, is a mixture of aesthetics and economics for which it is difficult to be ungrateful. We pay willing tribute to the men of vision and enthusiasm who planned and planted them.

But it is our duty to see that that vision be not betrayed by the cold-eyed exploiters, that promise be not trampled by the Beast. The Forests of Wales belong to the People of Wales.

The Welsh Republican (December 1955-January 1956)

The Murder of Blaenafon

BLAENAFON IS A pleasant place in its green valley of Gwent. One of the older towns of the industrial South – not a raw growth of the Coal Age, but with the sense of history and tradition that you get in other communities along the Northern Outcrop. Here, indeed, in the earliest ironworks, the Industrial Age first dawned on Europe and the world. And today Blaenafon faces a crisis few would believe possible. In the very first number of *The Welsh Republican* we called attention to Blaenafon's plight. It is nothing less than the deliberate murder of a community.

Some would say that such towns are doomed anyway, as their natural resources dwindle. But Blaenafon's resources, particularly coal, will last a long time yet. And, as Aneurin Bevan himself has pointed out, the existence of a settled community – with houses, businesses large and small, services public and private – is as much an investment as a privately owned factory, and is entitled to protection. Such were his reasons for opposing the closure of Ebbw Vale steelworks. Such indeed would be the action of any government which had the welfare of Wales at heart or believed in the elements of just planning.

But, believe it or not, the worst blows fell on Blaenafon while the late Labour Government was in power. True they ratted on the 1945 promises to introduce an integrated plan for Welsh industry, but they were doubtless bragging about the 'Dalton Plan' to stop forced migration by 'bringing the work to the worker'. While all the time the deadly drain was going on from Blaenafon.

During the period when public control was strictest, Blaenafon's three major steel undertakings closed down one after another. The closure of the solid wheel and axle foundry was perhaps the most significant and dramatic. Atlee's government openly admitted that they were in no position to help this 100% Socialist community against the speculative manipulations of the debenture share-holders who forced closure in the interests of their own pockets. To read what went on in those days is to imagine that it was happening in some Company town in America, not under the administration of a government whose first action had been to sing the 'Red Flag' in the Houses of Parliament.

Blaenafon protested with demonstrations, one led by the colliery band and parading the banners of 20 ex-servicemen's organizations. Even the local MP, Mr.Granville West, was stirred into activity. But nothing it seemed could be done. Blaenafon was too far from the sea (14 miles – Ebbw Vale 22 miles!), it was too high up (the same height as Dowlais, to which new factories were directed!), and similar wretched excuses. Anyway, there was plenty of work in the district. What exactly would steelworkers suffer in loss of earnings, starting as learners in the rubber factory at Bryn-mawr or the nylon factory at Mamheilad? What of the excessive travelling time, with its evil effects on family life and leisure? Welsh workers, we take it, should be grateful for any crumbs that are flung to them. With so many of them working at the nylon factory you might expect an improved bussable road to

Mamheilad to cut out the congested detour via Pontypool. No such luxury!

Meanwhile, opencast mining further up the valley at Waunafon imperilled the whole drainage system of the permanent pits. When anything was to be got out of Blaenafon, it was taken with both hands. But not a finger has been raised to save a community – and a very closely-knit, proud and self-conscious community (typically Welsh, in a word) – from draining away to nothingness.

Indeed, Blaenafon is playing the part of Banquo's ghost at the continuing feast of the post-war boom. The whole of Wales was once in Blaenafon's case, and may well be again. Look well, Wales, at the Ghost Town of Gwent, and be warned.

The Welsh Republican (April-May 1955)

Welsh Water for Wales

Our Homes and Industries have First Call
Not another Drop over the Border

AT LAST the whole of Wales is united on one point. Not another drop of Welsh water across the Dyke until the needs of our own country are satisfied.

The latest attempts of Liverpool to filch our great national asset have triggered off a nation-wide reaction that is nothing short of epoch-making. Even Saul is among the prophets. Even the Cardiff Kemsley Press has demanded a Welsh Water Board that will defend our interests. Even the cartoonist of the *South Wales Echo* lampoons the Liverpudlian sneak thieves. The shade of Ann Griffiths watched over Dolanog. But a living nation has leapt to the defence of Tryweryn. It seems that never again shall we see the scandals of Fyrnwy and Elan repeated in the heart of our land. For make no mistake about it, Wales has come to its senses with a crash and let our enemies and exploiters beware. All Wales, from Cardiff with its humiliating memories of drought restrictions among the rainiest hills of Europe, from Ebbw Vale facing shut-down and unemployment at the great steelworks because of water shortage, up through Mid Wales, where the great reservoirs mock the waterless farms and farm-kitchens, to Anglesey, where water riots have not been unknown, all Wales, we say, presents a solid front to the invader.

A few snivelling sentimentalists (we have those in Wales too) are concerned that Liverpool will go without water. Let it. For this is not drinking water they are after. It is industrial water. Water is one of the great raw materials of modern industry – as Ebbw Vale knows only too well!

This drain on our national resources must cease forthwith. It is idle to talk about reviving the deserts of rural Wales, it is useless to plan and blueprint if this sort of thing is allowed to go on.

In cahoots with our old friends the Forestry Commission, Liverpool has its flocks and forests in Fyrnwy, whose handsome profits help to keep its rates down and its citizens prosperous while Welsh local authorities struggle as best they may, for a dwindling population follows the water and the forest products over the border. Elsewhere in this journal we comment on the paper-mill scandal, all part of the same process which condemns Wales to hard graft and economic susceptibility in primary production, while the lucrative secondary industries are syphoned off to England. Perhaps they will tell us that the paper-mill for our forest products could not be built in Wales because there is not enough industrial water available! The contribution which English cities pay into the rates of Brecon and Radnor and Montgomery are hardly a compensation on this wholesale looting.

Indeed, recently Birmingham successfully appealed against Radnor's assessment of the rates on Elan, and £10,000 of rateable value was slashed off.

Now we have seen through the water swindle, now that we are all united on that one easily-grasped point, it cannot be long before we see through the other swindles

– coal, tinplate, chemicals, wool, forests, cement, and biggest swindle of the lot – father of them all – London rule. The way lies open for a tremendous advance in Welsh public opinion. As we have said, it is epoch-making.

It is perhaps fitting that God's commonest and least appreciated gift to the Welsh people, 'water of the rain of heaven', should have brought us to our senses and revealed the stark reality of our economic and national position. When we have successfully defended our resources against further encroachments we must reorganize the distribution of the great reservoir supplies we already possess. When we are satisfied, others may take the surplus – at a fair price.

Until then – not another drop!

Remember the Fron Aqueduct.

The Welsh Republican (February-March 1956)

The Welsh Establishment

THERE EXISTS IN England an undefined but very real nexus of interest and attitudes – the Court, the Church, *The Times*, the FO, the MCC, the SCR, the right clubs, the right ties – which is generally referred to as 'the Establishment'. It embodies all the hidden sources of power and patronage which control English public life behind the façade of democracy.

Our readers will hardly be unaware that there is an analogous ethos in Wales: the Liberal-Nonconformist petty bourgeois poor relation of its opposite number in England. The career of the late Dr.Thomas Jones exemplified to perfection the close link between these superficially dissimilar rackets. It need hardly be said that both 'Establishments' are equally archaic and out of touch with the masses, on whom they blandly but ruthlessly impose their attitudes: as witness the self-righteous gloom and furtive law-breaking of the so-called 'Welsh Sabbath'. Historian R.T.Jenkins tells us that as long ago as the beginning of the last century, denominational magazines would be more concerned over the troubles of a handful of sectarians in Cardiganshire than with the wholesale squalor of the industrial Valleys which were even then the centre of gravity of our population. In this century a guidebook by a Welsh minister (occupant of a Birmingham pulpit) can contain these phrases about our Valleys and great ports – 'These awful spots... in no true sense belong to Wales... Nevertheless, Cardiff people insist upon regarding themselves and their city as Welsh... It is the head of one of the busiest industrial areas to be found on our planet and it would seem to all reasonable beings that Cardiff's claim to be the capital city of a land of poets, preachers, dreamers and farmers has been proved to the hilt!'

Here, for once, we have the Establishment with the white gloves off – sarcastic exclamation marks and all. Here is the Wales that exists in the imaginations of these people – and nowhere else. The Wales to which Dowlais Top and Barry Dock and Abersychan 'in no true sense belong' – thank God! This is the Wales that has produced a *Dictionary of National Biography* in which the most space is occupied by Thomas Charles! He gets more even than Prince Owain Glyn Dŵr, whom the same publication generously admits 'was considered the most important character in Welsh History *before the Methodist Revival*' (our italics). What a grotesque and humiliating distortion of values.

The bastard eunuch pacifism which mutilates our true history and poisons certain sectors of the national struggle today is another emanation of the same smug gang of social profiteers.

Let them be warned.

Wales is a militant, industrial nation not to be deterred by empty sentiment or false piety from a virile and vigorous future.

Editorial, *The Welsh Republican* (February-March 1956)

Tory War on Wales

As ENGLAND'S EMPIRE staggers to its doom, the Tory Government unleashes war on Wales. The flashy façade of post-war prosperity is cracking under the hammer blows. Young Welshmen are conscripted, not for the defence of Wales, which would be acceptable and indeed desirable, but to spend their lives in propping up a disappearing Empire, which is intolerable.

The Birmingham businessmen and London finance crooks who have plundered our country for generations are having their way with our industries. The credit squeeze has forced the closure of barely established firms. The increased bank rate has crippled our local authorities, vainly striving with a legacy of squalid housing left over from the earliest days of the Industrial Revolution. Capital restrictions have hit at the Blaenau Ffestiniog Hydro-Electric Station which was to have meant so much to rural Gwynedd. The factory at Nantlle, into which so much local effort was put, has closed down after three years working.

In the South, just struggling to its feet again after the bad years, the cold blasts of redundancy are blowing though the narrow valleys. Factory after factory is laying off men. The ugly truth, which so many Welsh people have refused to realize, is now staring them in the face: these factories are branches of English firms, and the branches are being lopped.

There is 'concentration' and 'rationalization' as there was in the 'twenties and 'thirties. Swansea has lost Stewarts and Lloyds, Aberdâr has lost Helliwells because Tube Investments is 'concentrating' back to Brum. The luxury goods produced in the smart new factories on the Trading Estates are the first to succumb to hire purchase restrictions. Councils are unwillingly obliged to increase rents. School building is threatened. Food prices, already high in the Valleys, soar as the food subsidies are withdrawn. The debt-collector is making his rounds. The motor-bikes and the radios are going back to the shop. Sinister finance companies with English addresses, masquerading as Hire Purchase Firms, reap a record harvest. Building materials and all the necessities for public works are in the hands of squalid rings of monopolist middlemen and the Tory Government is either inactive or openly connives at all these antisocial activities.

Slaughter abroad and starvation at home – the Tories have learnt nothing and forgotten nothing. But the people of Wales have not forgotten either, and they have learnt plenty.

All these evils befall a nation which has not got control over its own affairs. This is no government elected by the people of Wales. Those in the Labour Movement who have set their faces against Welsh Self-Government have a heavy load pressing on their consciences. The time is ripe for a great surge forward of progressive opinion, such as Wales has seen many times in the past, and we are confident that under the new pressure of circumstances, the people of Wales will at last take the right road, and the decisive step.

Wales must build up her own integrated economy, based on her own great wealth. Wales must cut loose from Birmingham big business and London finance. The people of Wales must control their own destinies. The Tory criminals of Westminster must no longer rule in our land. Let those who try to throw sand in our eyes be warned. Whatever political label they may wear, they can no longer be tolerated for they are the hirelings of Imperialism and the accomplices of assassins.

There is only one solution for the predicament into which we have been delivered by bad leadership and bad faith: the establishment of the Socialist Republic of Wales.

The Welsh Republican (April-May 1956)

Welsh Labour Must Wake Up!

AT A TIME when England's Tory Government has revealed its unmistakable intentions towards the workers of Wales, what is the Welsh Labour Movement doing to rally the forces of the people?

With housing standards threatened, with food subsidies withdrawn, with emigration still going on, and the threat of unemployment growing daily, what is the answer of the Labour Movement?

It would not be true to say that there is no answer. But the holding of conferences at Porth-cawl and Cory Hall, Cardiff, is a very inadequate comeback, totally unworthy of the movement which represents the militant traditions of our proud people.

Delegates who sacrifice time and energy to attend these conferences are finding them meaningless, fruitless and repetitive. The formula is always the same. 'National' speakers came down from London, Mr.Cliff Protheroe beams like a Sunday School Superintendent at a Whitsun treat, the delegates are confronted with a 'resolution' which they can in no wise challenge or modify, however wishy-washy it may be. The platform speakers perorate, the floor calls for a lead. Ah, says the platform, we are not here to give you a lead. You must give us a lead. Then somebody like Dan Jones gets up and calls for industrial action. Oh, says the platform in shocked tones, that would be undemocratic! Questions are answered en bloc and evasively. The Tories are criticized in great style, but there is a lack of constructive alternatives to their programme. Often the flippancy and superficiality of these 'national' speakers who have no knowledge of Welsh conditions is deeply shocking. There was Victor Feather, Assistant Secretary of the TUC, for instance, at a recent conference on redundancy. This well-known Yorkshire comedian was never at a loss for an answer. When a delegate criticized the policy by which the Welsh economy was being made dependent on 'dolls-eye factories', Victor was ready for him. 'What's wrong with that?' came the answer, quick as a flash. 'Children like dolls with eyes.' Talk about laugh. Our spies report that the same gentleman, going back as quick as he could to London on the train, is supposed to have said that he did not think redundancy in Wales was very serious and didn't really see the point of a conference at Porth-cawl to discuss it!

It is possible to criticize our Welsh MPs for their bad record of attendance at these functions but at least one militant miners' lodge has given up sending delegates because they consider it a waste of time.

And when the resolution is finally passed, nobody seems to know or care what happens to it.

Amoral flippancy, contempt for the working class, evasiveness and shoddy generalities have all been noted at these conference platforms, noted and deeply resented by delegates whose job it is to go back to the branch or the lodge or the ward and get something done. These characteristics are not merely deplorable. They are criminally degenerate.

Of course there is no widespread unemployment just yet. But as the engineering firms pull out of the Trading

Estates north and south and the Cardiff suburbs, they are being replaced by servicing concerns which offer employment, it is true, but very often with wage agreements at the 'national' minimum – in direct relation to the cost of living index. In other words, you lose a job at which you earn four to five shillings an hour and get one at 2s 10d an hour. Not to speak of Automation. Our scientists have invented wonderful machines to lighten labour, but our politicians are not showing half as much energy and inspiration in facing the consequences.

What is needed if the Welsh Labour Movement is to meet its responsibilities?

A more flexible and democratic conference procedure. Fewer generalities and more detailed research and documentation into the changes in employment that are going on. Less complacency. Fewer 'national' (i.e. English) speakers on the platform and more Welshmen, in touch with the problems of the Welsh worker, and with a feeling of deep responsibility to Wales. Above all, a Welsh national policy on the lines consistently advocated by the Welsh Republican Movement.

As it is, the Communists in the industrial sector and Plaid Cymru in the electoral field score petty triumph after petty triumph.

There is only one redemption, as there is only one duty for the Welsh Labour Movement: to work for the liberation of our country and our people economically and politically, and towards the establishment of the Socialist Republic of Wales.

The Welsh Republican (June-July 1956)

Alien Rule the Road to Ruin

EVERY DAY brings fresh evidence of the grievous state to which the economy of Wales is being brought by the ineptitude of England's government.

Every day brings fresh evidence that only by means of her own government can Wales achieve an efficient and equitable economy.

The Tory Government in London was decisively rejected by the people of Wales. It was freely elected, however, by the people of England and, under the present arrangements, forced on the people of Wales. It is a government of financiers and imperialists, fighting needless wars all over the 'Empire' at the price of Welsh blood. It is a usurers' government, giving free rein to record booms in dividends and profits, while penalizing and inflicting 'economy cuts' on socially necessary undertakings, such as council house building, schools and hospitals. It has no moral claim to the allegiance of any Welsh citizen, and its moral bankruptcy is emphasized to the full by its practical shortcomings.

To the pressing claims of rural Wales, as urged in the latest authoritative report, it turns a deaf ear. Linked with this problem is the future of our tourist industry. In Welsh hands this can be a dynamic asset, as the continuing triumph of the purely home-grown Llangollen International Eisteddfod abundantly demonstrates. But our Tourist Board is a body with little power and few resources. The London Government will not relinquish its claim that the 'United Kingdom' is one and indivisible, yet its financial provision for this important source of revenue is so niggardly that it has led to widespread protest. 'British Unity' is thus revealed as a strictly one-way proposition. And so rural Wales goes without its amenities and improvements for farm-house and guest-house alike, while Birmingham and London pile up the profits from the loot of our forests and water.

In the industrial sector there is not a community in Wales which is not trembling under the shadows of redundancy, automation and the credit squeeze. 'British' salesmanship in highly competitive overseas markets is a byword for inefficiency. And when we need new machinery for automated plants, it does not come from 'British' industry but has to be imported from Sweden and Switzerland – small, well-organized industrial democracies to which an independent Wales would be similar in many respects. And on top of that, while the 'Empire' blunders to its doom, itinerant Tory claptraps have the nerve to tell us that an independent Wales 'could not last six months'!

The publicly-controlled sector is just as irresponsible. The Coal Board, answerable to no one, thanks to the wisdom of Shinwell, and now the passive instrument of Tory policies, has just managed to stumble out of the Gwauncaegurwen imbroglio relatively unscathed. But further west, they have, all unnoticed, closed the small colliery at Hook. Now the Milford fishing fleets find themselves hit by the rising price of coal. They ask for workings to be reopened. The Coal Board turns a deaf ear. Indeed, Welsh deep-sea fisheries are almost a vanishing industry. The Cardiff and Swansea fleets feel the same draught to a lesser extent. Here is an obvious example of the case for a unified Welsh Industrial Policy, as demanded by a section of Welsh Labour. Here is the sabotage of alien rule at its most ruthless. When it comes to ripping opencast coal out of the heart of Aberdâr and ruining even the scanty amenities of a better-than-average valley town the Coal Board are not so backward. The fate of this infamous proposal is in the balance but it is symptomatic of the Tory-industrialist mentality now ruling the roost, which regards Wales as a mere field for exploitation and a rubbish dump when the profit is all gone.

The criminal irresponsibility of the system now inflicted on Wales becomes daily more apparent. 'Big deals' are rumoured for Milford Docks and land along the Haven, mysterious prospecting for steel sites ranges between Llanelli and Newport, and the elected represent-atives are in no more position to inform or be informed on these vital matters than the man in the moon. Meanwhile these same representatives waste everyone's time nattering for a Severn Bridge when Welsh internal communications, and especially the Great Central Highway, are first priority and should be their chief concern. Whom the Gods would destroy, they first make mad...

A people gets the leaders it deserves and much that has happened to the Welsh people in this century, and is still happening, is largely their own fault. But on the leaders themselves a heavy burden of responsibility must rest. In this number of *The Welsh Republican* we commemorate the greatest of those leaders during this century [Keir Hardie]. Those who have come after have betrayed his work and taken his name in vain. And the Welsh people have suffered in direct proportion to the distance which separates the actions (or inactions) of our Labour leaders from their great exemplar. Let our readers of this number scan the man's words, the charges he delivered and the examples he set to those who would follow. Let them compare this man with the malignant dwarfs who ape his creed today. The time has come for these creatures to be swept aside and for the Welsh People to resume their historic march toward Independence.

The Welsh Republican (August-September 1956)

The Night of the Fire

IN THIS NUMBER of *The Welsh Republican,* we take the opportunity of recalling yet another glorious anniversary. Twenty years ago this autumn, three men, in the name of Wales, fired the huts on an airfield at Penyberth, in Caernarfonshire, which was being built by the English government in defiance of the wishes of the Welsh people. Those three men were Saunders Lewis, D.J.Williams and Lewis Valentine. When apprehended, they defended themselves in court to such good effect that in order to secure a conviction the English were forced to move the trial to London, where a jury of alien cosmopolites sentenced these brave men to imprisonment and shame. The most conspicuous among them, Saunders Lewis, was disgracefully treated by the so-called University of Wales, and has only comparatively recently been accorded the academic acknowledgment to which his gifts entitle him.

At first glance, nothing distinguishes the action of 1936 more than its complete isolation from anything before or after it, both in the careers of the three protagonists, and in the movement of Welsh opinion in general.

The anniversary went uncommemorated in the paper published by the body of opinion which these men once led. The action nevertheless remains a tremendous uprush of archaic force, sweeping aside the mildewed weeds of academic respectability and white-gloved liberal hypocrisy. It was an action in the hidden and unrecorded

159

tradition of our history, for when law and order offer no defence, the Welshman has never scrupled to use other methods. Our readers will be familiar with some of the highlights and some of the heroes in that endless battle, as we have chronicled them. All Welsh citizens will be familiar with events in an endless list of countries today, when the twilight of empires is the dawn of new hope for those bold enough to press their claims. Many will remember an occasion, four years ago, when the apathy of our country was shattered as unknown patriots attacked the Fron Aqueduct. Elsewhere in this issue, we focus attention once again on the Tryweryn Valley and the shameful fate that confronts it. We salute the men of 1936 as we saluted their predecessors – the men of 1831 and 1839, the quarrymen, the miners, the dockers, the farmers, all of whom have played their part in a glorious resistance. We salute them in confidence and pride that the Welsh of today will not be lesser men than their fathers.

The Welsh Republican (October-November 1956)

Wales and Hungary

ONCE AGAIN, the imperialist powers have plunged the world into chaos. The Middle East is aflame and the Danube runs red with the blood of Hungary. The ruthlessness of these actions is rivalled only by their recklessness, their bestiality is paralleled only by their stupidity.

The whole world must by now be heartily tired of both Russia and England. Both countries by their irresponsible actions have brought the world to the brink of war. Whatever sympathy and support Russia ever had outside her own ramshackle boundaries is gone for ever. As the *Daily Worker* shrinks in size, we may greet the disappearance of Communism with a sigh of relief, but this is a modest gain, for they never amounted to much, and now many unworthy reactionary elements are cashing in on our feeling of solidarity with martyred Hungary.

Meanwhile, the slick, penny-wise opportunism of the English Tories seems for the time to have consolidated their position internally, at the price of leaving the Middle East in an ulcerous state of resentment. The long-term disastrous effects of Eden's policy will remain for the next Labour Government to clear up if, indeed, England ever does elect a Labour Government again, which at the moment seems doubtful. Labour slipped up badly by banking on a prolonged Anglo-Egyptian conflict, which would have been generally unpopular, and tried to isolate

Eden. Eden had only to wave the cease-fire order and his position was secure, while Mr.Gaitskell was left gaping. The English Left have in fact been just as much at sea about the Middle East as were the Comrades in Moscow, who presented Nasser with all those arms, presumably under the impression that this would-be Arab Imperialist and his comic-opera army could make effective use of them. The appalling show the Egyptian Army and Navy put up against Israel, long before there was any question of Anglo-French intervention, only reveals a complete lack of capacity both in Transport House and the Kremlin. Both relied on Nasser being a much bigger force than he actually turned out to be, and he got them both in the cart.

The only people who have come well out of all this are the heroic Israelis, who were quite justified in their original action against Egypt. It is only through the folly of the 'great' powers that this clash has assumed world dimensions.

Nationalism is revealed as wisdom, and Imperialism the nadir of folly.

This too is the lesson of Hungary. Here a Socialist regime (of sorts) was intimately tied up with exploitation by a foreign power. The 'national' leadership of English Labour has come off badly, by its miscalculations about the Middle East and by the faint-hearted attitude of the National Council of Labour towards strike action. It is obvious that they do not want a radical change.

But the leaders of Welsh Labour would be better advised to turn their eyes towards Budapest. For they themselves have not yet come to the knowledge that Socialism is meaningless without national independence.

There is no difference at all between the Hungarian demand that Russia shall no longer exploit Hungarian mineral deposits and the Welsh demand that English industrial centres shall keep their hands off Welsh water, and that Wales shall build her own secondary industries on the coalfields, instead of seeing our raw materials cross the border to keep Birmingham booming.

As we write, the last miserable chapter in the tragedy of Blaenafon is reported. The last industrial plant in the town is being carried off lock, stock and barrel to Sheffield. All the time this wholesale looting of Welsh resources was going on, certain of our leaders go around preaching the myth of a 'unified British economy', that 'Wales is a poor little country living on English charity' and similar claptrap. Their proper place is with the Comrades who are preaching substantially the same doctrine from the turrets of Muscovite tanks in the ruins of Budapest. No wonder, either, that they did not support industrial action to overthrow the Tories.

They have utterly forfeited any moral authority they ever had. The leprosy of Gehazi is upon them. Worse, they have deeply infected Welsh Labour with their own hypocritical double-think. All the little jackals who have discredited Labour in so many local councils can only hunt under the protection of the pack-leaders – the Union Jackals.

Let them be warned. We do not anticipate seeing Mr.Dai Dirt MP strung up on a lamp-post, nor Alderman Whitehead-Sepulchre hurled from the windows of the Town Hall, as happened to their opposite numbers in Hungary, but at all costs, they must go, and the Welsh Labour Movement must add to its already great record by bringing off the crowning achievement – the Socialist Republic of Wales.

The Welsh Republican (December 1956-January 1957)

Tryweryn

THE FATE OF the Tryweryn Valley must now be the chief matter before us. Every aspect of the scheme to drown Tryweryn in the interests of Liverpool has its significance. Even those individuals and bodies which have in the past held aloof from national feeling and activity are stirred to protest. Indeed, the proposed Liverpudlification of this stronghold of Welsh life is a loathsome prospect, which has given rise to strong feelings, and the strong feelings may well, under unfavourable circumstances, give rise to strong actions. The emotional tone of much of the protest and comment is understandable and justifiable. The nation would be the poorer if this ready and generous response were not forthcoming. Nevertheless, the Welsh Republican Movement adopts in this, as in all other matters, its customary attitude of stern realism. The northern province of our land, historic and romantic Gwynedd, offers but a poor living to too many of its sturdy sons and daughters these days. Industries remain static or decay, rural depopulation proceeds apace, communications and facilities are primitive. Under different auspices, Tryweryn Lake would be welcomed as a vast storehouse and as a source of power. Piped water to farmyard and cottage kitchen would alleviate the domestic lot. As one of the basic raw materials of modern industry, the great supply of water would do much to remedy the deficiencies in the economic pattern of

Gwynedd. In fact, if Tryweryn Dam were to be built in the interests of Wales, we would welcome the scheme, as we would welcome the installation of any other valuable item of capital equipment. But if Liverpool has its way, this will not be – the story of Elan, Claerwen and Fyrnwy is being repeated. Not entirely repeated, however. There is a new and significant element in the Tryweryn story. Whereas these other schemes were accepted by all except a few doughty recalcitrants (*The Welsh Republican* alone has published the story of the shotgun resistance of the Lloyds of Elan), opposition to the Tryweryn scheme has been public, prolonged and vehement, nor does it show any signs of abating. Following Liverpool's hubristic decision to ride roughshod over the will of our people, the support of the Welsh MPs has been enlisted to obstruct the passage of the bill through Parliament. We congratulate the seven who have already swung into action. But we demand that the other 29 bestir themselves also. They are being keenly watched. Westminster itself is on trial in this matter. We also demand that the entire situation be reviewed with reference to the establishment of a Welsh Water Board, with real powers. If the problem is faced realistically, and not in a foredoomed romantic spirit, much good will result.

Editorial, *The Welsh Republican* (December 1956-January 1957)

The Company of the Living

IT IS POSSIBLE to be Welsh and not have any feeling or concern for Wales. There are probably many more such people in Wales than in a healthy country; but, in the nature of things, they must of necessity be in a minority. Anyone who is so concerned is potentially a nationalist. But it is also possible to be a nationalist of sorts and not be a member of Plaid Cymru. For many years this was my position, and it is possibly still the position of the majority of Welshmen today.

For this reason, a consideration of why I joined Plaid Cymru may be of interest to other potential nationalists who have not yet made that decision. There are many ways of serving our country without being politically active or declaring any political allegiance to Wales. But man, as Aristotle says, is a political animal, and most thinking people feel themselves obliged to take up some political position, indeed, an impressive majority of the Welsh people have already made such a decision and declared their allegiance to the Labour Party. If what follows is mainly a criticism of that party, I can only say that I have been asked to write from personal experience and, moreover, my personal experience is one that is probably shared by many thousands of my fellow-countrymen.

Without in any way discounting the strength that the idea of nationality derives from historic continuity it may be said that modern nationalism and socialism are twin products of the industrial era. Science and technology have unleashed forces, morally neutral in themselves, which can be used either to degrade or uplift humanity. Socialism and nationalism both sought to harness and humanize the potentialities of the new age, and both ideas have a great deal of common ground. Until recently, socialism has seemed to offer the more tangible dividends. The socialists tended on the whole to confine their activities to the economic sphere, and the abuses they tackled were so obvious and so monstrous that the early pioneers were able to generate an impressive moral and intellectual dynamic, and to accumulate a heroic saga of defiant resistance to evil. The very narrowness of their field of activity, corresponding to the constricted circumstances of most people's lives, was a source of concentrated strength. This is the moral capital on which the movement is now living.

Sooner or later, however, the socialists had to come to terms with the central problem of politics – the problem of power. Here, in most of the larger formal democracies, they failed. The events of the 1920s in this island showed that the socialists were not psychologically prepared to take state power, and the capitalists called their bluff. They have resigned themselves to working inside an overall framework which perpetuates the order they seek to subvert, and to effect what marginal fragments of their national programme they may. The inner tensions produced by this untenable position are manifested in the perpetual state of uproar and schism which is such a familiar feature of the Labour Party today. In order to maintain their precarious foothold on what little power they have, they are obliged to jettison most of their ideals. Power in itself has become an obsession with them (there are some classic examples at local council level), and the power status quo, as represented by the domination of the Labour government in every corner of this quite large and densely populated island, is bedrock of their thinking.

To add to their predicament, the compulsions derived from the clamorous urgency of the empty belly and ill-clad body have been attenuated almost to vanishing point – except among the old, who are not organized, and do not therefore count in the power game. The breakdown of economic and political power to a scale more consistent with the claims of the individual – what is meant by decentralization and co-operation – has been discreetly ditched; the moral bankruptcy of the Labour Party is complete, and well-attested by its increasing unconvincingness, its failure to attract the post-depression generation, and its dismal record in local government. The party's shameful double-dealing in relation to the national claims of Wales is of a piece with the foregoing and, for the responsible Welshman, decisive.

But Nationalism is not merely an attempt to carry on the job that socialism has fallen down on. It has a prior and independent validity, and wider terms of reference. The inevitable failure and falling away of socialism has, as it were, invited the fuller and more exciting potentialities of Nationalism. The narrowing of the gap between the socialists and their power rivals, their abandonment of a firm basis of morality, their tinkering with problems they are incapable of solving, their obsession with the narrow horizons of the past, their crude, mechanistic nineteenth century philosophy, all these have combined to deliver socialism into the hands of embittered old men, unscrupulous petty careerists and visionless apparatchiks.

The initiative is firmly in the hands of Nationalists, who stand firm on the rock of moral standards and the worth of the individual, who are concerned with real, living people in a real place, who look to the future not the mere past, who seek to enrich every aspect of life. The Welshman who speaks and thinks in terms of Wales is branded as a Nationalist whatever his formal political allegiance, and is pursued by hatred and suspicion. He may as well make a proper job of it. The progress from socialism to Nationalism is the progress from tutelage to maturity, it is a coming to terms with the real world, it is a coming of age, bringing with it acceptance of the responsibilities of adult citizenship. In joining Plaid Cymru, I forsook the company of the dead for the company of the living.

Why Nationalist (1961)

The Main Motion at Plaid Cymru's 1961 Annual Conference had as its subject 'The National Integrity of Wales'. In proposing this motion Harri Webb said that it sought not so much to 'set forth a proposition for debate', it sought rather to focus attention on 'the national crisis' and to emphasize 'the burden of our responsibility at this juncture of our country's history'. The remainder of the speech is printed in full.

We Stand for the Integrity of Wales

THE PHILOSOPHY OF Nationalism seeks to anchor our aspirations, ambitions and ideals, and to give them territorial limitations – which, like the canons of art or the disciplines of science, are a source of strength rather than weakness, a source not of restriction but liberation. This is where Nationalism is superior to other well-meaning creeds. It provides easily comprehensible terms of reference for testing the validity of ideas; it provides a concrete, everyday context for the implementation of schemes of human betterment, however humble or however ambitious these may be. It makes immediate and intimate what would otherwise be merely abstract and visionary. By evoking the background of the homeland and all that it means to us, our common experiences, traditions and memories, our ways of thought and action, our community of destiny, everything that raises life above the merely animal or merely mechanical. Nationalism provides the only setting against which it is possible, clearly and completely, to offer a valid criticism of the antisocial and anti-human tendencies of the present age. Only against this background is it possible to highlight the distorted pattern which alien power and alien greed force upon community and individual alike.

But while it sets the scene it also provides us with the motive force for vigorous and determined action. For Nationalism is essentially a philosophy of action. Therein too it differs from many other well-meaning creeds, whose terms of reference are often so general and remote that they either remain utterly ineffective, or, if put into practice, neglect the human factor entirely and easily degenerate into soulless bureaucracy, harden into outright tyranny, or become corrupted, collapsing into humbug. As Nationalists, the path of our duty is clear, the challenge is so intense, and the tasks before us are so multifarious that there need be no fear of any one of us remaining undeployed in the national struggle, or moping in disuse.

The motion offers us a view of Wales as she is today. We can distinguish the different areas, each with its own aspect of the national problem. There are the Northern and Southern coastal strips where the underlying threat to our country is overlaid by the appearance of stable and progressive development. From Hawarden to Llandudno, or from Newport to Swansea, or from Spencers to Prestcold, some of us have never had it so good. But in between, between Hotpoint and Prestcold, there stretch first the intermediate zones – the twilight zones of unstable economy and uncertain prospects – and, back of them again, the Green Desert. At one time these seaboard towns had an organic relationship with the industrial communities in the hinterland that nourished them, and these, in turn, drew strength and nourishment from the rural heart of Wales. Today that organic relationship is being disrupted. The busy urban centres are theatrical façades which can be dismantled at a moment's notice, held up by rusting struts – the intermediate zones of slow decay, which are patched and spliced here and there by minimum, and decreasing, industrial diversification.

Going north from Merthyr or south from Wrecsam, you come through ever more abandoned country, the ultimate emptiness, and in the midst of the emptiness, the Calvary of Epynt. All Nationalists – indeed, all Welsh citizens – should go to Epynt, for in the desolation of Epynt we can read the final destiny of our country if we in this generation are not upstanding in her defence. Obviously each of these different areas demands different approaches, and it is our duty, as a movement and as individuals, to provide the arguments, the policies and, above all, the actions, which will puncture the complacency of the apparently more prosperous areas, restore the shaken confidence of the twilight zones, and put fresh heart into rural communities resigned to extinction and despair. There is certainly no lack of opportunities for agitation, for political pressure at both local and national level, and for activity outside the purely political field. This is a great challenge to the movement and to each and every one of us. It demands flexible thinking and imaginative appreciation of circumstances different from our own immediate surroundings. It is a job to keep us on our toes, to redeem us from the appalling provincialism and parochial narrowness that character-izes our so-called internationalists!

This motion, enumerating certain outstanding heads of discontent, was compiled early this year. We make no claim to peculiarly prophetic powers, but every threat adumbrated in the motion has been more than fulfilled. We are informed, for instance, that the great Severnside complex is to be linked by pipeline with Fawley on Southampton Water. Certain sections of the Nationalist press were drawing attention to the potentialities of pipeline transportation – which can be used not only for liquids, but for solids – some years ago. With the unification of Europe in sight, overland transportation not only of oil from the Middle East, but a vast variety of commodities to the shores of Southern and Eastern England is well within sight. The tanker may well become as obsolete as the clipper ship. What then for Swansea and Milford? There is lack of vision, foresight and initiative on the part of far too many of our local authorities and industrialists.

It must be the duty of Nationalists to take the lead in pointing out the dangers – and the opportunities – that the future holds. The motion refers to the financial penetration of our bigger towns. Since it was written, Eton and Cotton have moved into Cardiff, and big deals are mooted for Pontypridd. There has been the shame of Merthyr Tydfil, sold by a so-called socialist administration to the financial speculators of London – an infamous transaction which is being vigorously resisted by the national movement.

Most striking of all, as we predicted, Welsh internal communications are under heavy assault. The railways of Monmouthshire – a dense and busy network – are to be virtually abolished, throwing a heavy burden on the already inadequate roads of the county, making its industrial valleys less attractive to badly needed investment and development, hastening the drift from the interior to the coast that is only the first step towards evacuating Wales altogether. At least such butchery proves one thing – that Monmouthshire is part of Wales. No major industrial area of England would qualify for such treatment.

In rural Wales, already the first shock waves are reaching us from the explosion of land values in the great centres of England. As farms fall vacant, and the soulless contributions of England contribute their quota of commuting refugees, as the Herrenvolk retreat from Kenya and Rhodesia, looking for land at fancy prices, it may soon be impossible for the average Welsh farmer or smallholder to compete with them. Already the pass has been sold in many areas. Already the *Manchester Guardian* can speak of the weekend cottage in Montgomeryshire or Cardiganshire as the latest status symbol for the Birmingham businessman. Social dereliction can be no less acute for being picturesque. The fate of Cornwall is no less distressing than the fate of Blaenafon. Both are dormitories, and the sleep is the sleep of death.

But there are encouraging signs. We must, for instance, congratulate the farming community of Glan-llyn, who have formed a consortium to buy their land, and to keep that part of Wales Welsh. We welcome, too, the initiative shown by those sections of organized labour who are demanding a Trades Union Congress on a Welsh national basis. And we can rely, too, on the deep and as yet untapped wells of loyalty in areas that might not, on the surface, seem to be all that promising. May I refer to a personal experience? Not long ago I spent an evening in an ordinary working man's club in one of the Monmouthshire Valleys – a drab, depressing village, exhausted and exploited, dominated by the slag-heap, the pithead gear and the ultimate insult of open-cast. Not an unusual night out; not an unusual scene. At the end of the evening's entertainment, the audience rose to their feet and sang 'Hen Wlad fy Nhadau'. Again, nothing unusual; social evenings in our Valley clubs never end in any other way, certainly with no other anthem. Why do I refer to this very ordinary experience? Because the name of that community was Six Bells, and, within forty-eight hours of singing the national anthem, dozens of the men who sang it had gone to their deaths underground. They had no doubt where their loyalty lay. Without any of the enrichment deriving from a vigorous linguistic or cultural background; without any material evidence about them that Wales was other than a place of restricted opportunities, narrow horizons and the labours and dangers of heavy industry, yet they affirmed their nationality with pride.

Instinctively, inarticulately, they expressed the whole faith that the National Movement exists to defend and which this motion seeks to define and make explicit on certain points: that the people of Wales belong to the land of Wales and to no other. It is perhaps possible to live elsewhere and be a good Welshman; but it is impossible to be a complete Welshman. And by the same token the land of Wales belongs to the people of Wales – to them and no other. Any divorce between the land and the people only leads to the deep impoverishment of both. Any actions, at whatever level and under whatever auspices, which furthers such unnatural separation is intolerable and must be resisted at whatever cost. Such actions happen every day and in every part of our country, with every colour of precedent and expedient, with all the excuses and justifications that come so glibly after centuries of sell-out.

Let there be some Welshmen, at any rate, who are not for sale, and who will stand and say that our country is not for sale either, and can under no circumstances be the subject of bargaining. Because this is our most precious possession, and if we lose it, we lose everything even unto our innermost selves, and if we were to gain the whole world in exchange it would profit us nothing. When the Russians first breached the frontiers of space, their announcement of this triumph contained the telling sentence that their spaceman landed safely again 'on the sacred soil of the Fatherland'. However far you go, you must always return home, and while the title to our land is in question, while the basic territorial integrity of our country is not respected and not asserted, while in fact we are homeless in our own homeland, we will never be able to set out on any great journey.

Welsh Nation (November 1961)

A Ward for Wales

THE PLYMOUTH WARD of the County Borough of Merthyr Tydfil stretches across the wide Taff Valley just south of Merthyr Town. It takes its name from an early iron works called after the prominent landowning family who, in our day, gave St.Fagans to the nation. But the name is the only English thing about this area. Around the iron works and their collieries there grew up in the last century three sizeable and separate communities: Troed-y-rhiw, Pentre-bach and Abercanaid. But they grew on old foundations.

The bridge at Pont-rhun in the middle of Troed-y-rhiw has legendary associations with the martyrdom of Saint Tydfil. In the wooded hills above Abercanaid, some of the very earliest Welsh dissenters met to worship in their own way in defiance of English law. It was from Troed-y-rhiw that Edward Morgan, the Jacobite, rode out in rebellion in 1745. It was to Troed-y-rhiw that he returned to face the gallows, declaring with the true reckless courage of the Taff Valley that he would rather go home to Wales and hang than stay on in Scotland and starve. Industry grew apace. Abercanaid was the home of Lucy Thomas, traditionally the Founding Mother of the Welsh steam coal export trade. And with industry, the tyranny of the alien ironmasters. The passing of time has not erased the bitter ancestral memories and family traditions of exploitation and humiliation. On such soil the radical ferment of the last century reached great heights.

The most revolutionary social doctrines were preached and backed up by vigorous action. From Troed-y-rhiw came Enoch Morrell who stormed up through strike and open riot to become Merthyr Tydfil's first Mayor. From Abercanaid came Noah Ablett, urging the miners to take the famous Next Step that has yet to be taken. The streets of Troed-y-rhiw witnessed memorable scenes of public emotion on that fine Sunday morning in 1915 when the crowds coming out of chapel were met by newsboys crying the death of Keir Hardie. When Plaid Cymru strode into an arena like this the whole of Welsh history was cheering us from the touchline.

Against this background, the hard facts of the present stand out starkly. Between Pentre-bach and Abercanaid, the great Hoover Washing Machine Factory glitters and sprawls – the one basket that still contains too many of our eggs. Opposite it, the old Kayser Bondor Factory, once hailed as the biggest plant of its kind, now a mere storehouse for Hoovers, and down the road the old colliery buildings that used to house the Standard Box factory, lost to the area by official stupidity. And from end to end of the ward, derelict collieries, defunct railways, weed-grown tips. Amenities and public services poor and threatened. Street lighting Dickensian. Roads? Well, Abercanaid was essentially a canal-side community, and when the Canal Age ended, it was stranded in the middle of nowhere. In 1962 a crumbling towpath is still its only communication with Troed-y-rhiw. The ward boundaries reach up the crests of the hills, and include that lovely mountain top community of Cwm Bargod – an almost unbelievable example of isolation, dereliction and neglect. Such has been the heritage of generations of rule by what some still call Socialism.

Here then, Plaid Cymru challenged the might of a well-organized machine and massive habits of loyalty to old ideas. On our side, youth and enthusiasm – and Wales. It was a cold weather campaign, fought in the teeth of freezing gales, but the wind that blew was the mighty wind of change. The personality of our candidate, Gwyn Griffiths, focussed the essential appeal of Plaid Cymru as the party of change, progress and self-respect. The Labour candidate was by no means negligible. He fought a thorough campaign and was dignified in defeat. But by age, and in all that he stood for, he belonged to a period that is passing. Gwyn Griffiths's young supporters swept through the streets like the brisk cleansing wind of those days. A vigorous battle of pamphlets and counter-pamphlets was waged. Spontaneous debates took place in pubs. From darkened telly screens the voice of Radio Free Wales took the air. Fantastic quantities of Plaid literature were sold. New members joined every day. The flaming presence of Glyn James swept us along. 'Wales is on the march,' he declaimed, and he never spoke a truer word.

From Cardiff and the Rhymni Valley, the South-Eastern Commando Brigade rallied, as always, to the call. To some of us, the result was never in doubt, but the size of the Nationalist majority was an undreamt of bonus. To some, it will raise problems and doubts. But when allowance has been made for every possible type of non-nationalist vote that came our way, Plaid Cymru is now the official opposition in the Council Chamber and the only possible alternative government of Merthyr Tydfil. Perhaps more important still, the old unquestioning loyalty to Labour has been shattered beyond repair – here in its birthplace and stronghold. Those mountainous majorities had once seemed as immoveable as the Great Tips of Dowlais, but by hard work they can be bulldozed away to reveal the enduring rock of nationhood. Through the breach in the enemy lines we must pour in and punch hard.

Looking back on every election, there is always one picture that seems to stand out. This time I think of a night in Harriet-town, a huddle of stone houses perched above the Taff. Framed in her doorway, a typical, cheerful Valley housewife, beaming maternally on a group of Gwyn Griffiths's young supporters in their jeans and duffel coats. 'The future we've got to think of, isn't it?' she called out. And waving a Plaid Cymru election address, 'These youngsters are bringing it to us'.

Welsh Nation (March 1962)

Instalment of Murder

TO MANY NATIONALISTS, the position of the Welsh language is that of a mountain peak which crowns the scene but is far beyond the bounds of their own journey, especially if they set out to rebuild Wales in an area from which the language has retreated. There are others to whom its challenge is insistent, and must be faced at once. Recently, the question has been well-aired. Saunders Lewis has spoken, and when the greatest living Welshman speaks, even the least worthy of his countrymen is forced to listen. Gwynfor Evans has published an excellent pamphlet outlining steps which can be taken at the administrative level. Educationists like Bobi Jones and Jac L.Williams have discussed the technical aspects of the problem in the press. But as far as it is a question of education, the brunt of responsibility for actually getting something done falls on the local councillors on the education committees of our counties or county boroughs.

In Merthyr Tydfil, the three Plaid Cymru councillors already in the chamber (there will be more soon) tabled a resolution calling for the teaching of the Welsh language, together with Welsh history and culture at all levels in the primary and secondary schools in the borough. These three men are: Bill Williams, a factory worker who left grammar school at the age of 15, Welsh-speaking; Tudor Evans, a building worker with elementary school education and no Welsh; Gwyn Griffiths, a brewery secretary and café-owner, college-trained, non-Welsh-speaking. They are a representative cross-section of the people, with no vested interests, no academic axe to grind, not culture-vultures. In tabling this, their first major policy motion, they were motivated by pure Nationalism, acting in the best interests of the Nation, putting first things first.

Once the resolution had been expounded, it was immediately assailed. Regretfully it must be recorded that the first attack came from the Rev.D.R.Thomas, a scholarly man of wide interests and sympathies but apparently baffled by this direct approach to an important problem. The Church having put the boot in, the Labour Party ran true to form: Councillor Dai Jones, Welsh-speaking but anti-Welsh (a conjunction which would seem paradoxical were it not so depressingly familiar) patted himself on the back on his knowledge of the language and taunted Tudor Evans for his ignorance of it. Alderman Charlie Webb BEM, said that he was proud to be Welsh: Councillor Tal Lloyd OBE spoke, as always, at some length and to no ascertainable purpose. Councillor Albert John said he knew people who didn't want their children to be taught Welsh. (Doubtless, but a thorough enquiry would probably be a nasty shock for him.) Councillor Donovan shed a tear over the fate of Irish, and called for an international language.

The Mayor thought that if we supported the National Eisteddfod everything would be all right. The Director of Education outlined what was being done already – nothing in the infants' schools, Welsh in eleven out of twenty-one junior schools, two out of seven modern schools, and first and second year teaching in the grammar schools, with continuation optional. A familiar picture, and, to be fair, better than some, but by no means good enough. Many of the problems stem from the bankruptcy of the educational system nationally, which has led to a shortage of specialist teachers and the difficulty of filling such posts as exist. The Director of Education is an able man and his heart is in the right place; the Welsh teachers of the borough have done good work over the years (the crowned bard of Llangefni was a Merthyr man), but no advance will be achieved without a change of beat – and of personnel – in the Council Chamber.

In a flood of crocodile tears and a fog of half-baked humbug the motion was defeated. The Labour Party, discredited in every other direction, will now strive to make what political capital they can out of the bogey of 'compulsion', though this meaningless point was capably demolished by the Director. There were, indeed, some in Plaid Cymru itself who thought that this was a motion which could have been left until after the May elections. But with our colours nailed to the mast, we hailed a triumph of principle over calculations of expediency. It is whispered by some that we have gone ahead of public opinion, and may lose seats. This is hardly likely, but, whatever the outcome, the branch has unanimously congratulated the councillors on their stand, and the Labour Party, not only in Merthyr Tydfil, but throughout Wales, stands revealed in its true colours.

Welsh Nation (April 1962)

Stooges in the English Political Game

JUST HOW DOES the average English voter look on Wales? What does he really know about Wales and her problems? Does he ever concern himself about conditions in Wales, and about what is troubling her people? If it came to the bit would he really care or would he just shrug his shoulders and say, 'I suppose something must be done about it?' Would his own interests and the interests and standing of England come first, would he not expect the party for whom he votes to place these interests first, and then if Welsh or Scottish or Irish interests needed some attention these could be dealt with thereafter provided he was not asked to sacrifice anything of his own well-being? Should the Welsh voter not admit that this is the truth and act and vote accordingly?

Every Englishman when anything happens asks himself, how does this affect me and my country, England? That is his chief concern. His chief fault is that he thinks of the English as superior to other peoples, and what he thinks is good for them, or their place in his scheme of things, must be best for them.

While demanding and accepting what he thinks – and in this he may be quite right – is his due from the Government and other bodies, and from society in general, he is, however, rather apt to forget the Welsh have the same or should have the same rights as himself; he grumbles and says why cannot the Welsh look after themselves, why should they mooch so much on me and look to me for so much help.

Let each Welsh voter ask himself just what part does he play in the present political party set-up? He can shout and bluster, but when it comes to the bit what influence has he on what takes place in London in his political party, his trade union or other society, body or organization to which he belongs? He is outvoted or ignored by the solid united English majority in their particular United Kingdom political party, or in their Westminster Governments.

The average Welshman has accustomed himself to be so dependent on his trade union or other of the United Kingdom political parties that he has abjectly subordinated himself to the rule and direction of the solidly united English majority in each. He cannot separate himself from the dictates of that majority, he just accepts this subordinate position, and Wales thus finds herself in the position in which she is today.

If all these parties and bodies, including the Westminster Government, had formulated policies and taken action to apply equally to meet the requirements in all the constituent parts, surely the benefits would also have been equal to everyone and to each area. Then why has Wales, why has Scotland or even Northern Ireland not received equal benefits from the results of the efforts of all these parties and bodies and of the Westminster Governments? Why has Wales not expanded as the Midlands and South-East England have? Why has Wales so much greater unemployment? Why have the rural areas become practically derelict and more remote as time goes on?

Shifting from one particular United Kingdom political

party and Government has not made much difference; the overall rot continues. To declaim against one particular party Government or one particular United Kingdom party has not got Wales anywhere, as past experience has shown. It might have got England somewhere, and may yet in the future, but the odds are heavily against much lasting improvement in Wales.

Wales in the past has been divided, one or more political divisions fighting against the other, and each blaming the English majority in another United Kingdom party for what has occurred and is occurring in Wales. The Tories, the Liberals and Labour are each but a Welsh subordinate section or branch of a United Kingdom political party whose policy and actions are directed by the solid English majority which must and does cater primarily for the interests of the English voter.

Where will the next Government be decided? It will be in the southerly part of the United Kingdom: the populous and prosperous Midlands and South-East England. It is obvious that the programme and policies of each of the UK parties (Liberal, Labour or Tory) must be directed to the voters in these areas.

All we in Wales will be doing if we vote for any of these parties will be to give them aid, by adding a comparatively few seats to the numbers from South England, and Wales will again be hopelessly divided, dependent again on the English majorities in each of the UK political parties.

The Welsh voter will be but a pawn in the English game of political chess, moved this way and that irrespective of his interest in order to conform to the particular tactics thought desirable to win the game for the Midlands and South England voters.

In Wales we must have a national voice which will speak clearly and independently for Wales no matter how the game goes in England. Wales's interests and well-being must not be sacrificed on the altar of English party politics. We must assert ourselves on Wales's behalf and on behalf of each and every Welsh man, woman and child. We can vote Plaid Cymru.

Welsh Nation (May 1962)

The Joys of Battle

WE OF PLAID CYMRU are concerned with Wales. We seek to advance the well-being of our national community in all its aspects. We are concerned with the economic problems of her industries and her countryside, the welfare of her people and the enrichment of her cultural life. We believe, on the evidence of past history and of contemporary developments, that the main obstacle to the full expansion of the potentialities of our country and people is that we lack the elementary right of self-government. We claim the freedom to make for ourselves the fundamental economic and political decisions which govern the life of every community. We believe that it is grossly irresponsible and childish to continue to allow these decisions to be made for us elsewhere. We claim the rights of nationhood; we claim the responsibilities of nationhood. If we do not exercise these rights and responsibilities then we will not be able to achieve our full stature either as citizens or as individual human beings, and our country will continue to drift into the shadows.

We believe that Wales is rich, not only in physical resources, but in human, cultural and spiritual resources, and that to fail to develop these fully is to impoverish not only our country and ourselves but Europe and the whole world. Therefore it is our duty to ourselves and to humanity in general to claim these rights and responsibilities. That is the meaning of Welsh Nationalism. To us, Wales is not merely a lot of romantic scenery, it is the home of a people – a nation. We are not concerned with abstract theories, nor are we a pressure group for powerful vested interests.

We want to take part in the building of a better world, based on peace, order and justice. But to do that, we have to begin by putting our own house in order. The aspirations of Welsh Nationalism are world-wide in their scope, but the daily preoccupation of Welsh Nationalists is with the down-to-earth, bread-and-butter problems which confront all of us in our daily life and work. While never for a moment losing sight of the overriding need for an Independent Welsh Government, making its voice heard in the councils of the nations, there is much that can be done in the mean time. Our sights are focussed on these immediate problems and possibilities, our aim is true, and where we have the resources to open fire, we have landed bang on the target.

Wales is not an abstraction, not a mere subject for sentimental rhetoric at eisteddfodau and St.David's Night dinners. It consists of seaports and industrial cities, mining valleys and quarrying communities, market towns and a varied countryside. Each of these has its own problems, and every local problem is part of the overall national problem. With every local problem successfully tackled, the nation is strengthened. With every national issue that goes by default, a town or a valley or a village – real people in real places – are the losers. Therefore the Welsh Nationalist can never be idle. Every parish or rural district, every borough and urban district, every county and county borough has its elected council. These councils have powers, they have opportunities. They are close to the people, so close that familiarity sometimes breeds contempt, and many of their functions are unsensational and humdrum. But the Nationalist, though proud of his nationhood, is humble before his sense of responsibility to the nation, and no task is too trivial for him.

Plaid Cymru representatives on local authorities have in a short time made contributions out of all proportion to their numbers. They have achieved these results because they are motivated by this sense of responsibility to the people and the nation, that is lacking elsewhere. Better local government could transform the face of Wales. In some districts, merely to have a clean, honest, moderately efficient administration would be a revolution in itself. And although the London Government has consistently narrowed local powers, if all these powers were used in a progressive and dynamic manner, the economy and amenities of our towns and countryside would show a great improvement.

The old parties have had generations in which to prove themselves, and in most cases they have failed, and in some cases have failed shockingly. The mentality of these organizations is unrealistic and irresponsible to the point of fantasy. The anti-Welsh parties with their irrelevant and outmoded theories and habits of thought, their humiliating dependence on London to do their thinking, write their policies for them, their timorous and servile unwillingness to offend Whitehall, their careerism and cynicism, their open contempt for the people, these are not the instruments of change and betterment. Only Welsh Nationalism can bring these things about. It is the movement of national self-respect, incarnating the national will to live.

As Gwynfor Evans has aptly said, Plaid Cymru is the Do-it-Yourself party. Not only is Welsh Nationalism relevant to the concrete and practical facts of daily life, both great and small, not only does it satisfy the intellect and the intelligence, it has another supreme advantage: it offers the fullest personal satisfaction to the individual. The Nationalist cannot be idle, neither can he be bored, because every aspect of life, however commonplace, seen in the light of Nationalism, becomes vividly significant. The Nationalist may become exhausted, but he can never be discouraged, because he knows that he is fighting the battle of a people that has never really given up, though they have come near to it at times. In some way or another, every single Welsh man and woman, deep down, is a Nationalist. The active worker for Plaid Cymru is like a pit-sinker, hewing laboriously through the hard rock of cynicism, defeatism and indifference but knowing that he will surely strike a rich vein of Best Welsh, and that Wales and Europe and the whole world would one day warm its hands in the glow of that fire.

Welsh Nation (May 1962)

Hustings in Paradise

IT MUST HAVE BEEN a long time since so much interest and speculation were focussed on Llanfihangel yng Ngwynfa and Llanfair Caereinion. Of all the provinces of our stormy land, Powys the Paradise of Wales has had the least eventful recent history. The Free Commune of Llanidloes, the Senate of Independent Wales at Machynlleth, the dreamer from Newtown, and the doer from Llandinam have come and gone, and it is a far cry from Owain Cyfeiliog to Emlyn Hooson, from the circling of the mead-horn in Mathrafal to a big Liberal vote announced from Welshpool Town Hall.

At first it may seem difficult for Nationalists to draw any lesson from the by-election which is not profoundly depressing. It can hardly be said that anything went seriously wrong with the conduct or organization of the campaign in the capable hands of Trefor Edwards and the party's officials. Workers there were in plenty from all over Wales. In Islwyn Ffowc Elis, Wales was represented by a candidate whose name alone was a guarantee of the highest standards of ability and integrity. Not even the most rigorous critic could fault the presentation of the party's message in terms of pure Nationalism ('Wales versus the Rest') or the cogent illustration of that message in terms of what was happening and would continue to happen to our water resources, communications, family farms, and small industrial towns under the present regime.

Yet despite all this, the electorate returned to Parliament a well-connected young man (Hooson-in-law to the wits of Llanidloes) whose undoubted abilities will lead him eventually, via the Commons, to some post of merited eminence in his profession, for it is unlikely that his party will ever be in a position to offer him high political office despite talk of a 'revival' in their fortunes. In fact, the Liberal 'achievement' in Montgomeryshire has been no more than to retrieve their losses of 1959 and to restore their 1955 vote. The position, then, is essentially a static one, and, if the Liberals have little cause for claiming an advance, the other English parties have even less reason for satisfaction. Tory and Labour alike lost a lot of votes, and this not to a 'reviving' Liberalism of the English type but to a well-entrenched county 'Establishment' on the defensive for the first time in a generation and with an immense accumulated fund of patronage, prestige, influence, connections and favours on which they made ruthless draughts. The situation in Montgomeryshire was, in fact, oddly like that in Ebbw Vale after the death of Aneurin Bevan. On both occasions the ghost of a famous man fought for his undisputed heir. In both places the appeal was to sentiment, tradition and loyalty, or what passes for such in modern Wales, not the real sentiment, the true tradition, the only loyalty. And this appeal was reinforced by the promise or reminder of material, social and personal benefits, inducements so subtle and pressures so intangible as never to incur the slightest imputation of the coercive, or the improper, and yet, inexorably herding the votes along the beaten highways of custom and habit. In green

Powys and the cramped valleys of Gwent, the Establishments bore all before them, and the disappointed English parties in each case are in no position to pour scorn on Plaid Cymru.

As to these Establishments, whether they be Labour, as in the industrial valleys, Liberal as over large areas of the countryside or Tory as in some peripheral districts, they are explicitly rooted in the denial of the Welsh claim to self-realization, and erect against it a rampart constructed of every possible variety of short-term material interest, mental inertia and psychological perversity, a barrier so huge that many live and die in its shadow without realizing that it exists, or that this very shadow is anything but the light of day. Nevertheless, breakthrough is possible, and perhaps the most significant thing about Montgomeryshire wasn't the result, which was predictable, but Mr.Hooson's victory broadcast in which he claimed that his success was due to the voters' dissatisfaction with the Government on three accounts: firstly, its handling of local Mid-Wales affairs; secondly, its handling of Welsh affairs; and only thirdly, its handling of more general problems. It is unlikely that anything like this has ever been heard before on the London Home Service of the BBC. Plaid Cymru, in fact, set the pace and pitched the key of the whole campaign, and if, for the time being, others reap where they have not sown, and spokesmen of alien parties make Nationalist speeches while attacking the Blaid, this irrational situation is unstable and cannot long endure. Plaid Cymru has the ball at its feet.

But we have been in this position too often before to afford complacency now, or to indulge in any but the most perfunctory felicitations. It is reported that while there is widespread sympathy for the party's aims, there is little in the way of concrete support. To convert the one into the other demands the unsparing labour of those concerned with day to day organization. It demands, too, vigorous self-examination on the part of those who call themselves Nationalists. If Montgomeryshire has its hopeful lessons for us, it also exposes weaknesses far more serious than shortage of money, machinery and manpower. There is a great deal of genuflexion in Nationalist circles before the Welsh language and all that it stands for. If there is one man who has taken the Welsh language seriously by proclaiming his faith that it is possible to make a living as a writer in Welsh, and by staking his livelihood on the prospect of setting up as a full-time professional writer in the language, then that man is Islwyn Ffowc Elis. Like all creative artists in whatever medium, he is, of course, a Nationalist, and moreover, prominently identified with the political work of Plaid Cymru. But if there is one man in the whole of Wales who could have been excused politics, who could have been told that with a clear conscience he could stay home and write his books, that man is Islwyn Ffowc Elis. And yet it was this man who came forward to carry the standard of Wales in Powys when no other could be found. He himself gains immeasurably in stature by his action. Honour too must go to Pennar Davies who also came forward at the last moment, and to the untiring energies of Plaid Cymru's President, Gwynfor Evans, who for years has been trying to persuade somebody to put up in the county. But the party will not be taken seriously by the people of Wales until it is first taken seriously by its own members, many of whom are all too ready to grumble at the 'indifference' and slow response of their fellow countrymen. Let this be the lesson of Montgomery to Plaid Cymru.

Editorial, *Welsh Nation* (June 1962)

Historic Judgement

THE CASE OF Gwynfor S.Evans of Betws has been generally recognized as of national and historical importance. As such it joins the list of crucial lawsuits of the past and as such it is a pointer to the future. The Llanfrothen case towards the end of the last century was a victory for Welsh Nonconformity, in its time and place a radical Nationalist movement. That judgement in favour of the Nonconformists anticipated by many years the disestablishment of the Church of England in Wales and the birth of an autonomous national Church in Wales on a footing of equality with the other denominations, but once the first steps had been taken, once the initial act of defiance had been made, the final outcome was only a matter of time – of time, perseverance and determination.

Similarly the Taff Vale case early in this century was an important milestone in the history of Trade Unionism. The verdict went against the Unions but this verdict was so much at variance with the spirit of the times that it was speedily reversed and by its very perverseness speeded the emancipation of the working man. Thus a secluded rural parish in northern Wales and a grim industrial battlefield of the exploited South lent their names to momentous decisions.

Llanfrothen, Taff Vale and now Ammanford.

For this is the present battle. The right to worship and to think in a way different from England's way was upheld at Llanfrothen, and is now the secure possession of all who choose to exert themselves in worship and thought. Taff Vale in a back-handed way saw the triumph of organized labour which endured even through the reverses of the 'twenties and 'thirties. No one would claim that it established any more than a modest instalment of social justice, but it secured all that can be secured under the present system. In this second half of the twentieth century we face far more fundamental problems. Independence and originality of mind and spirit on the one hand, the dignity and security of labour on the other, both essential to healthy society, are now dependent on the survival of Wales as a viable national community. And the language, even to those (perhaps especially to those) whose command of it is weak or non-existent, is a symbol and a guarantee of that nationhood which is the last defence of spirit and body, of individual and society against the horrors of uniformity and centralization, against the 'brave new world' of docile, conditioned, rootless mobile labour units, the ultimate destiny of man as envisaged by big-business Conservatism and soulless bureaucratic Socialism alike.

The very nature of man cries out against the condition decreed for him by his masters or would-be masters, and this is the basic strength of Welsh Nationalism. Indeed, we in Wales, despite our manifold troubles, are fortunate in that we have this sense of belonging to and being responsible for a very special place – 'this corner of the earth' – and every attempt we make here to vindicate the true nature of man as a being with rights and responsibility is a blow struck in defence of human dignity throughout the world.

We have referred to the judgements of the past. Doubtless these too were arrived at in open court and with due respect to the precedents and technicalities of the law. But it cannot be doubted that both these historic verdicts were in fact political decisions: the one against ideological intolerance and privilege, the other inopportunely upholding and thereby undermining the inhumanity and irresponsibility of the capitalist system, gaining everything and losing nothing in force from being made by courts which by and large sustain the status quo. And as these famous cases of our fathers' days and their consequences were victories in themselves and heralds of further victories for freedom of thought and the rights of labour and were so hailed by the progressive movements of those days, so today we boldly claim, with the President of Plaid Cymru, that the Ammanford Judgement is a political victory for Plaid Cymru and the herald of further victories for the cause of our nation.

The electoral reverse that followed the High Court judgement – not unexpected by those versed in the oddities of the Welsh temperament – while it pales into insignificance in comparison with the main issue, suggests two considerations. The first is the wisdom of Mr. Saunders Lewis's recent counsel that in Welsh-speaking areas action on behalf of the language could do more for the nation than more directly or conventionally political action; though it must be remembered that in this battle there can be no spectators and that every such campaign in northern or western Wales must be complemented by vigorous exertions on more familiar lines elsewhere, and that, throughout Wales, elections, as well as court decisions, must be won. This brings us to the second and perhaps most important point: it is not the slightest use having the Welsh language recognized by the High Court of England if it is not recognized, respected and cherished by the people of Wales.

In his article in this issue, the President of Plaid Cymru names some of the winning Welsh team. Others could be mentioned. The President himself played his usual captain's innings, but it is perhaps particularly significant and encouraging that the historic nomination form that began it all was drawn up by the champion of an earlier battle for the language, Mrs.Eileen Beasley, whose protracted ordeal at the hands of the bureaucrats should never be forgotten. The example of people like these needs to be borne continually in mind and acted upon with vigour if it is to become effective. Our forebears took on an easily identifiable handful of bishops and bosses. Today's enemy is far more sinister and pervasive. He lurks, not unseen but all too often unrecognized for what he is, in every public and private sphere in our land, and his exposure, humiliation and ultimate defeat and expulsion from Wales will demand unceasing vigilance and unflagging energy. It is more than a merely political task, as Nationalism is more than a merely political creed. The Ammanford case serves notice on the enemies of Wales to quit; it serves notice too on all who call themselves Nationalists, of the necessity for total commitment to the cause.

Editorial, *Welsh Nation* (July 1962)

Broadcasting in Wales

IT WOULD BE tempting to pursue a great many of the hares that have been flushed out of the alien corn by the reverberations of the Pilkington Report. We could comment acidly on the manoeuverings, protestations, recriminations and exculpations of various interested parties both in Wales and in London; we could spare a moment to gloat over the heads that are rolling against the wainscot in the Tory back-room responsible for selecting the Committee which came up with such a devastating criticism of the basic assumptions of the Tory Utopia; we could even join in the chorus of comment on the more immediately sensational aspects of the Report, but our duty as Nationalists is to deal with fundamentals, and with implications which will have been understandably neglected elsewhere.

The first point to be made with all the emphasis at our command, is that the Pilkington recommendations concerning Wales, coming hard on the heels of the Ammanford Judgement in the High Court, represented yet another triumph for Plaid Cymru.

While the Report does not go all the way to meeting the just demands of Wales, and while the White Paper on the Report imposes, as was to be expected, further demur, yet so much of Plaid Cymru's requirements have been conceded as to represent a major breakthrough, and that in the field of mass communications, one of the most important arenas of our age.

That Wales is to have priority in the allocation of the third channel, that Wales is to have its own television service unencumbered by the demands of an English region, that the powers of the national Broadcasting Council are to be enhanced (though not to the status of an autonomous Corporation) vindicate many years of apparently fruitless effort by Plaid Cymru. While it is true that Plaid Cymru has not laboured alone in this field, its was the first voice to be raised and, on some points, the only voice.

That the shameful ban on political broadcasts for Wales is to be reconsidered represents an even more significant breakthrough. Consider the terms in which the Committee treated this point, the very words of the question they asked themselves: 'Should the United Kingdom as a whole remain the Unit for party political broadcasts?' (p.16 of the Abridged Report). And the answer, by recommending separate political broadcasts for Wales (and Scotland) even though these are to be additional to those for the United Kingdom as a whole, admits as clearly as we could ever expect to be admitted at this stage of events, that United Kingdom unity is not the sacrosanct formula, the mystic, sweet communion so often lauded by Labour and Conservative politicians.

Some years ago the Labour Party argued, 'If we allowed Plaid Cymru to have separate broadcasts for Wales, we would be conceding the truth of their argument that Wales demands separate consideration.'

It is difficult now to see how such zealous upholders of London authority can dissent from recommendations emanating from a source they consider sacred.

Neatly hoist with their own petard, they are at last morally obliged to practise the democratic virtues they preach.

We would be less than human if this situation did not tickle us, but our satisfaction derives from a much greater cause than the discomfiture of a handful of elderly diehards. We repeat: the doctrine of a monolithic, homogeneous 'United Kingdom' has been severely modified, and not in any remote administrative sphere but in the world of TV and radio that reaches into every home. The consequences could be incalculable.

The recommendation loses nothing from its occurrence in a report which elsewhere takes the predictable attitude to the demand for a separate Welsh organization, which makes excuses about shortage of money and technical resources (but who invented the microphone, Sir Harry?), and which blandly proclaims that 'the dangers of Londonization are less than the dangers of isolation.' Since those words were written, Telstar has arisen in the sky, and 'isolation' is no longer a viable concept.

Which brings us to the fundamental problem of mass communications as they affect Wales. Possibly, soon there will be masts covering the whole of Wales, with a network of sound and vision programmes which could be of good quality, in Welsh and English, and it would still be on the cards that too many sets would be tuned in to Granada, Westward and Telefis Eireann, to Luxembourg, the Light and AFN.

The challenge here is twofold. Most obviously it is thrown to those who originate our programmes. Judging by past offerings, some of which have been magnificent and others downright dreadful, we can safely propound that for a small nation to concentrate on quantity at the expense of quality is suicidal. It has proved disastrous in other spheres and the overproduction of banalities would exhaust our available talents (not to mention the patience of the audiences) as surely as the overproduction of raw coal crippled our economic life. To speak for and to the Welsh nation is a privilege which demands infinite originality and inventiveness, a rigid avoidance of the phoney, the modish (which in Wales always turns out to be not quite the latest thing), the false sentimental distortions of our national life and downright reactionary ignoring of so much activity and so many individuals who display genuine creativity.

The other challenge is to Nationalists to create a Welsh audience with the Welsh mind, to whom the emanations of Telstar, Alexander Palace and Eurovision will be no more than an occasional distraction, who will take their nurture (as far as this may be derived from radio and TV) from Welsh sources, who will absorb outside influences naturally and without detriment to their status as citizens of Wales and trustees of her heritage.

Editorial, *Welsh Nation* (August 1962)

The National Will to Live

IT IS TO BE welcomed rather than regretted that Plaid Cymru has come under a particularly heavy barrage of criticism recently. However crapulous and contemptible much of this criticism has been, it is at least preferable to the alternative response of the challenge of Welsh Nationalism – Silence.

Silence has until recently been a very effective weapon, the perfect defence, one demanding no effort and so particularly adapted to the use of the enemies of Wales, who would be hard put to it to justify their position in any active or constructive manner. It is a weapon, moreover, that has been brought to perfection by continued practice, long before it became the instinctive reflex of those who had nothing to say, or nothing they would dare say publicly. One can almost imagine that no sooner was the last of the Tudors safely off the English throne than the directive went out: 'Ignore Wales'. For despite the pretence that the two countries had been united on grounds of equality, the so-called 'Act of Union', which we are now learning to call the Act of Annexation, in fact abolished Wales, and in as far as this move was inaugurated and supported by certain influential groups inside Wales itself it was as much an act of suicide as of genocide. Since the passage of that fatal Statute, as Wynne Samuel, the Vice-President of Plaid Cymru, has recently reminded us, only four acts concerned particularly with Wales have reached the Statute Book, and this legislative neglect has been paralleled in every sphere of human activity – with the important exception of the exploitation of the economic wealth of our country. And always the response to any vindication of Welsh claims has been this bland silence – not only from our rulers in London, who have at least the excuse that we have connived at our own non-existence, but from the heirs of those first Unionist suicides, the living dead in Wales itself, the zombies whom no quickening breath of national revival can ever reanimate.

Fortunately, this defence is wearing thin under the repeated assaults of the national will to live, as incarnated in Plaid Cymru. No longer can it be pretended that the forces of Welsh revival are inconsiderable. The leaders of the English political parties in Wales have been cut down to their small and shabby size by the recommendations of the Pilkington Committee which would give Plaid Cymru access to radio and television time. The press, even at its most hostile or indifferent, is now obliged to take note when Plaid Cymru speaks or acts, and many local papers, dependent for their existence on a prosperous local community, have begun to realize on which side their bread is buttered, and are fair, or even favourable, to Nationalism. The ostrich-like attitude of a certain Gwynedd newspaper is an exception which is rapidly becoming ridiculous to the point of fantasy.

The alternative to silence is – the Scream. This deafening explosion of hate is triggered off by any and every display of the instinct of self-preservation on the part of Wales. It can be a militant and aggressive action as recently at Tryweryn, or a modest insistence on the rightful place of the Welsh language. Whatever the stimulus, the reaction is always utterly irrational and disproportionate, fountaining up from the depths of guilt like a geyser of stinking mud in some contorted volcanic landscape. Nobody who takes Wales seriously should be alarmed by such manifestations, however unpleasant they may be. If the Blaid were to pursue some decorous course dictated by nothing more than sentimental regard for '*yr hen iaith*' or 'the Welsh way of life' or any of the other superficial and evasive attitudes which must inevitably flourish in a subject nation, then undoubtedly it would earn more praise than blame. And every such tribute would be but a wreath on the coffin of Wales.

But because Plaid Cymru takes Wales seriously, because there are men in her ranks who are prepared to strike a blow for the nation, are prepared boldly to diagnose her illness and bluntly to lay the blame on the quacks who have brought her to this pass, to plan and work for her welfare, then the party automatically incurs not only the enmity of the professional purveyors of dubious remedies but stirs up feelings of unease whose historical and psychological roots go very deep. We have all, at some time or other, failed our country; the stain of ancestral guilt is almost part of our natural complexion, and those of us who are trying to redeem not only ourselves but past generations are a standing reproach to those who have compounded it with an ignoble and servile acquiescence.

To take a transiently known name, no more or less important than that of many such, we have been denounced in the most unmeasured language by Mr.Alun Talfan Davies. That a spluttering Socialist or a shrill, scolding schoolmistress in *Y Faner* or tatty Tories in the *Western Mail* should rage like the heathen and imagine vain things is to be expected. But Mr.Davies in another of his capacities is a cultured man and a benefactor to Welsh literature. He takes the Welsh language at least seriously enough to want the Honourable Society of Cymmrodorion to do something about it. As a publisher, we respect him; as a politician, we can only point him out as the most perfect current example of the split Welsh personality. The agonized wretchedness of mind which has driven him to compete with the most degraded of our Socialist traitors in his search for off-colour adjectives and snide insinuations about Plaid Cymru represent a shocking disintegration of standards – a complete moral collapse which invokes a sort of horrified pity rather than any desire to swap recriminations. But even from these pathetic ravings we can salvage something significant and encouraging. Mr.Davies fears that 'our sons and daughters' – presumably the sons and daughters of decent-minded Liberals – will fall under the spell of Plaid Cymru. This at least is something that can be said about Plaid Cymru that cannot be said about any other party. The old parties have failed Wales, and the sons and daughters of Liberals, Socialists and Conservatives are all justifying Mr.Davies's worst fears, and are leaving these obsolete ideas to perish, and are proclaiming their allegiance, not to this or that English-made illusion, but to the abiding reality that is Wales, whose sons and daughters they are.

Keep you silence as best you may, scream as loud as you like; nothing can alter that.

Welsh Nation (November 1962)

The Breed of the Sparrowhawk

ELSEWHERE IN THIS number of the *Welsh Nation* our readers will have enjoyed Peter Hourahane's lively presentation of the proudest days in all the long history of our land. No excuse is needed for the retelling of this tale. No excuse is needed to justify the custom of celebrating the 16th of September every year as Glyn Dŵr's Day, a custom which it is gratifying to record has caught on and is likely to take root. For too long the Welsh have not had the moral right to commemorate such a day or to invoke the names of our national heroes of the past. But there are signs that, decadent as we may seem to have become, blood and not watered milk runs in the veins of at least some Welshmen. And it is not September 16th, 1400 that is in our minds as we write these words but September 23rd, 1962 – the night that Dai Pritchard of New Tredegar and Dai Walters of Bargod redeemed the honour of Wales.

Not the least significant detail in the story of Owain Glyn Dŵr is the episode of the Cardiff citizen who was executed for declaring, in the heart of that alien garrison town, as it then was, his loyalty to the rightful ruler of Wales. His name, John Sperhawke (or Sparrowhawk as it would be spelt today), is not only picturesquely medieval, it is wildly and unmistakably un-Welsh.

His roots in our land must have been recent and shallow, and his environment as foreign as his forebears.

One doubts that he knew much Welsh beyond the jargon of the market-place, and the rich cultural activity then in full flower could have meant little to him. Yet he threw in his lot with his country even though it meant death.

Not the least significant factor in the latest developments at Tryweryn is that the two young patriots concerned hail from the Rhymni Valley. Welsh as to their ancestry they may possibly be, but people from other, more recognizably 'Welsh' parts of Wales, even from some of the neighbouring coalfield valleys, who find themselves in New Tredegar and Bargod often find it impossible to acclimatize themselves to the environment and will only grudgingly concede that such places are Welsh at all, and that in a sense so restricted as to be meaningless.

Yet it is from shallow-rooted, recent and hastily run-up villages like these, that the men have come who have made us all once again proud to be of the same blood with them.

Walters and Pritchard are Welsh enough names as names go, but what little of the language they possess between them has been painfully acquired in adult life, after it had been lost in their background for the usual count of generations. Yet in making their stand at Tryweryn they were acting in defence of that language as surely as they were acting in defence of Welsh land.

As part of the Land of Wales, Tryweryn is, of course, inalienably Welsh, whatever laws may be passed elsewhere, whatever notice-boards and fences be erected by bandits and plunderers from over the Dyke. But added force was lent to the argument against its rape by Liverpool because it was so unmistakably, typically and essentially Welsh in its language and way of life. And when every process of law had been exhausted, when every democratic device had been worked to its fullest extent, when public opinion had been mobilized on the issue to a unanimity almost without parallel – and all in vain – then, when both land and language seemed lost, there arose on their ruins that without which land is but soil and language mere sound – the rebirth of our National Honour in the determination of two young men that evil and wrong should not go unresisted, and men, at that, from an environment so dissimilar economically and culturally from Merioneth as to have made many despair, in the past, of ever welding such unlike communities into a united nation.

But now the nation lives as never before in this generation, united as never before. All this is above, beyond and outside politics. Plaid Cymru pursues its course with the untiring relentless patience that has always been its strength, along the dull and dusty highways of electoral activity, but a highway lit now by the torch of high resolve kindled by the men of the Rhymni Valley. For while such a spirit exists in its ranks, who can doubt that Wales is worth fighting for?

Our readers will already know that there are plans afoot to enforce the official recognition of the Welsh language in areas where it is the language of the majority. The *Welsh Nation* is written for and, we hope, read by those who have not got the language but who hold themselves morally responsible for its continued vitality in exactly the same way as we hold ourselves morally responsible for the territorial integrity and social and economic health of our country; the two considerations cannot be divorced. Obviously, a place like Aberystwyth is the most expedient starting point for militancy about the language, just as Tryweryn is the obvious place to strike a blow for the land. But there are no mutually exclusive fields of activity. Welsh is ours of the seaport cities and industrial valleys as it is of the rural village and market town, it is ours of the border fringes and odd enclaves of proud and ancient Englishry from the cliffs of Gower to the sands of Dee. It is ours in the same way that the Land of Wales is ours, because we are hers, we, the disinherited children of the neglectful and misled generations of the recent past, we, the breed of chancecomers from England, Ireland, Italy, Germany, Poland and Greece (to mention the ancestral provenance of but a few Welsh patriots known to us), on whom the land of Wales has laid her unbreakable spell.

And in her name a collier and an engineer went to a valley of farmsteads and sheepwalks, in the same way as a citizen from the streets of Cardiff five hundred years ago rallied to the banner of a mountain prince. There is an appropriateness about so many of the details of Welsh history that is as inspiring as it is poetic. John Sparrowhawk was well-named for his historic role. Its eye that marks down the slightest movement of its prey, the serenity of its hovering vigilance and the suddenness of its pounce to kill make the sparrowhawk a bird to be feared. Its claws are of steel and the drive of its bill irresistible. And there isn't a single white feather in its plumage. It breeds as readily in the cities as in the hills and has survived all attempts to exterminate it as a foe to plump pigeons.

Today when the old Wales is dying and a new Wales not yet come to birth, suddenly the spiritual descendants of the old Cardiff patriot strike again, and in the spirit of his name.

The royal eagles have fled from Gwynedd, the kite is a lonely wanderer over the spreading green desert of the Empty Centre. But the breed of the Sparrowhawk are on the wing.

Welsh Nation (October 1962)

Farewell to the Old Year

IT IS NATURAL, as the year draws to its close, for a mood of retrospection to set in reinforced by the customs of the seasons which bring together separated families and old friends. At such times, the framework of tradition by which all men must live is revealed and acknowledged more clearly than at any other time, and it matters but little by what particular avenue of human thought the sum total of our observances has reached us. The calendar is a mathematical convention. Christmas can be steeped in mystical speculation about the meaning of life, or, more likely, it can be a Norse eating and drinking festival or a Celtic tribal reunion, or an Anglo-American commercial racket. But, at whatever level, the season brings more pleasure than pain, and this alone, in terms of human experience, makes it a welcome and untypical interlude. For purely physiological reasons, in these northern latitudes, as the sun sinks and energy dwindles, we have less strength left to pursue actively the quarrels and hates that, to unregenerated humanity, give life so much of its meaning and savour. Soldiers fraternize in the trenches, Socialists are polite to Conservatives and even to other Socialists. Each of us individually relives his own past, as a child, uncritically receptive of the accidental loot of the season, as a young man or woman eagerly anticipating the social pleasures that have survived even the gloom of the long Welsh night.

And so retrospection is in order, a faculty which tends to overflow the bounds of the calendar and range effortlessly afar. The welcoming of old friends still with us reminds us of those whom we miss, and it will seem to many that this last year and the last few years before have borne heavily on the close family circle that is Wales.

Only to mention the names of some whom we will never see again is to sense a loss amounting almost to impoverishment, and each name stands for so much beyond the bearer: ways of life, channels of national self-expression stopped up for ever. Bob Owen, Croesor, surely the last of the great self-taught scholars, sprang from the peasantry, already an anachronism in the days of the county school and university scholarship, but a precious living testimony to the vital and attractive personalities who kept alive the Wales of the bards and scholars in the seventeenth century and the emergence, not long before our own lifetimes, of the new sponsorship of colleges and national institutions. Bob Lloyd – Llwyd o'r Bryn – the finest example of what people used to mean when they claimed that the Welsh country man was a natural aristocrat, a farmer who could turn from his crops and beasts to dominate an audience of thousands with story and rhyme, and then turn back again to his hillside farm – the last of the minstrel princes. And not long before them, Bob Roberts, Tai'r Felin, another last man. In him the ballad singers ended their song, who have wandered from fair and market throughout our history. Others, too. The late Archdruid Tre-fin, a man who had made his way in the world by his own efforts, yet had no trace of anything but gentleness in his make-up. Jubilee Young, perhaps the last of the pulpit giants. Tom Nefyn, possibly the last man whose name and frame will be associated with acute theological controversy. Cynolwyn Pugh, another of the generation who rose from the coalface to versatile and lively prominence. William Jones, the shy poet of hopeless love, last of the pure lyricists, and in sharp contrast, Aneurin Bevan, the last Welsh Socialist.

It is perhaps significant that with the exception of the last, many of the names in this muster will be but names to those of our readers to whom the Welsh language is a closed book, and perhaps not even names. With every one of them a little of the old Wales died, and this is a process that is taking place everywhere throughout the land, as inevitably as the falling of the leaves. In our town streets, our straggling valley communities, our scattered countryside, there cannot be one of our readers who does not look back at the recent passing of a relative, an old friend, or a neighbour whose going has meant that something has been lost: perhaps a store of vivid memories, a treasury of tales and rumours and rhymes, perhaps something more intangible but more real: a way of behaving and believing, of acting, feeling, and ordering their own life and influencing the lives of others.

In a finely imaged poem, Eirian Davies (who should write oftener) has personified death as a bailiff, taking away the human treasures of the nation like Bob Tai'r Felin and Llwyd o'r Bryn, because the nation has become bankrupt. It is difficult not to agree in some ways, but a stricter accounting would reveal assets undisclosed and unrealized, bonds not yet matured.

Against this melancholy roll-call, the year 1962 proudly sets out its triumphs: the Ammanford judgement – a Welsh advance; the Pilkington Report – an astonishing

English climb-down; and, towering above all, the Action of Tryweryn – in the very area so lately impoverished by the loss of Bob Lloyd and Bob Roberts – an action undertaken in the name of Wales by two men to whom Tai'r Felin and Llwyd o'r Bryn were names, if that, and who could not have understood or appreciated the songs of the one or the stories of the other. In such ways does a nation renew itself, unpredictable but never failing. One such action can outweigh a myriad losses, as the sword of the proud barbarian, plunged into the scales, outweighed the ransom of a Roman senate.

1962 will be notable as the year in which all Wales was brought strongly face to face with the realities of alien rule. For a long time now it is the more defenceless parts of our land that have suffered the most – the thinly populated rural areas and the smaller industrial communities. The Valleys were getting their breath back at last after the hangover of the Depression, and the coastal areas had never had it so good. But first came the chill breath of factory closures, always a nagging possibility, now in places like Hirwaun and Nant-y-glo and Dowlais and Wrecsam, a grim reality that has to be faced. And then, the activities of Dr.Beeching and the threatened disruption of the transport system. And as if that was not enough, the Rochdale Report, bringing the humiliation of our seaports. All Wales now drains the bitter dregs of truth. Proud Cardiff, resting on the most diversified and apparently prosperous regional economy in Wales, is undergoing an agonizing reappraisal, Bristol casts its shadow, and all over Wales the ghosts of dead communities: Dylife and Llanwddyn trouble the thoughts of living men.

It is an ambivalent season, and an ambivalent period in the nation's history. We take then the courage of the season and the comfort of the season. Between Christmas and the New Year the daylight lengthens *'cam ceiliog'* – by the mere stride of a cockerel, but all renewal is in those few added minutes, the hope of spring and the promise of summer. So in the dark of the year, we keep each one his Christmas in his own way. For some the incarnation of the Word. For others the innocent pleasures of an older faith. But for all, respite and then renewal. The Christian worships at the cradle of a child under the sign of a new star in the heavens. The Welsh patriot could do worse.

Editorial, *Welsh Nation* (December 1962)

The Plastic Leek

As St.David's Day approaches, the Welshman who takes his responsibilities to his country seriously tends to wish himself elsewhere. The festival has come to stand for everything that is utterly intolerable in our national life, from the emasculated history re-enacted in the schools, via tedious recitals of phoney peasant culture, to those heights from which the 'leaders of the nation' bore us with sentimental and sanctimonious platitudes about our way of life, our heritage, and what a wonderful lot we are. It is no good trying to escape from it, however, by catching a train over the border (those are the trains that will never be taken out of service) or taking wings to the uttermost ends of the earth, because wherever you go you are likely to find a group of well-placed expatriates (who on this day and during Eisteddfod week label themselves, with lachrymose dishonesty, 'exiles') having the same meaningless seasonal attack of emotional hiccups that is ravaging Wales itself. And rhetoric about the matchless qualities of our sturdy *gwerin* and our unique attachment to the hills and valleys of our homeland is even more insufferable in an hotel dining-room in Croydon or Karachi than it is in Wales itself.

It would be churlish to begrudge the children their holiday, however (even if it is the wrong time of the year for it, and a national festival at a more suitable season should be a priority in the free Wales), and the fun of dressing up as Arthur or Owain Glyn Dŵr (but not Edward of

Caernarfon or Henry Tudor), and probably most of us have carried with us from that age of comparative historical innocence some consciousness we would not otherwise have, that we are members of a nation and heirs of a tradition. It may seem hard, too, to carp at the one established custom which permits us to take some notice of our nationality and to make it the occasion of social enjoyment. Perhaps it could even be claimed that the roistering that goes on under the sign of the Plastic Leek is a factor of some survival value for the continuance of national consciousness. At a fairly low level this may indeed be the case, and perhaps we should ignore nothing that reinforces this consciousness, however shallow and meaningless a lot of it is. It is only safe to exercise this tolerance, though, if we keep clearly in mind the distinction, which it would be fatal not to make, between the easily aroused emotions invoked by St.David's Day (and international sporting events and the National Eisteddfod and Plaid Cymru rallies) and the deeper and more serious commitment which is becoming increasingly necessary if the nation is to survive. And this, perhaps, is the real value of St.David's Day.

Wales has never (we have said this before) deserved her great men, and has nearly always let down those who have striven hardest for her. It is particularly fortunate therefore that a race like ours should have for its patron saint one who exemplified all the virtues of which we stand in most need. The outstanding characteristic in the life of David as it has come down to us was that of total commitment to the cause he believed in, the complete subordination of every other consideration to the betterment of the lot of his people, and above all, the utter willingness to pay the price that this course of action demanded – a price measured in hardship, poverty, laborious toil, unceasing diligence; no small undertaking for the son of a king. The ascetic features of David challenge across the centuries all to whom he is more than a mere name or a date in the calendar. Most of all they challenge those of us who call ourselves Nationalists.

Perhaps there are individuals and groups in the Wales of 1963 who can, with a clear conscience, keep March the First as a deserved relaxation from their efforts on behalf of the country. There would be those who have consciously laboured to refurbish the battered fabric of our Nation, repairing some of the yawning gaps in the structure of her economy by establishing industries or safeguarding her land from the stranger, by enriching her language or by standing as witnesses to the resurgence of her self-respect; those who have been diligent in furthering the Welsh Schools Movement, certain industrialists and trade unionists, some (though by no means all) members of Plaid Cymru. But none, even of these, especially the last category, have any cause for self-satisfaction or complacency. The more that one does, the more one sees that needs doing. And the worthiest commemoration of St.David is to share his understanding that the redemption of Wales demands total commitment.

Since the last anniversary we can at least record signs that Nationalists (or some of them) are coming to grips with this necessity and are steeling themselves for the truly superhuman efforts involved. No sneering critic can say any more that Plaid Cymru is a party of dilettantes who engage in mild protests and endless nagging but are not really serious in furthering their cause. Since last March we have seen men risking impoverishment, loss of liberty, the break-up of their normal lives and all the weighty vengeance of the non-Welsh state. We have seen the senior exemplar of modern nationalism, Saunders Lewis, hounded once again for speaking too plainly against the politicians of the English parties, we have seen Gwynfor Evans of Betws, a man of status in his community, go before the courts, and students and young people courting arrest (but, paradoxically, not appearing before the courts), both in vindication of the status of the Welsh language; we have seen David Walters and David Pritchard going to Capel Celyn – to be followed by others, whose names will not be known this side of Independence. And even with all this, the inexorable demands of our country have not been satisfied. English law has been challenged, broken but not yet removed, and while it remains, there will be this suspicion of undeserved ease attached to the most well-earned relaxation.

For it is obvious that we are on the eve of a far more strenuous phase in the battle, and that before all is done, the Welsh patriots of today will need to display just as much moral and physical courage as were ever called upon at any time in our long history. Plaid Cymru alone makes insatiable demands on its members. The sensational improvement in the party's finances (to take the most humdrum aspect of the matter) cannot have been achieved without a whole series of sacrifices in homes throughout the land. The striving dissatisfaction manifested in the continuous attempts to better the party's organization speak of an urgency that is felt to be overwhelming. And outside of Plaid Cymru, moving parallel with the strictly constitutional path which the Blaid must follow, sharing most of its ideals and a lot of its members but impelled inexorably along other tracks – tracks that have led to Trefechan Bridge and the ill-fated transformer at Tryweryn – other forces are gathering. Those who know, in their deepest hearts, that the constitutional paths are not for them have made a choice that may – nay must – lead to hardship and suffering. Those who take their stand in the beaten ways of politics know that they must tread an exhausting road without any of the emotional gratification that attaches to dramatic action. Both types of patriot demand and deserve from the other mutual respect and mutual sympathy.

But neither path is easy and Plaid Cymru can offer no bribes and no inducement. Nations have never been redeemed by speeches and tea-parties. Whichever choice the Welsh patriot makes, it is a hard road he will have to travel. He will travel under the patronal protection of David, whose day falls in the worst of the year, when it is neither winter nor spring, and the few first flowers are buried in the last snows, when the sun's delay is least tolerable and all strength seems to be exhausted, when the wind is keenest and the ground hardest. This is the weather in which we are called out of doors, and he who flinches from it let him sulk by the fire. There is no joy comparable with the joy of battle, be it against the unfeeling enemy – 'the beast from the windowless forest' – or against the well-heeled Welsh traitor; there is no exhilaration like striving against the wind. These, the pattern of David's life, are all that we offer on his day. For we are told that his reward is without end, and his sign is the dove.

Editorial, *Welsh Nation* (February 1963)

A Letter to Gwilym Prys Davies

Garth Newydd
Merthyr Tydfil
April 1963

Dear Gwilym,

After our conversation yesterday I felt it necessary to put down on paper a clarification of my attitude and to offer a critique of yours. I have been doing this with various people, by letters and in conversation, for some time, and it has always produced some sort of result. When I was appointed editor of the *Welsh Nation*, Huw sent me a nice note in which he said, '*Gobeithio clywed llais cenedl*'. I asked him to write for the paper and he refused. This led to a correspondence in which we thrashed out whether Plaid Cymru's standpoint – and indeed Plaid Cymru's existence – was justified, he writing in Welsh and I in English as I am afraid I always must at this level. On our tour of Wales, Legonna collected both ends of this correspondence – my letters he took from Huw and Huw's letters from me – and declared them to be a very good summing up of the different points of view. He still has them and you may find them worth consulting. Some of the points I made now seem to me to have lost none of their validity and in particular my contention that the growth of Plaid Cymru into its present

Gwilym Prys Davies, Arthur Williams Incorporated
Photographer, Cardiff

form has been inevitable, that it is a factor that cannot be eliminated or discounted, and that it could be the basis from which all future advances can take place.

Let me first of all define my own position. You may find what I have to say exaggerated, oversimplified and melodramatic. These are criticisms I am used to. I claim that my point of view has validity not despite the limitations of my temperament but because of them. That is how a lot of the Welsh people think and feel, and I am merely making articulate what thousands have to leave unexpressed. There are other points of view, I know, less emotional, better disciplined, perhaps, and we all need to be able to appreciate and work with one another. That, incidentally, is one of the things that has been and is wrong with the Blaid – they are cold-blooded, or at least the people who have set the tone in the Blaid do not seem to possess any capacity for judging the emotional reactions of people. All the faults both of the Blaid and the Labour Party stem from the unhealthy state of the nation – the 'pacifism' of the Blaid, which is not the strenuous non-violence of Gandhi but merely a polite name for lack of moral fibre, and the sheer scoundrelism of the average local Labour Party, are both the characteristics of a nation which has reached rock bottom. And I feel that the development of my own ideas gains validity from this parallel at least with the course of our national history: we have got to start from where we are, and where we are is rock bottom.

I see the idea of national sovereignty and independence as something that has been safeguarded by different strata of society, and as one class has fallen, another has stepped in. I think the line of descent from the princes, via the rebel chieftains, the gentry, the middle-class of the eighteenth century right down to the *gwerin*, is pretty clear and unarguable. What we must face now is that the last of these social bulwarks has fallen. The *gwerin* has given up. The *Gweriniaethwyr* manned a barricade that had already been overwhelmed. In the industrial areas the *gwerin* have become what it was once said they would never become – a proletariat. Oddly enough, it has taken 'affluence' rather than depression to make this transition quite clear and unmistakable. The idea of a Socialist order intimately related to, inspired by and springing from the national heritage – a sort of folkloric Celtic Socialism – has failed to stand the test of reality. I believe Keir Hardie had this idea, although as you pointed out a long time ago in *The Welsh Republican*, he wasn't a systematic thinker at all. Certainly James Connolly had it, and Connolly was a very systematic thinker indeed. But it was James Larkin who led the masses in the end, both before and after independence, with a more direct bread and butter emphasis.

The Republican failure could perhaps have been foreseen, in any case, it was definitive, final. But it contained the seeds of renewal. If it brought one phase of Welsh history to an end, it began another. We saw then the *gwerin*'s final rejection of Wales. We saw also the assumption, by a few individuals, of an unparalleled responsibility. As Legonna wrote in *The Welsh Republican*, 'We set ourselves apart as founding fathers'. That, the positive side of the Republican episode, cannot be overestimated. With the *gwerin* – and make no mistake about it, the rural *gwerin* are in full flight from their heritage and responsibility just as much as the people of the Valleys – with the *gwerin*, I say, a panicking rabble, running in all directions or cowering waiting for the kill, a few people took it upon themselves to assert the absolute and unconditional independence of Wales, in terms which are, I believe, without parallel in the whole of our history, and were able to maintain a small but coherent group together for a number of years on that basis. For me there can be no going back on that declaration: no acceptance of anything less than the maximum claim, no compromise.

I had, I suppose, much the same reasons as yourself for joining the Labour Party, but perhaps lacked the tenacity and self-discipline to stay there. I do not regret that sojourn. It opened my eyes and taught me a lot. But it became more and more obvious every day that I was playing a false role, trying to be something I wasn't. I lack sympathy with people who do not seem to be able to do anything for themselves or think for themselves, who have only got themselves to blame for everything that has happened to them, all the appalling infantilism of the Welsh left. This, I will agree, is a temperamental limitation of mine. I like to be surrounded by people I can talk to and who can talk back at me. I am quite uninterested in welfare work, rescue work, charity and helping the underdog. Human progress has always depended on a minority of intelligent and sensitive people, and to think otherwise is mere sentimentality or political cant. So deeply did I feel the degradation of the Welsh people as expressed in the mental bankruptcy and moral rottenness of the Labour movement, that it seemed to me that anyone who had originally taken what Henry Edwards would call the maximalist position of the Republicans must sooner or later get out or suffocate;

that he owed it to himself to remove to a position in which he could be himself. And the only possible public position was, for all its defects, Plaid Cymru.

But behind the public position there is the private position. I straightaway found myself in the anti-leadership group in the Blaid who were pressing for a much firmer line – people to whom the offer by the Blaid of compromise proposals over Tryweryn, and the failure to take action over Tryweryn, were a betrayal of that particular cause and of the national cause. I did not feel myself personally tainted by that particular guilt because I had not been in the Blaid at the material time, but I shared the unease of those who did feel that the Party's policy should become more vigorous and that the leadership should give a lead. The issue is still in doubt, so I will speak no more of it just now except to say that the retirement of J.E.Jones a year ago (April 28, 1962, to be precise, I have good reason to remember the date) and the simultaneous resignation of Dr.Tudur Jones as editor of the *Welsh Nation*, were both (although veiled in diplomatic lies) forced resignations. J.E. was got rid of by Emrys Roberts standing up to him and Dr.Tudur by a mass revolt of the whole party against his inept handling of the paper, and the way is now clear for fresh advances. I believe the appointment of Ray Smith, for which I was largely responsible, is another great step forward. Ideologically he has no contribution to make, but as a practical and realistic organizer he will tidy up the mess left by J.E. and blow away a lot of cobwebs and mirages. I feel the Blaid is already a better place to be: the younger men and the inexperienced older men who are coming into it are not likely to get the same frozen mitt as you and Cliff Bere and Huw Davies got in the late '40s. If they get it from one quarter they know there are other quarters in the party to which they can turn. The leadership know this. Gwynfor Evans is exceptionally anxious to make me his man, and I am ready to back him up a long way, because there's no successor and we need somebody at the top if it's only King Zog. Elystan Morgan is I think now very much the ex-Crown Prince; Wynne Samuel would be at best only a competent caretaker; Trefor Morgan just wouldn't get the support; and I don't want the job anyway.

This brings me back to my personal position. I feel that in my present position I am at my maximum usefulness, and indeed, devote all my time to the paper and do very little in the way of addressing meetings, helping at elections etc. I am trying to bring into my part of the work what I hope Ray Smith will bring into the organization as a whole – the professional attitude – an end to the 'anybody can do anything' attitude which has long lost whatever merit it had. It is also, for myself, a phase in the progress toward total commitment which I see to be the chief need in Wales today. What we need is not a Blaid with ten times more members than it's got at the moment: they would be recent converts and bring a lot of poison with them. No, we need, if anything, a smaller and stronger and more resolute party, or at least a party which will precipitate inside itself a newer and stronger distillation of the spirit of nationalism – a movement which will have in it, not necessarily in publicly prominent positions but leavening the whole mass, a body of men who accept no limitations to their nationalism and no limitations to the demands nationalism makes on them. There are perhaps only five hundred nationalists, real nationalists in this sense of the word, in the whole of Wales. That is enough. They would leaven the party and the whole inert mass that is or was the Welsh people, and make it a people and a nation again. To these men, in this age, has the sovereignty of Wales fallen. They and no other *are* the Welsh nation. The others have sunk so low, are so deeply stained with the guilt of servitude, that their condition may be likened (as Pearse likened it) to that original sin in which theologians say the human race is lost. The act of redemption can only come through the sacrifice, if necessary – and I believe it to be necessary – of the lives of the best. This I think goes beyond the old Republican doctrine. The Republicans said that they would not accept the self-imposed trammels of pacifism with which the Blaid leadership disguised its lack of moral fibre. The Republicans said that they would not shrink from shedding blood if necessary. They said that shedding blood would probably be necessary. I say now that such sacrifice is not only probably necessary, a predictable statistical likelihood, but absolutely necessary. Without it there will be no wholeness or health in any of the other actions that lead us forward. It is necessary, secondly and on a slightly lower level, to sweep aside all the appeals to reason, which have fallen on deaf ears, all the arguments which have failed to convince, all the inducement which can be countered and out-bid. It is necessary to keep the surviving leadership true to their purpose and to avoid compromise. It is necessary to commit our people to the struggle, to shame them into the struggle, to inspire them for the struggle.

A status which is achieved in any other way, however legally and practically satisfactory, will not be psychologically satisfactory. The great justification for independence is that it would allow us to be more ourselves and lead to a release of energy that is now wasted or perverted.

Independence achieved without such a release would be a purely legal fiction, much the same sort of 'independence' that Stalin gave Byelorussia and the Ukraine – puppet statehood, another voice backing up England's, another vote in the UN in accordance with orders from Downing Street. The break, when it comes, must be clean and painful. This of course is not Blaid policy. They too are anxious to avoid what Saunders Lewis called *'bawgwaed'* and to get as far as they can along the path of concessions. I do not despise this approach. I regard it as essential that there should be some people working along those lines, making valuable preparations for the final transfer of power. But without the other thing, the concessionary approach is meaningless and could be harmful.

I think that for men of my generation there is a remarkable parallel between recent Welsh history and pre-war English history. All the time I was growing up, people were saying 'We've got to stand up to Hitler sooner or later'. Nobody wanted to draw the logical conclusions from obvious facts. Nobody, after all, wants war while there is a possibility of other ways out. England (and English-Welsh opinion) averted their eyes from Hitler's accumulating record of aggression and were content to pass pious resolutions. Then came Munich and England was shamed and England knew it was shamed and from then on the days of appeasement were at an end. So in Wales Tryweryn was our Munich. Clywedog may be our Poland. But Wales – or those few voices who speak for Wales – has come to the end of the period for appeasement. That happened when David Pritchard and David Walters went to Tryweryn. And just as the craven mood of the Chamberlain-Baldwin era was succeeded by a grim determination to fight the Nazis, some change has come over Wales. I for one, during the Republican period, was a mere theorist of possible or potential or desirable action. Today, although only on the fringes of things like that, I am quite psychologically prepared for anything – jail, disruption of personal life, hardship, the lot. I am on active service. I have been called up. This is something that is reflected in all sorts of ways. The English parties are taking Wales very seriously in the Swansea election – all their election addresses have a slant dictated by the presence in the fight of Plaid Cymru. You will notice that no heavy denunciation of action at Tryweryn has come from our enemies: only that ass Elystan Morgan has done that, and he's completely ruined himself by so doing.

You may say that none of this is within the terms of reference of politics as generally understood. You will be right, of course, but this cause is above 'politics' in that sense. You may say that this high-flown talk of sacrifice, commitment, dedication etc. is meaningless to the *gwerin* of the bingo-hall and the betting-shop. My contention is that there must come a time when it will mean something to them – perhaps everything to them – and that time may well come hard on the heels of the time when people seem utterly to reject it. There is an elementary psychological calculation here, which the Blaid are utterly unwilling to face, which may be best illustrated from the history of Ireland. The Easter 1916 Rising failed, and as the leaders were being marched off by the soldiers, the Irish people of Dublin, whose lives had been disrupted by the battle, and who had been put in terror by the firing, spat on Pearse and Connolly and cursed them. But within a year that mood had passed, the true significance of events had sunk in, and the battle of Ireland was as good as won. If, of course, the people of Wales fail to respond to the events of the next few years, if they cannot be moved by acts of resistance, then they are lost and the nation is at an end (though that, too, is something that was probably said in 1415).

You may ask why, if I believe this, I am in the Blaid. A fair question. But the Blaid is changing, and even Gwynfor is beginning to take a far healthier attitude. Last *Ysgol Haf* [Summer School] the *Pwyllgor Gwaith* [Executive Committee] were in almost continuous session about one thing and another. Gwynfor Evans said then that matters of party discipline were perhaps even more important than Clywedog. Anyway, we came to no decision about Clywedog at all, were absolutely paralysed. Then, in November, we took the decision which has just been published to buy land in Clywedog. This is something I had been preparing for a long time. When the legal possibilities of this manoeuvre have been exhausted, some of us are going to defend our bits of land in other ways. The action at Tryweryn really broke the ice.

I believe the Blaid to be the ideal instrument for effecting and initiating all sorts of activities quite apart from its function as a political pressure group. It is under the impulse derived from the Blaid membership that companies have been formed to promote the manufacture and distribution of Welsh goods. I am a shareholder in a small engineering company (and potentially a very prosperous one) founded directly as a result of meetings in the Blaid offices, with a view to diversifying the Welsh economy. There are all sorts of developments in North Wales – firms, shops etc. – that I don't know much about

Plaid Cymru Executive Committee

but are all the same sort of thing. Political nationalists are behind the Welsh Schools and (the Talfanite gang apart) the revival in Welsh publishing. There has been a movement in existence for years called *Urdd Siarad Cymraeg*. It has done nothing. Recent militancy on behalf of the claims of Welsh was started where? In a Blaid paper, and an English-language one at that! If I never do anything else for Wales, at least I published the article by Gareth Miles that started the chain of events that led to Trefechan Bridge. I don't honestly know of anything going on in Wales today that is advancing the life of the nation and making us more of a nation, that is not somehow linked with the Blaid, or at any rate sponsored by people who if they are not in the Blaid, are probably regarded with grave suspicion in whatever party they belong to because of their interest in Welsh affairs.

If there were no Blaid, I cannot see that any attention would be paid to Wales by the other parties. This, as I say, is obvious from the tone of their propaganda. It is so in Swansea, it was so in Montgomery, and even to some extent in Ebbw Vale, and this, not the fewness of the votes actually cast for the Blaid, justifies its intervention in these contests and its whole existence. Also, the Blaid is the only party that can possibly understand the course of action I described earlier as 'illegal' action. Not all the Blaid, of course. Far too many, in fact, might just as well be in the Liberal Party. But the Blaid is the only party that possesses the capacity to vibrate in sympathy with such actions and interpret them to the public. I cannot agree with criticisms of Gwynfor which say that he cannot disown these actions and at the same time sympathize with them. It seems to me that is just exactly what the

Blaid must do. It must not be so deeply compromised with direct action as to incur proscription, but it must be in emotional sympathy with this current, act as an amplifier for the subliminal echoes that such actions set up. It was rather odd to hear you utter the same criticism as the *Western Mail*. May I ask you to rethink your attitude on this point? For once, the Blaid may be acting with real political acumen and may show signs of developing as a real political arm of the independence movement. For me, at any rate, the possibilities of Plaid Cymru are intoxicating, and I can put up with quite a lot of its weaknesses – except inefficiency in practical matters, which I am doing my best to remedy.

So far we have discussed (i) direct action and (ii) action through an independent political party. I have gone into the first from a personal point of view because it involves personalities and not many of them, but of these it demands total commitment – the complete opposite, by the way, of J.E.'s jingle, 'To win for Wales self-government, Of time and cash I'll give one per cent', a doctrine I have found myself denouncing at every public meeting I have spoken at this year.

The second course of action I have dismissed nothing like as fully or as clearly as I should have liked, because it is one which is always being discussed and you have probably thought about it as much as I have, so all I have done here is bring up one or two salient points. We now come to the third possible course which is the one you have chosen – working within a party controlled from outside Wales. In practice, only one such party could ever have been considered as a field for pro-Welsh action. The Tories are by definition hostile, the Liberals, for all the hoo-ha, don't count. So I am going to put forward my criticisms of the wisdom of working within the Labour Party purely objectively and impersonally, I hope.

We must first of all consider the long-term prospects of the Labour Party in the light of those factors which it itself considers as important. Taking first the overall world situation. The climb-down over Cuba showed that the US-USSR deadlock, which began at Korea, is with us for another decade – indeed, may stretch on into all the foreseeable future that matters. The only factor which may disturb it is the emergence of China as a nuclear power, with no inhibitions. I don't pretend to know what's going to happen then, but until then, global strategy will be based on fear of global war and avoidance of large-scale conflict. 'Europe' will probably emerge as a sort of composite nuclear power, throwing isolated England more and more into the arms of the US – in other words, an indefinite prolongation of the situation as we have it today. The US have found that the Conservative Party are their best bet as a puppet regime. The disastrous record of the Labour Government in respect of US loans is forgotten here, but remembered in the dollar-conscious US. As US control of England is, at its worst, considered by most people to be preferable to the only possible alternative, client status of the USSR, England will swallow any insult and humiliation at the hands of the USSR. The Tories can get away with this better than any Labour regime could. It has only to be made known that the US are backing the Tories for them automatically to win an election. The US, as in Italy where it made loans conditional on a Christian Democrat victory, will probably finance a Tory victory one way or another. I think they will be more open about it than they have been. It is significant that they now have a President from a traditionally anti-English segment of their country, who will probably initiate a way of looking at England coolly and cynically, and England will get treated more and more like Italy. (All this bodes no good for any English political party.) Even apart from the support of the US, the Tories are in a position to manipulate the economy so as to be able to go to the country at the time most favourable to them. By their contact with big business they can influence commodity prices, by their contacts in the money market they can do what they like with bank rates, interest rates, sterling etc., by their control over the civil service and the decision-making sectors of English society in general (the 'Establishment') they can so manipulate the life of England that I do not see them taken at a disadvantage or fighting an election on any terms but their own. They have absorbed just enough Keynesianism to be able to keep the capitalist system afloat indefinitely, giving rough and ready satisfaction to nearly everybody. They are having a bad press just now, but a lot of that is the professional anger of Fleet Street for the Vassall case sentences on journalists. It is Harold Macmillan who is the villain, not the Tories as such. His purge of last year may (nay, must) be reserved by a putsch. The old man gone, a new leader will emerge – a clean vigorous young man (Edward Heath?) who will run rings around Wilson and, with a new team recruited not from the ducal houses but from the hard-faced meritocracy, we'll be in for another twenty years of Tory rule.

This is the strength of the opposition the Labour Party must face, and they face it disunited, with the cracks very thinly papered over. I don't know that the loss of Gaitskell was all that significant. I don't think the rift is so much between the intellectuals and the pseudo-workers, although that little feud must not be ignored, as between the dogmatists, whether middle-class Fabians or trade unionists, and the opportunists. If the party is to survive at all, the latter must win, thereby further hastening the process of transforming the Labour Party into a permanent alternative party in a set-up of 'Ins and Outs'. Much of the liturgical reverence paid to Gaitskell by 'the House' was because he set the seal on this process. Really speaking, we are now back in the pre-Keir Hardie period – an impression strengthened by the incredible Victorian jingoism of Harold Wilson's speech at Cardiff and his message to Sean MacBride. In order to counter the US subservience of the Tories, Labour is obliged to resurrect a 'British' patriotism and White Man's Burden theme that is a bit laughable these days, as a substitute for their previous mission.

I don't know whether you read what I had to say about the Labour Party in the pamphlet *Why Nationalist*. My basic criticism went deeper than their obvious tactical weaknesses. I said something to the effect that their whole position was inherently self-contradictory, that they suffered from the tension and instability innate in the position in which they find themselves – working within the framework of a traditionalist society whose mores they have had to adopt in order to exist at all, while proclaiming that they exist to overthrow that society. They are in the same dilemma as the Social Democratic parties in all the large centralized countries; they have a melancholy record – Jaurès, Hardie, Bebel, Blum, Prieto,

Largo Caballero, Macdonald, the men of Weimar, Mollet, Bevin, Ollenhauer, Nenni – all doomed from the start, ground between the upper and the nether millstone, snuffed out by the aristocratic embrace or the storm-troopers of the right, or forced into an alliance and gradually eaten up by the Communists. You could say, of course, that Plaid Cymru is in much the same ambiguous position and that it too has stresses and feuds that derive from a rather analogous situation vis-à-vis the British constitution. But whereas the Labour Party can only recover its dynamic and raison d'être by going to the left, i.e. Communist, which is unthinkable and would be disastrous, Plaid Cymru has access to the dynamic provided by nationalism and by those nationalists whom I discussed earlier. This is by no means unthinkable and could be the reverse of disastrous. There may be not much future for Plaid Cymru as it is now (or rather, as it has been since the war), but its potential function as a sort of midwife of new life is most important.

On top of the weakness of the Labour Party 'nationally', we must all consider the special and peculiar malaise of Labour in Wales. This again is something that could be gone into in detail. The tragedy of Welsh Labour is part of the tragedy of the Welsh people. But we cannot allow ourselves to become involved in that tragedy. Movements have their days: the nation must go on. The most significant symptom of its condition is the fact that since the war every Welsh seat becoming vacant has either been filled from outside (Swansea is the latest example) or, if home-grown candidates have been found, they are utter nonentities or worse. Leo Abse and John Morris (who was dead lucky) and Llywelyn Williams, although technically Welsh, are really outsiders to the mainstream of Welsh Labour that produced Morgan Jones, Jim Griffiths, Aneurin Bevan etc. When a movement is unable to renew itself from below, it is dying; it is, in the precise, non-rhetorical sense of the word: *degenerate*, and it is no good looking for anything healthy to come out of it.

Even before this decline took place, the Welsh, for all their contribution to the growth of the Labour movement, did not really count at the top. Individuals counted, of course, but the Welsh element as such do not figure largely in the official histories of the movement. I imagine that Clement Attlee's attitude to the Welsh Labour contingent was rather like Ben Gurion's attitude to the Bedouin sheiks who took the right side in 1948. As for the present generation of Labour leaders, many of them were my contemporaries at Oxford. I remember Michael Foot well and at one time had quite a lot to do with Desmond Healey. Their attitude to Wales is, if Healey is anything to go by, uninterested, incurious, slightly contemptuous, basically hostile. There is no reason why it should be otherwise, and much of the contempt is merited. Even if this very ancient English attitude did not exist, I cannot see that the Labour Party are under any obligation to give Wales any special consideration or priority, and I do not believe they are likely to do so, whatever they may say before an election. In other words, I just don't trust them. This is a very ancient Welsh attitude. You will have noticed that Labour has always been led by a Londoner, or that there has always been a very powerful deputy leader from London; George Brown has taken on the historic role of Morrison, who, you will remember, was bitterly hostile to any attempt to move things away from London. There is nothing wrong with this in an English context; it is quite legitimate. After London and the South-East come the Midlands, then the North, then a long way behind, Scotland, then Wales, perhaps – all neatly graded according to the un-exceptionable principle of the greatest number – if we were one nation, but we aren't. The next number of the *Welsh Nation* contains a comment on a speech by Brown at Corby which is most revealing.

The above are some of the reasons why I find it difficult to believe that any good will come to Wales via the Labour Party. They aren't going to win any more elections (or if they do, it will be 1924 and 1929 all over again), and if they do they will go back on their promises. And even if they did do what they promise, then it isn't necessarily any better a deal than we'd get from the Tories. Labour may have a pretty good programme for Wales, but I have it on good authority that the Tories are always prepared to go a long long way, administratively and economically, to keep us quiet, for more concessions are on the way than would have been conceivable a few years ago. And even if these concessions do come, it will not do us any fundamental good because they would be something that had been given us, not something that we had forged for ourselves, something that came to us from the outside, not something that we had created from within ourselves.

As I say, on one level, administrative concessions are not to be despised, but at the deepest level, which is what counts, we cannot operate according to the plans of others, or be dependent on the luck of the draw in a country which is not our own. I am not for one moment trying to divert you from the course of action you have chosen; I am merely giving my impression of that course and its chances of success as they seem to me, and giving also my reasons for following the course I have chosen.

Best wishes,
Harri

This letter was written in April 1963 to Gwilym Prys Davies and is published here with his permission.

© Gwilym Prys Davies

Emyr Llew Has Gone to Prison

On March 28, at Swansea, Chris Rees received 1,600 votes in a by-election. On March 29, at Carmarthen, Emyr Llew Jones received a year's imprisonment for his action at Tryweryn. It is tempting to link the two events causally as they are linked in time, as they are linked indissolubly in the minds of those many Nationalists who, in a crowded week, contrived to be present on both occasions. Behind the crush-barriers outside Carmarthen court-house there were those who had tired themselves tramping the streets of Swansea. To these the drab grind of the election and the high drama of the trial were but contrasting chapters in a continuous tale. On both occasions there was a sense of waiting, of expectancy. In Swansea, expectations were disappointed. At Carmarthen, a verdict was given and sentence was passed, but it was a result as inconclusive in its way as was the Swansea election. Wales is still waiting. Historic movements are building up which have not yet come to fruition. We are waiting as those crowds waited. And in such an atmosphere there are always those who play on heightened feelings, who confuse the issue, who darken counsel.

The Swansea result is naturally disappointing to Nationalists and gratifying to the upholders of the status quo, and the temptation to link it with 'irritation at recent exploits' is irresistible to the glib pen and the shallow mind. In fact, it is the consequence of a completely different chain of cause and effect. Plaid Cymru is in much the same position as many a small firm that finds that an increased demand for its products brings not prosperity, but financial difficulties, with production costs and the necessity for capital investment outstripping income. By now, a by-election anywhere in Wales without Plaid Cymru's participation would be unthinkable.

These are challenges which must be accepted, even if the arenas are those with which the party is almost totally unfamiliar and where the opposing forces have all the 'ground advantage'. Such has been the case in pretty nearly every by-election over the last few years. And in the General Election the party extended itself as never before, with the same disappointing results. For we are still in the pioneering stage. When J.E.Jones recently addressed those assembled to honour him on his retirement after thirty years as Secretary of Plaid Cymru, he told them that, when he took the job on, he knew that thirty or forty years would not see the completion of his labours. And the estimate of this sagacious, untiring man does not seem to have been far out. For only now are we beginning to see the first few scattered results of years of back-breaking labour, and all too often it seems that much of that labour has been wasted on stony ground. In his retirement, J.E.Jones stands for all those who have borne the heat and burden of the day. At Swansea, it was Emrys Roberts who was in charge for the first time, and with him Ray Smith, a young man at the beginning of his career with the party. J.E. and his generation performed the incredible task of making an independent political party viable from its small beginnings in front rooms and vestries and keeping it in being during the aftermath of depression, the upheaval of war, the false dawn of a Labour Government in London and the equally false Vanity Fair of Tory rule.

Until now, Plaid Cymru has been a pressure group and a not ineffective one. The London government has itself admitted that nationalist pressure alone has been responsible for such concessions as Wales has been granted. Many will call on Plaid Cymru to resume its role of indirect persuasion, and to ignore the possibilities indicated by those areas where there has been something of a breakthrough and where the party is a direct participant in the politics and machinery of government. But a pressure group can only function if it exerts pressure. And the very presence of Plaid Cymru in any political arena constitutes such pressure. Not only in the affair of the nomination paper in the Welsh language did Plaid Cymru score a success unrecorded in any count of votes. As in Montgomery and Ebbw Vale the Welsh Nationalist challenge virtually dictated the presentation of their cases by the other parties – from Conservative to Communist. Indirectly, perhaps, and with painful slowness, the electorate are being led to think in Welsh political terms. In every way, Plaid Cymru's participation in this by-election was justified, as will be its participation in every other election that it is humanly and financially possible for it to fight.

What the party does, it often does brilliantly. What it fails to do is just as often catastrophic. There are reasons for this, but no excuses. Now that the party is firmly established as 'a fleet in being', its deployment calls for attention to elementary matters of organization. It will be the task of the party's new generation of organizers to see to it that Plaid Cymru goes to the polls as least as well organized as its resources allow; and that the closely-knit network of poll organization which is the chief basis of the Labour Party's high vote in Wales is duplicated in a better cause. Attention to mundane details like these will, we are convinced, bring about a substantial improvement in the Welsh vote, and at the cost of much hard work, remove much criticism. Swansea has proved that the random miscellaneous protest vote is no sure basis for a national cause.

Swansea has not shown that the party has somehow come to grief because people operating independently of it have resorted to direct action. As we make abundantly clear elsewhere in this issue, and as has been made abundantly clear all along, political activity and direct action are 'clean different' and by choosing to stick to one path, Plaid Cymru automatically rejects the other; even at the cost of incurring much reproach. Plaid Cymru is accused of "sitting on the fence" in dealing with direct actionists, and is exhorted to give enlightened leadership to "young hotheads." The men in question have gone their own way, and if Plaid Cymru is sitting on a fence, these men have left it far behind. Those who have been identifiably engaged in direct action have acted in accordance with their own consciences and convictions. They do not seek to influence party policy and take no part in much-publicized debates on whether or not the party shall espouse direct action – they act.

They act in such a spirit that when Emyr Jones stood in the dock at Carmarthen, the very judge who sentenced him was moved to refer to 'an injustice to your country' and to pass sentence with every mark of reluctance. It was left to the journalists of the Cardiff and Swansea press to smear him with their venom, to offer gratuitous comparisons with acts of loutish vandalism perpetrated by young men of the same generation, to refer to 'juvenile heroics', and generally to yap like curs. When, by a strange irony, the duty of prosecuting Emyr Jones fell to Tasker Watkins VC, two brave men faced one another. The one had been honoured above all Welshmen of his generation for bravery in battle, the other's action carried with it the possibility of no reward but jail. If there is one man who can be accorded the right to bring the calibre and courage of others into question, it is a holder of the Victoria Cross. But this prosecuting counsel carried out his duties with an apologetic reluctance which, in the context of the situation, amounted to respectful recognition that here was a man in his own class.

When the prosecutor for the Crown, and that prosecutor such a man as this, attenuates his attack to the utmost; when the very judge on the bench is visibly tortured by the necessity of having to pass sentence, is Plaid Cymru to raise its voice in condemnation of Emyr Jones and his companions? God forbid. We would sink to the level of the poison pens of Thomson House and Castle Bailey Street if we did. It may be difficult for these gentlemen to appreciate that there are occasions when considerations of human decency and instinctive national pride outweigh the calculations of political expediency, and this is one of them, even if we have no part in these actions and are bound to follow other paths. We would, in the last analysis, rather lose votes than lose our self-respect.

Emyr Jones has been reviled as a 'young hothead' and referred to in more than one headline as a 'youth'. Encased in English uniform and fighting in some foreign field he would have been spared that reproach. He is, in fact, much the same age as were those Battle of Britain pilots who 'left the vivid air signed with their honour' in the service of their country, and like them, he is one of a few.

In Swansea there were thousands of people too bored to vote; those who did vote threw their votes away. In Carmarthen, the police tensely awaited a riot that never flared out and the crowds around the court were too full of emotion even to sing.

In Swansea, the election result with all that it contained of disappointment and waste was announced on a night of pouring rain after a day of chill gales. In Carmarthen, Emyr Jones went to jail on the day that the Tywi Valley greeted its incomparable spring.

The political weather in Wales remains unsettled. We are waiting for things to happen. They will.

Editorial, *Welsh Nation* (May 1963)

The Failure of the Labour Party in Wales

IN THE APRIL number of the *Welsh Nation* we compared the present Conservative regime in England to the state of affairs in that unhappy country during the reign of Charles II. The point of our comparison lay in the political irresponsibility of the Conservative Party, not its moral depravity, and the revelations with which we have since been regaled may be regarded as at least some compensation for having to put up with such an inept lot. To some of us, the news that Conservatives were human enough to have human weaknesses might have come as something of a surprise. The Conservatives, from Baldwin of the Depression to Brooke of Tryweryn, have behaved towards Wales with such flinty and bloodless lack of feeling that it is almost reassuring to know that at least one of their number has something in common with the rest of the human race, even if it's only common women.

Now that its initial impetus is spent, the complicated imbroglio of illicit assignations, switched stiffs in the morgue, glamorous dolls, double-crossing double agents (it mystifies us why this activity is still referred to as 'security'), flights to Majorca and all the rest of it, is getting a bit tedious. The recent history of England could well be handed over to Ian Fleming for a re-write, with additional dialogue by Henry Miller.

We are candid enough to admit that we are amused

rather than shocked by the whole business [the Profumo affair]. We are not so naive as to believe that unlicensed dalliance and administrative incompetence are any more less prevalent in high places in England or anywhere else at this time than at any other, and the virtuous attitudes now being struck in various quarters are almost as grotesque as the goings-on that have inspired them. The country whose evangelical Liberalism culminated in Lloyd George and whose crusading Socialism produced Jimmy Thomas had better keep silent in such matters. And we fail to see why the Conservatives in our midst should be so censorious of a Minister who exercised the divine right of his caste and breed to get away with the biggest lie he could manage, or of young women who regard even the pleasures of love as subject to the laws of the market place, for these surely are logical Conservative attitudes.

The real significance of current scandals in England lie not in themselves but in the public reaction to them. In a strong, confident society, such peccadilloes would pass unheeded, and even grave incompetence would be seen in proportion against a background of progress and constructive achievement. But in a once-powerful nation now in decline, such matters achieve a neurotic significance out of all proportion. The Conservative politicians – still the only logical rulers of England – behave like Restoration fribbles and libertines because they too, like their historical parallels, are not really responsible. Standards matter little in a puppet government, and when all the real decisions are taken in the Pentagon and the White House, it is of no consequence how the underlings carry on in Admiralty House and Whitehall as long, of course, as they do as they are told.

The relationship between responsible self-government and elementary efficiency and basic self-respect has never been more clearly demonstrated. And if England is ruled by puppets, Wales is ruled by puppets – the Labour hangers-on of Uncle Sam's pensioners. And here in Wales, even more vividly than in England, we see the inexorable law in operation which decrees that those who accept office without responsibility must rot inwardly and become a hissing and a byword.

We admit that the Labour Party in Gwynedd is not what it is in some of our southern Valleys and that there is a world of difference between, say, Goronwy Roberts and Iori Thomas. But the Gwynedd tail has never yet wagged the Labour dog, and it is where Labour is most powerful and longest established that we must look for its true image. As Plaid Cymru has been invited almost en bloc to join the Labour Party we must ask ourselves what it is we are being asked to join – and why.

The not unexpected invitation was made by Mr.Cliff Protheroe at a recent conference of the Welsh 'Regional' Council of Labour, at which certain elements in Plaid Cymru were accused of the usual picturesque catalogue of crimes – and this by Socialists, whose dogmas have plunged whole continents into bloodshed! But despite their lawless record, it seemed that Plaid Cymru were enough of a problem for the Labour Party to spend most of their time discussing how to cope with them.

First of all they put forward a Welsh policy – far too Welsh a policy for some of the powerful local bandit chieftains, to whom the idea of national loyalty and wider horizons would spell the end of their own little racket. If any of the more naive members of the Labour Party start taking this programme seriously, the flick-knives will be out in real earnest. But this is unlikely; Protheroe is just as adept as Profumo in making statements which bear no relation to reality.

Assuming, however, that the party which, when in power, succeeded in antagonizing every Nationalist movement from Ireland to Iraq and from Ghana to Guiana has had a change of heart and that they really mean what they say this time, would Nationalists be justified in abandoning their independent position and joining the ranks of the Labour Party? In support of this it is argued that there are already many good men in the party whose attitude is very close to ours, and who are doing good work. This we readily concede. Few in numbers they certainly are, and beset by all sorts of difficulties. And it is precisely for their sake, among other considerations, that we must refuse to join them. For if Plaid Cymru ceased to function these patriotic spirits would have nothing to threaten or reproach Labour with and their influence would be even less than it is now.

For these men, isolated and frustrated, are in a very small minority in their party. And, obstinate realists that we are, it is the majority image of the Labour Party that keeps getting in our way, whenever we try to find the patriotic minority in their ranks. Once again we must stress that it is not corruption and incompetence in themselves that we reproach Welsh Labour with. As with the English Conservatives, these are merely surface manifestations of a far deeper moral failure.

While we attack fiddling and jobbery whenever we

encounter it on the local level, and recognize its prevalence as one of the many factors which cause our fellow countrymen to doubt whether they have the capacity to govern themselves fairly and efficiently, we look rather ironically on the current campaign to elevate a long-standing scandal into an item of hot news. The circles in which this campaign originated and those which subsequently ventilated it at greater volume are hardly in a position to pass judgement on anybody.

It is for a far more fundamental and simpler reason than any of these that we must refuse any offers from the Labour or any party. We are Nationalists. The whole point of our corporate existence as a political organization is to place the claims of Wales and the Welsh people before all other considerations whatsoever.

We are lent strength, by that decision, and by that decision alone, to wage a battle that to ourselves often seems endless, and to those untouched by the same spirit, must seem pointless. The transient ebb and flow of English-style politics will not divert us nor overwhelm us. We began this article with a comparison with Stuart times. Let us end on the same note. Let those who will cast themselves in the role of Cavaliers or Roundheads, reformers or revellers. These postures may well satisfy those who wish to cut a figure on the stage of English politics. But, now, as in those days, the true future of Wales is being shaped by those who put the needs of their own country before the easy lure of compromise programmes and opportunist politics. In full consciousness of its historic role, Plaid Cymru, this summer, meets in Caernarfon, at a place still called

Segontium, where, at the beginning of Welsh history, so the Mabinogion tells us, a dream became a reality. And there we shall fashion a second beginning.

Editorial, *Welsh Nation* (August 1963)

Building a New Country

This summer saw two family visits that attracted a great deal of attention. The President of the United States called on his relatives in Ireland. Obliged by the laws of vassalhood to chronicle the activities of their overlord, the English, in some natural embarrassment at the circumstances under which so many Irish people had to leave Ireland, decided to treat the whole episode as a sentimental journey, an interlude in the real business of the President's European tour. But the United States, for all that it has succumbed to temptations which it would be difficult for any nation to resist, is still in touch with its own best traditions and the ideals on which it was founded. Its leaders are clever men, but not tired cynical opportunists. Confronted with social evils, they at least recognize them for what they are, and do not try to pretend that they don't exist. And in Kennedy's speech to the Irish Dail and Senate, there is more genuine understanding of what is going on in the world and of the potentialities of the human race in small countries as well as in great, than any English statesman has shown in centuries. We can quite understand why the English Press did not publicize this statement. And we hope our readers will understand why we are giving it so much prominence in the *Welsh Nation*.

For we wish to draw a contrast between the happy circumstances of Kennedy's visit to his cousins and another cousinly visit involving another Head of State in these West European Islands. (This, by the way, is now the generally accepted designation for what were once called the British Isles.) The true nature of the English state was mercilessly revealed under all its theatrical pseudo-traditional trappings when virtually martial law was imposed on London and a reign of police intimidation swung into ruthless action against what was, after all, a handful of demonstrators. In case anybody thinks that this was an altogether exceptional outburst of panic on the part of the authorities we refer them to a comment in the Conservative *Daily Telegraph*, welcoming the construction of a huge new military barracks in London on the grounds that the time is rapidly approaching when the police alone will not be able to enforce order in the English capital.

And while this reign of legalized terror is in preparation, slum racketeers amass fortunes, high persons of State creep around the brothels, and a whore is cheered by a crowd of hundreds on the steps of the Law Courts. England is going down into the darkness quicker than anyone would have thought possible. It is as if all her crimes against other nations are to be expiated in our lifetime. 'The sky is dark,' said a Chinese statesman just before the war, 'with the wings of chickens coming home to roost.' The rape of Africa, the ruthless exploitation of the Caribbean, have brought Lucky Gordon and Edgecombe and their like to wreak a vengeance on behalf of their kin, in which ministerial reputations are determined by perverts and degenerates.

England has sown the wind and must reap the whirlwind. We refer to her plight in no spirit of involvement. For Wales, and other plundered dependencies, are paying for all this, as we show in another article in this issue (adapted, as we must here gratefully acknowledge, from the *Scots Independent* – our opposite numbers in that equally submerged nation). The bluff features of John Bull have for far too long been a mask to hide the real visage of predatory and parasitic England – Rachman, Profumo and all the rest of them. Decisions affecting our people are taken in the infected atmosphere of this society, and plans drawn up for our future which enshrine the sordid and cynical values now prevalent in London.

There is usually a note of comedy, however wry, to lighten the scene, and the recent royal progress through Gwynedd was a gift to the connoisseur. Happily unencumbered by their more embarrassing relatives, the visitors were welcomed at the National Eisteddfod by a children's choir which had been schooled to sing, without any apparent *arrière pensée*, a song about grandfather's old penny-farthing bicycle. The same day Caernarfon was made a 'royal borough'. The dream-city of Macsen and Helen, the capital of Gwynedd and well-spring of poetry and song for generations, thus achieves parity with Kensington and Kingston-on-Thames. We hope the monoglot 'Cofis' are enjoying a good laugh in those Welsh-speaking back streets. It is difficult to imagine them as 'royal burgesses'! Later in the day, the seal of royal approval was placed on Mr.Butlin's holiday camp at Pwllheli. It should not be forgotten that this camp was cynically sold to Butlin by the Admiralty at the end of the war, contrary to express authority, who wanted to develop the site for sorely needed industry. To use royalty to make this wretched transaction socially acceptable is surely improper by any standards.

But the crêpe-bordered *Draig Goch* flag, among the

decorations at Pwllheli, displayed by the wife of Owen Williams, now in jail for his country, must bring us back to reality and must make us ask ourselves what we are doing about it all.

Nobody could pretend that the debates at this year's conference reached a high level except occasionally in terms of rhetoric. And one doubts the sincerity of much of the response to Emrys Roberts's astonishing address. For those who were not there, he roundly accused the Party of not taking its job seriously, from the *Pwyllgor Gwaith* to local branches. Rarely can any gathering have been addressed in terms which reflected so badly on the majority of those present. The proper reaction would have been shocked silence, but, of course, the speaker was warmly applauded. Our grandfathers presumably got the same kicks out of listening to hell-fire sermons, for we are a masochistic race. It is to be hoped, however, that the message has got home in some places at least.

The effort of those who seek to perfect the party as a political instrument were not helped by the course of the debate on constitutional reform. At Llangollen in 1961, the party rejected involvement in Direct Action not by such a huge majority as all that, but decisively nevertheless and, probably, irreversibly. All the more reason then for stern application to the political arena. But, with the next election getting nearer every day, and with literally hundreds of seats in local elections to be fought, both for their own sakes and for the sake of the more publicized parliamentary battles, the party escaped into a nirvana of fatuous optimism that survived even Montgomery and was only recently punctured in the grey streets of East Swansea; to be succeeded, one fears, by an equally barren stoicism, and a phoney stiff upper lip in the face of anticipated further maulings.

None of this is constructive. None of this is good enough. The revision of the party's constitution and machinery has consumed the precious time and effort of able servants of the party and of those leaders who really care. The revised constitution was allowed to reach the floor of the conference without any comment or opposition from those who were hostile to its provisions. It was then assailed on all possible grounds and 'referred back' – to limbo. Such tactics as these do no credit to those who employ them, however permissible they may be in more cynical parties. Neither do they help the party to evolve the more flexible and representative framework necessary for political effectiveness.

The truth must be faced. Wales is up against an enemy grown desperate with age and weakness. We have our internal weakness to eradicate before we can face the external threat with any confidence of success, and the national movement will of necessity reflect some of the weakness of the nation itself. That is why Nationalism demands more of the individual than any other creed. It demands more of the just as it offers more. Out of the darkness of England's rotting empire we seek to build the New Country, and those who build it must be as clean and as hard as new steel.

Editorial, *Welsh Nation* (September 1963)

An Open Letter to Goronwy Roberts

Dear Mr.Goronwy Roberts,

Ten years ago I heard you speak in the House of Commons in support of the bill for a Welsh Parliament. This summer, in a sunny tent on the Eisteddfod field at Newtown, I heard you give an account of your stewardship as Minister of State for Wales. As a member of *Undeb Cymru Fydd*, that impeccably non-party organization to which you spoke, I would agree with many of the claims you made. At the same time, I couldn't help feeling that in ten years none of us had got very much further.

The establishment of the Welsh Office undoubtedly changes the scene. Many minor advantages will accrue to Wales, and perhaps some very considerable advantages. Plaid Cymru takes all this into account and is prepared to make adjustments accordingly. But it makes no difference to the basic situation by which Wales is ruled from and by England, and Welsh resources are at the disposal of England. Let us take your most weighty and positive claim: there will be no more Trywyryns. You base this statement on the fact that the Secretary for Wales now shares authority for water resources with an English minister, and that Welsh interests will have to be taken into account in any future schemes. On paper this sounds like equality. In practice (and you are a practical politician) what happens? While men like yourself and

Jim Griffiths hold office we look to you to do your best. But your party only holds office at rare intervals and for short periods. There is no guarantee that the traditional and natural party to govern England will be equally vigilant for Wales when it returns to power. Already, in their shadow cabinet, Wales has been downgraded to its original subsidiary position, and our watchdog is Mr.Thorneycroft! But even assuming that a Welsh Minister, in an unchanged Welsh Office, is still there when the next big water decision has to be made, how will he fare in any real difference of opinion with a colleague representing English interests? Really, the question has only to be asked to be answered. Indeed, it seems to me that the only role he could possibly play would be a rather unworthy one. If I named it, I would be accused of impropriety. Of course there will be no more Tryweryns. Already there is Clywedog. The next instalment of aggression will probably be even less clear-cut, giving even more room to wrap up in political manoeuvre the final inevitable sell-out. May you be spared the harsh judgement which will fall on whoever has to go through these motions. If I understand you aright you act according to a consistent strategy and philosophy of gradualism. You say that it will take generations to undo the work of centuries. This, it seems to me, is all the more reason to press on with advocating maximum claims untrammelled by allegiance to alien interests or dead dogma, for what could happen in those intervening generations does not bear thinking of. You advocate a wide measure of inter-party or supra-party agreement on many matters of immediate concern, and this is reasonable. This is why you and I can both be members of *Undeb Cymru Fydd*, which, it is to be hoped, will increasingly concern itself with such matters. At the same time, as a politician, you know that parties must exist in our society. So please do not expect Plaid Cymru to forgo one fraction of its witness, or stint one ounce of its energy in the task which it has set itself, merely because the chances of English politics have allowed for a space one well-meaning Welshman to report back to a society concerned for the welfare of the nation. At the end of your discourse Mr.Alun Talfan Davies spoke briefly to the same effect on behalf of another English party in Wales. There is obviously something to be done on this basis, by those committed in the last analysis to England but marginally concerned for Wales. You are nearer the corridors of power, whose polished walks have before now attracted fainthearted defectors from the national cause with no stomach for the stern battles ahead. Politics is politics and I do not expect you to concede that your efforts and tactics would be meaningless and pointless without the existence of Plaid Cymru to give perspective to the picture, and to set the ultimate terms of reference by which all other labours must be measured. But such, I am confident, will be the judgement of history.

Wishing your efforts every success,
Yours sincerely,
Harri Webb

Welsh Nation (September 1963)

The Miners' Next Step

WITH THE BEST WILL in the world, the antagonism that exists between the NCB on the one hand and miners on the other cannot be resolved. Under nationalization, the miners have been granted the rights of 'consultation' – after the major decisions have already been taken by the NCB. In effect 'consultation' simply means the right to be told what decisions have been taken. In essence, the present form of nationalization is a rehash of the combine v. miners, boss v. worker approach to the conduct of the mining industry. There has been one fundamental change – the combine has grown bigger. It is now called the State.

A perusal of the old coal company reports, before nationalization, has revealed a striking similarity with modern pronouncements of the NCB. In making the charge of 'absenteeism', criticizing miners for 'not pulling their weight', 'letting their colleagues down', and complaining that production is lower in the Welsh anthracite area than in the English Midlands, the mantle of the former chairman of Powell-Duffryn or Amalgamated Anthracite has fallen squarely on Lord Robens. The only difference is that the Chairman of the NCB has a professional publicity department, and therefore receives a wider press coverage. The complaints, the allegations, the excuses, remain the same.

The truth is that under the present system of nationalization, the Welsh miner has no power, no authority, no responsibility, no equality, and no control over his industry. On vesting day, Mr.James Griffiths said: 'We as miners have looked forward to this day. I am glad that I have lived to see it happening. The miners are now owners'. Mr.Griffiths is still alive, but any Welsh miner will tell him – 'the miners are *not* owners'. The Welsh miner is still only a cog in a vast impersonal, industrial machine, now centralized in London.

An inquiry was held into the 'swear word' dispute which caused a strike at the Deep Duffryn Colliery, Mountain Ash, which brought out nearly half the colliery workmen in the Southern Welsh coalfield. The subsequent report is a pathetic attempt to restrict comment to 'Who-said-what-when-first'. In fact, the strike was only one symptom of a wider malady that besets the whole NCB admin-istration. It affects not only miners, but managers and officials whose ultimate powers of discipline and management have been taken away from them to a more remote body of officials in Cardiff, who in turn are subservient to an even remoter body of officials in London. To hold an inquiry confined to a 'swear word' incident was farcical and an abuse of process. What is of more importance to the Welsh coal industry, in this period of crisis, is an inquiry into the whole working and administration of the NCB. After nineteen years of nationalization, it is time that the centralized and London-dominated NCB should be decentralized, reorganized, with the devolution of responsibility and control to a Welsh Coal Board, the setting up of four regional boards in Wales, with the added necessity of giving the miners themselves responsibility in the control of their own industry. Why not? Let the Welsh miners study the administrative pattern of nationalization in Holland, where miners are treated as responsible human beings, sharing responsibility and control. And for forty years there have been no important strikes in the Dutch coal-mines.

It is true that this is Plaid Cymru's policy – but the Blaid go even further. As the Miners' Next Step we advocate the decentralization of the administration of the NCB with a diffusion of responsibility, which would give the Welsh miner real and effective control in his own industry.

Lest prejudice should ruin the appeal, let it be said that the urge for responsibility was implicit in every call for nationalization made by the old South Wales Miners' Federation. It was a principle advocated by the Sankey Commission. It was a declared principle in Mr.James Griffiths's Welsh publication, *Glo*. And lest the Labour Party should again be allowed to forget its roots, let us quote from a publication of the Labour Research Department, *Britain's Coal* (page 173): 'In a nationally owned industry, when the conflicts are removed, the working miners will have to play a very special part in the control at every level, from the pit and district to the central organization, planning output and development.' The conflicts have not been removed in the Welsh coalfield, because the miner is still only regarded as a producing machine.

In the immediate crisis, we join with the Welsh miners, with the insistence that there must be a full investigation into every potential pit closure. We oppose the massacre of whole Welsh communities, or the transfer of a single Welsh miner to work in English pits.

We believe that alternative industries must be set up.

We advocate special research into the mechanization of Welsh pits, with their particular geological conditions. We press for intensive research into the manufacture of by-products from coal – a sphere of activity which has almost been forgotten. The future of coal is not in the grate, but in its by-products. Such a policy would ensure better diversification of our economy, and the setting up of new light industries.

But outside these necessary preoccupations, the Miners' Next Step must be the structural and administrative decentralization of the present NCB. The time to begin is now. The whole future of the Welsh coal industry is in the balance.

Editorial, *Welsh Nation* (November 1963)

To the Young People of Wales

IF SELF-GOVERNMENT is not achieved within the lifetime of those who have not yet reached middle age, then, sometime in the twenty-first century the Welsh nation may well cease to exist. It will not have succumbed to force of arms, nor yet to economic rapine nor to political pressure, weighty though these factors may be. It will have been undermined by its own inner rottenness. It will have gone down because those Welsh people who are alive today were base. It will have died because it did not deserve to live.

Much that we see around us is already far gone in decay, and for much of it, improvised over the last few generations, we need shed no tears. Talk of a 'Welsh way of life' which must be 'preserved' is for the most part meaningless. For no such way of life has been possible for centuries, except a way distorted by all the desperate shifts necessary for survival under conditions designed to obliterate, a way tainted with servility, evasiveness, mysticism and lack of moral fibre, a 'way of life' which, on closer inspection, often turns out to consist of nothing more than the anxious proprieties of English lower middle class existence as practised at the beginning of the century.

But there is still much in Wales that is seemly and strong, and a concern for the future gives us no licence indiscriminately to reject our past. We can leave the tasks of insensate destruction to others, and can even learn from them, for any feature of our national life that is derided by Tory snob or Labour scut is probably well worth defending. Chiefly, there is enjoined upon us a critical and judicious attitude to the Wales we see around us.

Our 'heritage' is largely a pile of junk, but it includes, like a treasure on a scrap heap, the Welsh language. The young people of Wales have a particular duty here. If they already speak Welsh then they can begin to speak it properly, and bring to a merciful end the corrupt jargon of their elders. If they do not already speak it, they can learn it more readily than most of their elders. If they have no ability in this direction they can contribute to a favourable climate of opinion, they can lend their moral support and, indeed, something more than that, like those non-Welsh-speakers who took part in the action on Trefechan Bridge.

But even here we must beware of sentimentality. That a language is old may mean nothing more than that its time has come to die. The existence of a great literature is an argument that the language will in some sort survive, though it cease to be an everyday tongue. But if the Welsh language is perhaps the only valuable thing that has come down to us from the past, it is not for reasons of beauty or antiquity. We honour it because it is placed in our hands, not as the Crown Jewels, but as the Ultimate Weapon: the one factor in our national make-up that neither enemy nor traitor has ever been able to ignore or come to terms with. It is not only a weapon to destroy alien rule, it is an instrument to build a new society: the New Country that must arise in place of the tourist-infested native reservation that is our countryside and the down-at-heel slum of our industrial scene.

When for a brief space, as in the recent history of

America or Israel, the natural order is suspended or reversed, and it is the old who learn from the young a language and a new way of life, then occurs one of those impressive moments when a new nation is born or an old one reborn, with all the vigour of youth in it and all the promise of youth before it. And it is for the young people of Wales to choose whether they will be the instruments of this transformation or whether they will passively offer themselves to the conveyor belt to be filleted and processed into docile futility.

Most of the older people in Wales today have made their choice and accepted their damnation. The young have still to choose. In many ways life is easier today than it was in even the very recent past. But life was never meant to be all ease and pleasure, and now that the bare physical problems of survival have been largely solved, even greater problems must be faced. It is with these problems, of the moral order, involving the ultimate meaning of life rather than its circumstances, that we, as Nationalists, are concerned, and there can be no softening the choice that must be made.

You can manfully shoulder the burden of the struggle for Welsh Freedom. It is a heavy burden and you are at liberty to shrug it off your shoulders.

But you will then find that you are borne down by a heavier burden – the burden of the guilt of betrayal.

You can say: 'Wales is finished. Wales is dead'.

Or you can say: 'Wales begins with us. Wales shall live'.

Choose then – life or death.

Editorial, *Welsh Nation* (February 1964)

The Only Way

IN A RECENT article in *Baner ac Amserau Cymru*, Mr.Gwilym Prys Davies persuasively states a case that may commend itself to many people. He notes that there has been a shift of emphasis from the purely political fight for self-government towards such activities as the Welsh Language Society, the Welsh Schools Movement and other non-political initiatives. He suggests that this shift springs from disappointment at Plaid Cymru's showing in the 1959 Election and that any further efforts by the party would be a waste of time and money, not likely to attract a new generation. He also seems to cast doubt on the claims made for Plaid Cymru as a pressure group, exercising indirect influence. Mr.Davies calls instead for a united non-party organization which will effectively safeguard Wales by preparing reports and, on the basis of diligent fact-findings, run campaigns to influence public opinion and the activities of Welsh MPs. This body would have ample financial and intellectual resources and would deal with language, culture, education, industrial research and development, unemployment in Gwynedd and the Valleys, water, forestry, transport, housing, local government and political responsibility. In ten to twenty years such a body could become an authoritative spokesman for Wales.

Mr.Davies notes that Plaid Cymru's leaders have not responded to Huw T.Edwards's appeal for the party to disband and feels that the Party's present role, which is divisive and estranging, will continue to be disastrous. Meanwhile there is *Undeb Cymru Fydd*, which has done much good work but has somehow not succeeded in establishing itself as a major force. He cites Carmarthenshire where three of the four Parliamentary candidates have made contributions to the life of the nation, and asks why they do not unite their forces in *Undeb Cymru Fydd*. Is this organization too vague and too respectable? Or is there some fundamental weakness in the idea of a non-party national movement?

Having stated his case, Mr.Davies is honest enough to end it on a question. This question we will try to answer fairly, by examining Mr.Davies's points one by one. No one would deny the disappointment felt at the results of the 1959 Elections, and this disappointment was not confined to Plaid Cymru. The development of other forms of activity, however, has not taken place instead of political action. They have grown against a background of far more continuous and extensive political activity by Plaid Cymru. Neither are they as non-political as Mr.Davies makes out. The instances he cites: the Welsh Language Society, the Aberystwyth and Bangor campaigners for official status for Welsh, the activity of the Welsh Schools Movement certainly transcend the bounds of party, but politically active Nationalists are prominent in all of them. It is doubtful if some of those organizations would have been born at all had it not been for Plaid Cymru, and no one with the slightest knowledge of the personalities involved and the course of events which led to these initiatives could ever claim otherwise.

As for Plaid Cymru's importance as a pressure group,

when the London Government itself admits this, albeit in the discreet obscurity of a PEP report, little weight need be attached to unsubstantiated suspicions to the contrary. Even so, let us take Plaid Cymru at its least impressive – in the last parliamentary by-elections. A comparative study of the literature and statements put out in both campaigns by all the other parties, from Conservative to Communist, will show an emphasis on Welsh affairs out of all proportion to the priority given by the general public to these matters if this is judged by the Plaid Cymru vote only. There is also the strange business of the Labour Party's Welsh policy which we analysed, as far as there was anything to analyse, in the July 1963 issue of this paper. As a policy statement it is unconvincing. It only makes sense as an apprehensive manoeuvre to contain a thrust by Plaid Cymru or to hold the internal balance between anti-Welsh and pro-Welsh elements in the party, the latter of whom would not have a leg to stand on were it not for the existence of Plaid Cymru. Politically alert elements in the community, at any rate, are under no illusions about the cogency of Plaid Cymru's case, and take it fully into account. In some ways the party is still paying the penalty of being ahead of its time. In the January issue of this paper we reprinted, as a contribution to the current discussion on the Welsh language, an article by Saunders Lewis which was hailed as apposite and timely, It was, in fact, written over thirty years ago! In respect of his own proposals, which we shall next examine, Mr.Davies counsels a gradualist approach and ten to twenty years of patient waiting for results. Why then does he decry the patience of Nationalists as a vain show of confidence disguising an inner despair?

As for Plaid Cymru's lack of appeal to the younger generation, this is a problem common to all political parties and Plaid Cymru's experience is probably, on balance, more encouraging than that of the English parties. Most of the regular contributors to this paper are in their early twenties. When young Socialist intellectuals at Aberystwyth founded the magazine *Aneurin* their elders must have been somewhat mortified to see it described by such a well-informed observer as Mr.Kenneth O.Morgan as 'more conspicuous for Nationalism than Socialism'. At least one of this gifted group has since left the Labour Party for Plaid Cymru.

To turn to Mr.Davies's own proposals: in themselves they seem sound. Many people in Plaid Cymru have been saying for years that Wales needs a fact-finding body of this description. It could be argued, though, that this research organization, a sort of Welsh Fabian Society, could not do anything that full-time specialists at a University could not do better, and that, as much recent work has shown, the way to get the facts is to make use of facilities and trained personnel already available. Even the Central Government's role in the realm of fact-finding is not to be despised. Some of its recent reports are praised by Mr.Davies himself. So far so good, but we are also asked to accept that the proposed body should also initiate campaigns and influence public opinion. How can it do that without intervening directly in the political arena and thus forfeiting its non-party status? Mr.Davies says that Welsh MPs should be regarded as representatives of Welsh interests rather than of their parties. This doctrine would strike at the roots of the English party system in Wales. We would, in fact, be back in our present situation. If Plaid Cymru stood down in favour of this new body, it would have to be resurrected immediately the new body came face to face with the realities of English power politics. Plaid Cymru, after all, was not founded in a fit of pique. It was a logical development from previous tendencies, as Dyfnallt and others saw clearly at the time. After the eclipse of the old *Cymru Fydd* movement at the beginning of the century, defence of Welsh interests went by default until gradually there came into being a league of like-minded organizations, known from its initials in Welsh as *Y Tair G* – the Three Gs. It was just such a body as Mr.Davies now has in mind. When H.R.Jones founded the national movement which was to become the Welsh Nationalist Party, nearly everybody who had been active in *Y Tair G* joined. Why Mr.Davies thinks that Plaid Cymru should now dissolve merely for these events of the 1920s to be re-enacted is something of a mystery. But there is a saying: a country which forgets its history is doomed to repeat it.

As for the possibilities of *Undeb Cymru Fydd*, Mr.Davies himself is only too aware of the limitations of this excellent body. It is cultural, middle-class, and Welsh-speaking. It has made no impact on the industrial areas or the rural *gwerin*. If Mr.Davies thinks he can transform it into a sort of dynamic Fabian Society-cum-Committee of 100, then good luck to him.

As a member of *Undeb Cymru Fydd* myself, I would welcome such a development. But when he asks members of all political parties to give over in its favour, he is being more selective than at first appears. The Conservatives hardly enter into this discussion. Their only Welsh-speaking candidate does not believe there is such a place as Wales. The Liberals are merely a transient phenomenon – a Jonah's gourd, if we may coin a phrase. The bulk of the Labour Party care nothing for much of what we and Mr.Davies hold dear, and those few Socialists who would sacrifice their politics to be active in defence of Wales would not be missed from the Labour ranks, so few are they and so uninfluential. Plaid Cymru, however, would be absorbed completely, and as we have seen, to no purpose but to be resurrected. Mr.Davies's proposals, however seductive they may appear, do not bear scrutiny. Appeals for unity can only be made when a will to unity exists. It is no good condemning Plaid Cymru as a divisive and estranging force. We did not create these divisions and estrangements. They are old in our unfortunate history and cannot be wished away. The really divisive forces in Wales today are the English parties. Mr.Davies would doubtless concede the antisocial and anti-national character of Conservatism. But the Labour Party, despite its paper *Welsh policy* is, in practice, equally hostile to the idea of Welsh nationality. No resolutions concerning Welsh affairs were submitted to its last year's conference, and the local parties are parochial beyond belief. Their Gwynedd supporters would be shocked if they could attend an election campaign in the Glamorgan Valleys and hear the insane hatred and contempt with which Labour speakers assault rural Wales and the Welsh language. Not only do they actively ferment division between different parts of our land, the notoriously low moral and intellectual standards of Labour politicians have bred deep doubt as to whether the Welsh people are worthy or capable of self-government.

Mr.Davies calls for a movement which will bridge all

divisions in our national life, and which, on the basis of known facts, will campaign to arouse public opinion. Such a movement exists. It is not a non-political movement for this is an impossibility. It has many weaknesses and limitations, but it is active in the Valleys of Glamorgan and Gwent, where *Undeb Cymru Fydd*-type operations would make little impression, as well as in Gwynedd and Powys and Dyfed. It bridges the gap between those who do and do not speak Welsh, and is the only movement making any sort of shot at this tricky task. It is called Plaid Cymru.

Welsh Nation (February 1964)

The Gathering Storm

Plaid Cymru in the light of the Election

THE LAST ROUND of local elections was fought in the looming shadow of October's Election. So that when voters went to the polls in May and June they had one eye on the town hall or county hall and another on Westminster. They voted for or against Harold Wilson as much as they voted for or against the local man. Plaid Cymru has felt the first draught from the stormy scenes that lie ahead.

On balance it has weathered the storm. Of course it will be objected that some hard-won beach-heads have been lost, and that some expected gains have not been registered. But this is no new situation. In the long-drawn-out battle to which Welsh patriots are committed, there are bound to be gains and losses. And Plaid Cymru's victories in the past few years have been, for the most part, by slender majorities, painfully susceptible to the polarization of English-influenced opinion in Wales rallying to one or other of the old parties under the influence of October's Election.

We do not and cannot minimize these losses. Their effect on the progress of the National cause is not encouraging. Their impact on the local scene can never be anything but painful. That able, honest and articulate men should be rejected in favour of hacks and worse is a measure of the tremendous task of social regeneration that confronts all who strive for the betterment of our country.

That vivid characters like Glyn James, doughty fighters like Dewi Wynne Thomas, strong clear-sighted young men like Ron Dawe should lose their places is a bad business that cannot be excused or ignored. And behind them, others as yet less prominent but of equal calibre, fighting perhaps not for the first time, have failed to win their rightful places.

But let us look at these matters in perspective. Let us set them against the background which matters: the scale of the struggle. In the past, Plaid Cymru has often made its mark because it has been able to concentrate its resources from over a wide area onto one particular sector; those days are gone. The front is widening. There are so many sectors now. Every local band of Nationalists must fight on its own.

This year the battle has raged sporadically all over Wales, from Deeside to the Cardiff suburbs, from the Valleys of Gwent to the coast of Cardigan Bay. In the less sensationally contested rural areas quiet consolidation goes on. In the smaller towns, which present special difficulties to the penetration of new forces, there have been one or two especially heartening successes of a calibre and character that compensate somewhat for their sparse distribution.

It is particularly pleasant to be able to refer to Councillor Millward of Aberystwyth and to Councillor Gareth Roberts of Holywell, and to do so knowing that they will make their mark in the council chambers of their communities.

Perhaps Plaid Cymru has not yet adjusted to this new scale of fighting, where every branch, from now on, will be wise to assume that it is on its own, and that it will not be able to rely on help from unengaged neighbours. The sooner this lesson is learnt, the better.

The other encouraging factor is this: it remains true now as it always has been that no Nationalist candidate has ever been beaten by a better man. What has counted every time has not been the man but the machine. In areas where Plaid Cymru has not been outvoted two to one, it has often been outnumbered twenty to one in terms of workers, cars and all the other apparatus of electioneering. Some of the men who made a good start in the Valleys of Gwent fought virtually single-handed. It needs very little arithmetic to show that if Plaid Cymru merely doubled its effectiveness in such cases it would begin to make substantial inroads even on the most massively entrenched enemy and begin to win seats at the level that matters.

Again the lesson to be learned is a severely practical one, having nothing to do with ideas, policies or programmes, but everything to do with hard matters of money, organization and efficiency.

The third consideration is basic: the wider historical perspective in which these clashes, and those of the coming October, are set. In the populous areas of Wales that are the centre of gravity of political power, the Labour Party still reigns supreme. In the rural areas, equally important in other ways, Liberalism is still strong. Plaid Cymru has been fighting them both for a very long time, and has made little headway outside of Gwynedd. But by the end of 1964 neither of these organizations will exist in its present form.

This is not a prophecy of what is going to happen at the General Election. After all, if everybody knew what the result of an election was going to be, there would be no point in having one. The English system is riddled with factors making for uncertainty, and we leave the crystal ball to others. Neither do we suggest that, even with their obsolescence staring them in the face, these organizations will vanish from the scene. That is not the English way of doing things; there are still men with spears guarding the Tower of London.

But the Liberal Party, at least, can have little hope of meaningful survival with the collapse of the narrow basis on which its opportunist manoeuvring is possible. As for the Labour Party, two possibilities confront it in October, both equally dreadful. It can lose the Election, in which case the discreet disengagement of the TUC from its unruly and often embarrassing parliamentary partner, which has not passed unnoticed by informed observers, may suddenly become very obvious and impossible to ignore. Not to mention the fierce recriminations which would break out inside the parliamentary Labour Party itself. All these stresses would shatter the precarious unity of the party beyond recovery. Or the Labour Party could win the Election. In this case its doom, though delayed somewhat, will be even more certain and complete. For even a substantial swing in its favour, which the sated and booming English centres who dominate the voting are unlikely to provide, cannot possibly convert a Tory majority of over one hundred into anything but the slenderest majority in favour of Labour. From a precarious basis they will have to implement unpopular policies. To back up the boastful and bloodthirsty imperialist utterances of Harold Wilson, and to prove to their American bosses that they are just as good little boys as the Conservatives, they will have to bring back conscription.

To implement their policies in this island they will be obliged to re-establish from scratch the dense network of controls which in 1945 they inherited from a wartime situation. As the realities of Labour rule emerge, the pretences will fall away. Their insolent pretence to be regarded as the party of 'science' in some semi-mystical (and totally unscientific) sense will then be regarded by the public with the same contempt as it is now regarded by scientists.

And so for all their other schemes. During their previous tenure of office, they were careful not to touch the rich, among whom they number many friends and backers. They financed their schemes by penal taxation on the most intelligent and productive members of the community. In the last decade this sector of society has expanded. Maybe Labour can now look forward to gaining the support of some of those suffering from natural frustrations: skilled workers, technicians, managers, and professional people. But under the impact of reality such support will disappear as rapidly as it did between 1945 and 1950.

For in the last analysis Labour's heart is where its treasure is, and its whole outlook is conditioned by the mental limitations of the least adaptable section of the community, a section which in England at any rate is dwindling both in numbers and importance under the influence of education and technical progress. Because

Wales is technically backward and economically stagnant and socially unbalanced by the forced emigration of her best people, factors making for continued loyalty to Labour are stronger here. And here, perhaps more so than in England, a small minority of sincere idealists in Labour's ranks keep up some semblance of a justification for the party's continued existence. But in all the countries of this island, these idealists, most of all, will never recover from Labour's term of office, if any.

There will be a lot of politically homeless people wandering around in the next twelve months. In England there has been a noticeable exodus of such disillusioned people out of conventional left-wing politics already, into such activities as the Campaign for Nuclear Disarmament, the Rank and File movement, the 'solidarity' and other types of 'grass roots' Labour organization, or into a concern with directly effective agencies offering scope for personal engagement and a sense of doing something worthwhile where it is most needed: voluntary service in the developing countries, War on Want, Freedom from Hunger, Oxfam and the welfare of refugees.

With none of these last-named can we have any possible quarrel, but to the desperate seeker after a valid cause that offers immediate engagement in real issues, which is, in other words, political in the best sense, what England cannot offer, Wales can. We do not pretend that Plaid Cymru is a perfect lodging. There is, in fact, quite a lot wrong with it. And it may well lose a few more slates in the coming storms.

But there is nothing wrong with it that good will and hard work cannot put right. In contrast to the shoddy jerry-building with which Labour has disfigured our national life during its long decadence, in contrast to the flimsy and collapsible edifice of Liberalism and to all the other ephemeral tips of a moment and a day, Plaid Cymru is a house built foursquare on the rock of nationhood. It will stand when the others are no more. And its doors are always open.

Welsh Nation (October 1964)

Showing the Flag

FROM CARDIFF TO Bridgend via Caerffili Mountain, Dowlais Top, Cilfynydd Common, Maerdy, Porth, Nant-y-moel and Abercynffig is not an AA recommended route. For the record it is 120 miles long and takes eight hours. But this was the route of the seven-constituency motorcade that set off from Cathay's Park to cover all the Nationalist arenas of the South-East in the uncertain weather of the Saturday before the General Election. From the steps of the National Museum, with the rain driving in gusts full of dead leaves, the first arrivals looked glumly at the possible waste of a day. The idea of a joint motorcade had been born back in the summer, from the success of the procession that had set out from Fishguard to carry the Flag to the three coasts of Pembroke: October in Glamorgan looked very different. But the abiding uncertainties of Wales saved the day, and the ambitious programme planned by Ken Spencer began to look more attractive as our numbers grew and the weather relented.

We got off to a brisk start through the crowds of a shopping morning in Cardiff, with the Red Dragons fluttering from the cars and Emrys Roberts's name on the posters. No loudspeaker work, the city police did not consider it advisable, and they had shown themselves so helpful in other ways that their wishes had to be respected. The press of traffic, in any case, rather scattered us, and we made our way through the main commercial arteries and well into the northern suburbs in twos and threes – but not unnoticed.

At a lay-by looking south from Caerffili Mountain over the rain-swept streets of the city, we stopped, reassembled and put up the name of Phil Williams. Then over the top, to a cheer from roadworkers at Cwmwbwb and down into the Rhymni Valley and the sunshine, with the loudspeakers opening up, not to fall silent till evening. The Valleys never look better than in clear weather after rain, and even the drabbest stretches of Victorian jerry-building seemed tolerable and clean. Phil Williams put over the message of a New Wales, a contingent from Gwent joined us at Ystradmynach, and we drove on through busy Bargod and Pontlotyn up to Rhymni Common and Dowlais Top. Here in the bracing weather that is special to the place, the Merthyr Tydfil contingent awaited us, near the confused construction works of the Heads of the Valleys Road, the most modern obsolete highway in Europe. Ioan Bowen Rees now took place of honour and by now we had acquired a cheeky blue convertible, a two-seater with just enough room for the candidate to perch standing in the back. So we took him on an open-air ride around the constituency, with many a detour for thinned Dowlais, neglected Abercannaid, out of the way Perthigleision, as well as the main centres, where lunch-time quiet reigned. At the borough's southern boundary, in a leafy dell above the Caiach brook, we changed again and put up the name of Dewi Wynne Thomas, before racing down to Traveller's Rest to turn up into Cwm Cynon.

Sandwiches were eaten en route, or hastily at the change-over points, between business with Sellotape and string. The long chain of colliery communities that lead up to Aberdâr were also quiet, but the Queen of the Valleys was her usual lively self. Up into Hirwaun (calling Trefor Morgan's name during a brief incursion into the Brecon and Radnor constituency), back down through Llwytgoed for a second traverse of Aberdâr, and up the steep mountain road where Glyn James awaited us, his vehicle visible from afar by reason of a huge sign on the roof. Here, as we put our Rhondda candidate's name up, the unbelievable view stretched northward from the rock of Blaen Gwaist to the stormy ramparts of the Beacons, all shining in the last of the sun. The Rhondda Valleys, though, generate their own inner radiance. From Maerdy down to Porth Square, out to Pen-y-graig and on to Ton-y-pandy, we had ample proof of that, as we hit the shopping streets of the strung-out townships at their Saturday afternoon busiest.

Gangs of boys gave us the thumbs-up sign, nice old women waved from their scrubbed doorsteps, even the senile Labour canvassers whom we encountered as they groaned their last up a steep street in Williamstown looked more human than they usually do, while Glyn James rode the convertible until it was Vic Davies's turn to take over in Ton-y-pandy for the long run under the darkening sky to the end of the valley. It was raining in Blaen Rhondda, the stone-built Welsh-speaking village under huge hills. Back down to Treorci and Cwm-parc for the spectacular climb over the Bwlch to the Ogmore basin and the even more spectacular run down into Nant-y-moel. Here, in central Glamorgan, is wild, tangled scenery equal to anything in Mawddwy or Deudraeth, and in a storm lit by a dying sun, inexpressibly moving.

We were few in numbers now, and daylight was ending but our flags flapped briskly in the wet wind, and by the time we had taken in Ogmore Vale, Melin Ifan Ddu and Abercynffig, we still had time to make a circuit of Bridgend for Margaret Tucker before staggering into Mr. Cavalli's crowded but hospitable restaurant opposite the Plaid Cymru campaign headquarters, where the realization at last hit us that we had been on the road since mid-morning with little to sustain us.

Was it worth it? Yes. As a piece of election publicity it gave a lift to the campaigning throughout the South-East. But there was more to it than any possible return in terms of votes. We showed the Flag – to the people of Wales, and to the enemies of Wales. We took the Red Dragon from the processional avenues of the capital to the windswept heights of Graig Ogwr, from Queen Street's Golden Mile to the crumbling disgrace that is Dowlais, from the suburban tidiness of Llanishen to the neglected and decaying communities of the coalfield. Some of us saw some of these places for the first time, all of us saw them anew in the light of the important decisions that lay before the people.

This was our country, and to know it is to love it. At its loveliest it inspires us with a pride that does not stoop to excuse or apologize. At its most befouled it invokes in us an implacable hatred of the enemy, be he the alien despoiler or any of his piebald native jackals. And in the name of that pride and that contempt we will stand when others have fallen. These words are written before the result of the election is known, but this is certain: when we paraded the Red

Dragon through the heart of Glamorgan on that moody Saturday in October it was a rehearsal for a triumphal progress.

Welsh Nation (November 1964)

The Loss of Cwm Tryweryn

THE INTERVENTION OF Plaid Cymru on Thursday, October 21, in the ceremony planned by Liverpool Corporation at Tryweryn was effective, thanks to the work done by the party during the previous ten years. It was Plaid Cymru which made Tryweryn a national name and issue and which towards the end of the campaign united local authorities, political parties, trade unions, the churches and public bodies throughout Wales. Although the Labour-controlled Liverpool Council had the power of the state behind it, on October 21 it was clearly very conscious of its weak moral position.

Despite its arrogance during the years of the campaign, the Liverpool Council had to defer more than once to the strength of the Welsh opposition. Having refused to accept a national deputation of the most distinguished Welshmen of the day, on the ground that it never allowed strangers to address it, it felt obligated to listen to the President of Plaid Cymru. When it called its statutory town meeting its weakness among the people of Liverpool themselves was proclaimed by the ruse which it was forced to adopt of postponing the start of the meeting for half an hour while it sent for enough corporation employees to give the scheme a majority vote. In the council itself it could muster only 90 out of 160 members to vote for the scheme. In Parliament its task was of course easier, for there it had the support of the vast majority of 600-odd Labour and Conservative MPs, as well as the Minister of Welsh Affairs. Nevertheless, Parliament at Westminster demonstrated dramatically how unfit it is to be the parliament of Wales. Yet it is the only Parliament the Welsh nation has.

Wales has lost a cultured community and a valley. Day by day it is losing scores of millions of gallons of water. But the effort to save these for Wales has been an invaluable education for the Welsh people. They have learnt how disgraceful their position is as a nation in the second half of the twentieth century. They have learnt also something about the duties of nationhood and of the need to give Wales their loyalty. The value of their natural and human resources has been forcibly driven home to them. Finally they know now that they have their own political party, identified with their interests, on which alone they can rely to fight for them.

Liverpool, too, knows who is the active force in Welsh affairs. It was generally noted that although the Council felt free to ignore the Secretary of State for Wales, it took public steps to make contact with Plaid Cymru. The meeting between the President of Plaid Cymru and the Leader of Liverpool Corporation, at the latter's invitation, was even more significant than his meetings, in 1963 and 1964, with Sir Keith Joseph and Mr.Edward Heath.

Its opponents in the English Parties often scoff at Plaid Cymru as being small and weak. Yet those in the best position to judge obviously regard it as the creative force in Welsh life. A party which has been able to do so much with comparatively slight resources could obviously make the Welsh people an irresistible power if they united behind it. We are edging forward towards that position. The Welsh nation is gradually growing into a political force to be reckoned with. That is what the English Parties know and fear.

Editorial, *Welsh Nation* (December 1965)

Compromise or Appeasement?

ONE OF THE FEW people in the Labour Party for whom Welsh Nationalists have any respect is Mr.Gwilym Prys Davies. For many years he has sustained an arduous role as the lonely Welsh Conscience of his party.

Recently in an important article in *Y Cymro* he bent his considerable talents to a defence of that party's record. As this has never been referred to in the English-language press, I will summarize it.

Mr.Prys Davies contends that the Welsh Office must be judged on the basis of three important documents: The Welsh Language Act, the White Paper on Local Government, and the Economic Development Plan. Few will dispute that there is ample basis here for passing judgement. Before passing to a detailed consideration of these policy statements, Mr.Prys Davies begs us to consider them in their context as part of the policies of compromise. This he says is essential to the democratic process. The more enlightened elements must move more slowly than they would like, in order to carry their opponents with them. This process, he suggests, is temperamentally uncongenial to poets, men of letters, and preachers. (The insinuation here is obviously a hit at the sort of party Plaid Cymru is alleged to have been some thirty years ago!) To the rash passions of these creatures, Mr.Prys Davies opposes an idealized picture of the democratic politicians, sincere, honest and brave, tough and unemotional. Their courage and devotion to duty have produced the three documents under discussion, which he then subjects to analysis.

The Welsh Language Act is welcomed, and its disappointing limitations frankly admitted. He believes that the language should not have equal status in all parts of Wales, and that the limited recognition guaranteed by the Act is the most that can be expected at the moment.

Mr.Prys Davies does not attempt to defend the Economic White Paper at all. It was a mistake to publish it, he admits, and urges us to wait for a better effort next time.

On the other hand, he is fairly enthusiastic about the Local Government Policy, and quotes the praise lavished on it by academics and political writers outside of Wales. He confesses his disappointment that it does not recommend an elected Council for Wales, something Mr.Prys Davies himself has worked heroically for over the years, but acquits Mr.Cledwyn Hughes of any blame. We must remember, he tells us, that there are many anti-Welsh elements not only in London but in our own country as well. Mr.Hughes, however, should not express his disappointment by offering his resignation. We are reminded (it hardly seems a necessary reminder) that he is neither a rebel nor a crusader. We must hope that in the long run enlightened opinions will prevail. The new Economic Council due to be set up in March 1968 would be developed into a democratic, elected council and Mr.Hughes is urged to make an early declaration of intent. The whole argument is set against a background struggle of the new Welsh Office to acquire strength and staff and status. In the circumstances, everybody has done very well, and should be urged to do better.

Mr.Prys Davies presents his case with eloquence and skill worthy of a better cause. It is obvious, to one reader at any rate, that this is not one politician supporting another, but a counsel for the defence trying to secure an acquittal on compassionate grounds for an offender whom public opinion has placed in the dock. Like everything Mr.Prys Davies does, it is superbly well done. The indefensible Economic White Paper is not defended at all, the Welsh Language Bill is given a moderate welcome which conceals its limitations, the full treatment is reserved for the Local Government White Paper which is hailed as a great advance. No mention of the shameful, shuffling hesitation with which this long-delayed document was reluctantly produced. No mention of the almost unanimous chorus of disapproval with which it has been greeted. The praise of pundits and academics conveniently distant from the scene is invoked to drown the condemnations of all practical men, councillors and officers alike, irrespective of party, whose daily bread is earned in this field. No mention either of the total and crushing humiliation of the Welsh Labour Party generally, whose support for an elected council counts for nothing in Westminster and Whitehall.

Despite expert manipulation, the evidence does not support the case. As for the doctrine of compromise of which these policies are the result, it must stand condemned if only because of the wretched inadequacy of its products. A tree is known by its fruits. If the documents are rotten, then the philosophy behind them is rotten. Compromise is all very well in its place, of course. In the affairs of a state, the different parties must compromise among themselves (though even here it could be argued that compromise can be taken too far, as when a Labour Government operates Conservative policies!). Inside a political party, various shades of opinion must arrive at a compromise, in order to operate effectively. But there are limits. These limits are set by the distinction between calculations of party advantage and the national welfare. Plaid Cymru, in taking its stand for Wales and her people, contracts out of compromise politics. The claims of a nation can never be the subject of compromise. *To traffic national integrity for short term party political advantage is not compromise – it is appeasement.* See where the doctrines of compromise have landed the Welsh Labour Party! The concessions are all one-sided: the voices that have prevailed with the London Cabinet are those of the anti-Welsh politicians, the evil old men of the Rotten Generation and their allies, the arrogant Fabian Fascist intelligentsia of the latest intake. To such compromise and to its dead-sea fruits, Plaid Cymru offers implacable hostility.

The Welsh economy and the Welsh language deserve better than this, and we are determined that they shall get it. There can be no appeasement of elements whose sole raison d'être is to obstruct the healthy development of our nation. One does not have to be a poet, or a preacher or a man of letters to sense the great change for the better that is coming over Wales and her people these days, a great wave of renewed national self-respect and self-confidence that will completely obliterate the policy of appeasement and dismiss its practitioners to a merited and merciful oblivion.

Mr. Prys Davies and a few able and well-meaning men like him seem to have somehow or other been caught on the wrong foot. We respect their efforts to make their political associates see sense and reason. It would be a tragic waste if men like these were swept away in the cataclysm that is about to overwhelm the English political establishment in Wales. There must surely come a time when they will realize that compromise can only take matters so far. After that point has been reached (and we are now well past it) only a movement advocating the maximum claims of the nation and the people will obtain a hearing. And there is room in that movement for all who love their country and have shown by untiring labour in unpromising soil, that they are worthy upholders of the cause of Wales.

Welsh Nation (January 1968)

Reactions to a Non-Event

Some Observations on the Investiture

FROM NOW UNTIL next July Plaid Cymru will sail through choppy waters. The Investiture of Prince Charles at Caernarfon has been a move kept in reserve ever since he was proclaimed Prince of Wales at the Commonwealth Games in Cardiff in 1958. The calculations behind the move are obvious, not least among them the political embarrassment of Plaid Cymru in the general election due for 1970 amid the likelihood of creating an internal difference in the party. To Plaid Cymru, the situation offers a challenge, and all shades of opinion must strive to meet it so that we weather the transient discomforts of the next two years and emerge in fighting trim to win the majority of Welsh seats in 1970.

It will be as well to set the whole matter in perspective. By the end of the eighteenth century, Wales could be referred to at Westminster as 'a phantom nation'. Its independence belonged so far in the past that its very identity was not apparent to outsiders. It was a 'non-historic' nation, like the Czechs, whose claims were not recognized even by opinion which supported independence for more well-known people such as the Italians and Hungarians. However, a national revival was in preparation escalated by industrialization from the culture and religious context of the eighteenth century to the significant political and social demands of the 1800s. But the ages of subjection had done their work well. The idea of autonomous constitutional status took a long time to develop, and by the 1890s it was formulated in relatively modest terms, bound up with local government reform. 'Home Rule' of the *Cymru Fydd* period as envisaged by Lloyd George and Tom Ellis, was based on County Councils, an elected national council of much the same sort as has just been withheld by Cledwyn Hughes. Shortly afterwards, the Investiture was invented. (It had of course, no historical precedent, even in the pageant-stuffed annals of England.) Its purpose was to make Lloyd George respectable after his mildly Jacobin budget of 1910. The First World War and the inter-war depression downgraded constitutional issues. Now the emphasis was all on economic matters and the Labour Party took the lead. Out of the cataclysm Plaid Cymru emerged in 1925. Of necessity it had to take over from where *Cymru Fydd* had left off, for this was the only recent precedent that existed. Their first proclaimed objectives were to establish the status of the Welsh language, to gain control of local authorities and work (in very general terms) for the economic prosperity of Wales. More far-reaching constitutional ambitions were only imprecisely envisaged. When Dr.D.J.Davies joined the party he found its leaders discussing a 'treaty with England'. Not the least of his services to our cause was to drag them sharply back to earth.

In 1931 the Statute of Westminster defined the relationship between England and the 'White Dominions', largely in order to weight the voting at the League of Nations. The new formula recognized their already de facto independence with the Monarch and the Privy Council common to all of them. Immediately an able group of Nationalists saw that this Formula could apply equally to Wales and succeeded in getting it adopted as Plaid Cymru's official policy. In the climate of the early 1930s this was a great step forward. It was the first precise and unambiguous formulation of Welsh constitutional claims since Glyn Dŵr, it had the merit of being ambitious and yet comprehensible, with modern and attractive precedents. It involved acceptance of the English monarchy at a time when the mystique of that institution was still unchallenged and was not thought of as in any way compromising to full statehood. But there was still some reluctance to go the whole hog. The phrase 'freedom not independence' was coined, permissible perhaps in a philosophical discussion among the intelligentsia of a minority party but, in terms of mass politics, savouring of evasion and double-talk. It is still occasionally heard, but the time has surely come to drop it.

The 'thirties were crowded with incidents relevant to the present situation. The party was wakened by dissension caused by all things, a civil war in Spain. There was the glory of Penyberth. The Union Jack was hauled down from Caernarfon Castle; its remains are still one of the party's official trophies. There was the fervour of George V's Jubilee and the embarrassment of his successor's Abdication. The utter irrelevance of this Ruritanian 'constitutional crisis' to the main course of events is well worth bearing in mind. The Coronation of George VI saw the Three Men of Penyberth in jail, and the party briefly led by W.J.Gruffydd who called for the Festivities to be boycotted. It is the unanimous opinion of all who were active in our cause at the time that this tactic was disastrous, and largely nullified the great impression made by the Action at Penyberth. This may seem very strange and contradictory, but we are dealing with people, not logical calculating machines. Gruffydd's political judgement was in any case thoroughly unreliable; he later defected and did enormous damage by successfully opposing Saunders Lewis in a parliamentary by-election for the old University of Wales seat, getting in on an anti-Welsh vote and delaying the parliamentary impact of Nationalism for a whole generation.

After the war the party emerged into an atmosphere of revolutionary change. In 1947 India expelled the English (who claimed, of course, 'we gave India her freedom') and India and Pakistan became Dominions à la statute of Westminster. This was obviously an interim arrangement attributable to the complexities of reorganizing a subcontinent; Burma, with less complex problems, opted out to become an autonomous Republic. In 1948, Ireland severed her frayed links with Crown and Commonwealth and became a fully independent Republic. Nationalist Wales, ever influenced by Ireland, was deeply stimulated. A Republican body of opinion developed in Plaid Cymru and by 1950 was strong enough to emerge as an independent movement. The constitutional issue was not the only stimulus here. The movement was fuelled by dissatisfaction with Plaid Cymru as it then was. The Welsh Republican Movement made maximal constitutional claims implicit in its name, and propounded the doctrine of the sovereign people, at a time when Plaid Cymru was pursuing the more moderate tactic of an all-party alliance to establish a more or less Northern Ireland type *Senedd i Gymru* [Parliament for Wales]. Both tactics were sound, both points of view were mutually respected and both could claim to have influenced opinion to some extent. After seven years of vigorous propagandizing in the industrial valleys, the Welsh Republican Movement felt that its mission was largely accomplished within the limitations of its capacities. Plaid Cymru had become much more of the left, had learnt to communicate with industrial workers, was not so obsessed with the language issue, was altogether more political and realistic. Most Republicans now felt they could join Plaid Cymru with a clear conscience.

For there had been yet further developments on the international scene. In 1951, India and Pakistan had become Republics, but unlike Ireland and Burma, remained within the Commonwealth, electing their own Presidential Heads of State, but recognizing the English Monarch as 'Head of the Commonwealth', a formula written into the proclamation of Elizabeth II in 1953. Since then the Commonwealth has continued to disintegrate physically and as an idea. Most of its remaining members are Republics with Presidents. It is an obvious calculation that by the 1970s the decade of Welsh Freedom, the Commonwealth will have ceased to exist. In the early 1960s Plaid Cymru's membership card still read 'to secure self-government for Wales, like Eire, New Zealand etc.', although by then these two countries had very different constitutional positions. This lingering hint of vagueness in the Blaid's approach to such matters was swept away in the general spring-clean of recent years so the Party's first aim is now clearly defined as 'to attain self-government for Wales' leaving us free to opt for whatever form of self-government we wish.

Obviously events are moving at an accelerated pace. It becomes clear that as the economic and psychological havoc of English rule piles up with ever-increasing weight on the backs of people now almost fully aroused to claim their rights as Welshmen and as men, then their rejection of the present system in all its aspects will be the more complete and their demands will escalate to the maximum.

It is against this deep current, moving inexorably towards Welsh freedom, that the English Establishment and their Welsh hirelings are now trying to erect the frail dam of a ceremonial musical-comedy, 'Principality', complete with flower-strewing chorus of loyal peasants and a Student Prince. But it will not arrest that current. All it will do is to throw up a certain amount of frothing surface eddies. We must be careful not to let them upset our navigation and throw us off course. The utter meaninglessness of this sort of jamboree cannot be too strongly emphasized. In 1947, George VI and all his family were wildly acclaimed in South Africa. A few years later, without any opposition, it became a Republic. Surveying the change, an English political commentator recollected the anecdote of Cromwell being acclaimed as Lord Protector, and looking out over the cheering crowds, saying, 'They would cheer just as loudly to see me hanged'. For last year we saw the Russian Revolution commemorated on our television screens, with newsreel shots of the Tzar appearing on his balcony and thousands of his loyal subjects sinking to their knees in homage, knowing that just three years later they saw him thrown down a mineshaft. Lenin knew how to bide his time. He accepted all sorts of apparent reverses, even the humiliating Treaty of Brest-Litovsk; he compromised with alien capitalists right into the 1920s. But because he kept his eye on the ball and refused to be distracted by side-issues, he laid firm foundations.

A regime is only tolerated and cheered while it is providing the goods. Once it ceases to do that, however picturesque and historic it may be, and if there is a credible and emotionally satisfying alternative, it is hustled off the stage of history. With the storm clouds of disaster already beginning to loom over Wales, who can doubt what the outcome will be? In 1911, nationally minded Wales seems to have been so grateful for any form of recognition that it welcomed the Investiture uncritically. Opposition came from Keir Hardie, who denounced it as a symbol of historic oppression and influenced Mabon and others not to attend. This feeling is much stronger in the aroused Wales of today and finds its focus in Plaid Cymru. (Official Labour is effusive in its servility, but ordinary people are estranged from them on this as on other and bigger issues.)

Plaid Cymru is thus confronted with a choice. But this choice does not lie between enthusiastic acceptance of the Investiture and outright opposition. The former alternative has never been considered by anybody. In welcoming Prince Charles to Aberystwyth, in expressing the hope that he will identify himself with Wales, in calling for a simple, *gwerinol* ceremony, with our language given prominence, Plaid Cymru is throwing the challenge back to the Establishment, a challenge they cannot possibly meet, and when this failure really to recognize our nationhood becomes apparent, the synthetic jubilation will turn to bitter disillusion, fuel to the flame it was supposed to smother. Meanwhile, the whipped-up hurrahing must be recognized as the trivial and superficial thing it is.

Pseudo-medieval pageantry is but a shadow show. Let us not lose the substance by grasping at those shadows. When we have our own parliament we can pass what laws we like. Then, and only then, and not in an atmosphere of candy-floss and mumbo-jumbo, will the great issue of sovereignty be finally settled.

A memorandum circulated among members of Plaid Cymru's
Executive Committee in 1968

Posturing in the Last Agony

'THE HISTORICAL TRUTH is that the existence of nations cannot be proved or disproved by objective characteristics, the presence or absence of which can be determined by the proper authorities. Nations exist when a significant number of people believe themselves to constitute a nation, and have the collective will to assert and maintain themselves as such.

It is not even possible to determine on preconceived principles what percentage of a population must possess this national consciousness in order that a nation may exist. It remains a fact that the process takes place and that linguistic or religious groups may or may not undergo a qualitative change and become transformed into nations.'

I take these words from a review in the *Times Literary Supplement* of a learned work on the break-up of the Hapsburg Empire. They seem to me an exact statement of the present situation in Wales.

We have, of course, been a conscious nation with the collective will to assert and maintain our identity, for longer than most. Specialists may argue about when exactly this identity crystallizes beyond question. Some would place it as late as Owain Glyn Dŵr, others might take it back to the dawn of history. The relevant thing, and the encouraging thing, is that this identity is becoming stronger and more distinct with every day that passes and that the will to assert and maintain it is now the dominant factor in the Welsh scene.

It is not just a question of politics. The growth of Plaid Cymru is the central, but by no means the only feature of what one can call the National Revival. One sees it on every side, in commerce and industry, in the arts, in entertainment and sport. Someone who is in a position to know, a high-up in the field of industrial development, told me recently that he expected that Welsh native talent would soon activate a major breakthrough in the field of Welsh-based secondary industry.

Our fathers knew only the heavy industries in which they were hewers of wood and drawers of water. It is only since the last war that our people have had much experience of a more diversified economy, still controlled from outside, of course. It takes time for an entire community to familiarize themselves with the technique of new development and to get the feel of a new situation.

But the period of apprenticeship is drawing to an end. Already there have been some encouraging initiatives. Given the legendary ability of Welsh people to get to the top in every sphere in which they choose to exert themselves, there is every likelihood that, once this ability is thrown into the industrial field, Wales will be transformed.

It is no accident that many of these new initiatives are closely linked with political nationalism, or inspired by sentiments not very far removed from it. It is a far cry from the days when 'Welsh Nationalism' was a mere romantic and cultural thing, considered completely irrelevant to the day-to-day business of earning a living and making money.

With England in its present mess, and no hope of getting out of it, the bread and butter arguments for Welsh Independence are strongly reinforced. As the Austro-Hungarian Empire crumbled, so will England's hold over the Welsh and the Scots.

In its last agonies, the Hapsburg monarchy made great play with pomp and ceremony and the personalities of the ruling family. In vain. Our Labourite politicians who are promoting the Investiture stunt don't seem to be able to learn from history. All the loyal Kikuyu who will be parading and posturing at Caernarfon belong to an age which is already dead.

Welsh Nation (July 1969)

History Passes Labour By

FOR ONCE, we can refer in all sincerity to our English friends, without the quotation marks. For their own reasons they got rid of the Labour Party and condemned it not only to at least 10 to 15 years (on form) of nailbiting impotence as Her Majesty's Disloyal Opposition, but, quite possibly, to extinction.

The always tense relationship between the unions, who found the cash, and the motley concourse of ideologists and opportunists who did all the talking, is more strained than ever.

The unions are beginning to realize that their real power is at the point of production, and that they don't really need these weird allies recruited from various dim and dusty conclaves dedicated to the perpetuation of defunct doctrines.

For the moment they are papering over the cracks, but the house is falling about their ears for all that. Mr.Michael Foot has been elected to the Shadow Cabinet.

Doubtless he will do his best to drag it kicking and screaming into the seventeenth century. Mr.Roy Jenkins is also there, as proof that Mr.Gladstone is alive and well and living in hopes.

But history is passing them by. In England and (in a very different way) in Wales, the living stream of ceaseless search for social and economic change is finding new channels. An Establishment is an Establishment, and even the crudest and daftest alternatives have more validity and more vitality.

In Wales, which is our exclusive concern, the alternatives are neither crude nor daft. Wales is a nation, and if there were any meaning left in the word Socialism, Keir Hardie's declaration that Wales is naturally Socialist would still be worth repeating.

But that great man's spendthrift heirs have so devalued his legacy that we may no longer speak in those terms. We must speak and think in terms of Wales and Wales only.

It may seem paradoxical to some, but this is the only guarantee that we will be in tune with the great world movements taking place beyond 'the sea that chides the banks of England, Scotland, Wales'.

The change of government at Westminster, and at the Welsh office, illustrates how low Labour had fallen. It is almost incredible, but the Tory, Mr. Peter Thomas, is on every count a welcome change from his ghastly predecessor [George Thomas].

The MP for Hendon, the Chairman of the Conservative Party, knows more about the real Wales than the drivelling clown whom he has replaced. Mr. Peter Thomas recently defended Sergeant John Jenkins, who is currently serving a ten-year jail sentence. He not only had the privilege of being associated with a very brave man, but he had the opportunity of getting to know what makes such men tick.

Being himself a real man, he did not feel it necessary to attend the National Eisteddfod at Ammanford this year surrounded by hundreds of policemen. The unclean hysteria injected into Welsh life by the Labourite regime has vanished with its discredited authors.

These so-called champions of the working class can

claim many achievements, the continued decline of our economy, the contraction of our labour force, the run-down of the local industry, the death of the slate quarries, the mishandling of our port potential, the end of our railways, the beginnings of a savage assault on our family farms.

It is an impressive record of sabotage and treason for which history (and the tribunals of a free people) will call them to account. Not to mention their crowning triumph, the Investiture of Charles the Last.

But it has all been in vain. The last UK election showed them on the brink of losing their overall majority in our country, while Plaid Cymru, for the first time ever, emerged as the main challenger. Now is the time to press home. The next few years are not going to be easy (but nobody ever joined Plaid Cymru for a rest cure).

Mr.Peter Thomas will have to pronounce on Bryncroes, Senni, Dulas, Cefn Sidan, on local government, the national university, Aber Hafren, the development areas.

He will not do so as an illiterate bigot like his predecessor, but how many votes will he carry in a Tory Cabinet? Despite his many personal qualities (something totally lacking hitherto at the top in the Welsh Office), he is in for a rough time.

For however decadent the Anglocentric Left in Wales, however bumblingly well-meaning the English Right, we, the Welsh, must find our own way and fight our own battles.

And there must be no compromise. The victory must be on our own terms. Labour and Tory are alike meaningless. The National Eisteddfod at Ammanford this year was notable for more than the mere absence of policemen and punch-ups (and some of the mountebanks who inspired them).

When Gwynfor Evans spoke (and he spoke as even he has never spoken before) the whole crowded pavilion and field fell silent.

This was the beginning of his personal comeback in Sir Gâr. And it was the beginning of something bigger. A lot bigger.

Welsh Nation (September 1970)

The Political History of the Cynon Valley

IN ATTEMPTING TO do justice to such a large subject as the political history of the Cynon Valley, and the landmarks in it which reflect and illustrate the history of the nation, one becomes only too well aware of how much, in the space at our disposal, has to be left out. In Wales in particular, politics has never been an autonomous activity, conducted by a specialist class of professionals remote from ordinary people. Politics everywhere is a working out of social and economic pressures which affect everybody directly. And in Wales it has always been something more, an expression not only of immediate necessities but of wider ideas and ideals, embracing such fields of human activity as religion, language and culture. In attempting to set the story in a manageable framework, much of this must be left out. In a political history, elections are the focal points, but it is well to remember that they are merely the broken wavecaps thrown up by deep currents of feeling and thought.

Certainly modern Welsh politics has its beginnings in religious and educational controversies, and in a very different world from ours, but it has always been characterized by a most impressive consistency of character, for which the most appropriate adjective is 'radical'. And this radicalism, this sense of equality and fair play, of concern for people as individuals, this opposition to the claims of mere brute wealth and power, seems to be innate in the very fabric of our nation. It was certainly here before industrial developments gave it such a powerful stimulus, and its earliest expression in modern times is to be found in the more attractive aspects of Nonconformity, the great formative force whose potential reached out from its purely spiritual mission into every aspect of personal and social life, and rapidly developed definite political implications.

In the Cynon Valley at the start of the Industrial Revolution we meet the attractive figure of Edward Evan of Ton-coch, above Cefnpennar, weaver, poet, musician, historian, preacher and radical reformer. He was one of the founders of the Unitarian cause in Aberdâr, and among his successors was numbered that Thomas Evans, (Tomos Glyn Cothi) who, as a young man, had spent two years in Carmarthen jail for preaching the principles of the French Revolution. It was men like these who educated and inspired the new population that began crowding into the valleys in the early years of the last century, organizing them into congregations where their own language was respected, where they learnt disciplined habits of thought and conduct, and where they were effecting autonomous religious, educational and even political establishment. Unrecognized and explosive, the first generation of ironworkers and coal-miners had no alternative but direct action. The explosive events of 1831, the great Merthyr Rising associated with the names of Dic Penderyn and Lewis the Huntsman, are among the great landmarks of Welsh radical history. What does not seem to be generally appreciated is that the rising actually began in Aberdâr, when the workers at Aber-nant besieged Fothergill, the ironmaster, in his mansion and made him disgorge bread and cheese before marching over the mountain to join forces with the Merthyr men. While the main confrontations took place in the Taff Valley, the men of the Cynon Valley were by no means inactive, staging a spectacular side-show by hijacking the London-bound stage coach at the Cardiff Arms in Hirwaun.

In the following year, 1832, and largely as a consequence of the Rising, Merthyr Tydfil was given its own parliamentary seat at the historic reform of Parliament. It was promptly occupied by Guest, the ironmaster of Dowlais, who is not known to have expressed any gratitude to his rebellious workers for having provided him with it. The miners and ironworkers of the Cynon Valley then being satellites of the Merthyr undertakings, the constituency boundaries of Merthyr Tydfil also embraced Aberdâr and this kingdom of the ironmasters was represented first by Guest of Dowlais and then by Bruce of Dyffryn, almost by divine right. They were not, personally, unbenevolent men, and Bruce, in particular, was interested in education and social welfare. Later in life he was to correspond with Karl Marx. But in the middle years of the nineteenth century, the state of Wales was too turbulent to be pacified by personal benevolence. The radical chapels of Aberdâr were active in propagating the ideas of the People's Charter, but their leaders believed in persuasion rather than force, and very few men from the Cynon Valley took part in the fatal march on Newport in 1839. Then came the hungry 'forties and the heyday of Rebecca, and the consequence was a government enquiry into the state of affairs in Wales, and the publication of the famous – or infamous – Blue Books in 1847. Here, it is generally considered, modern Welsh politics, the politics of national identity, really begins.

In the furious controversy that they sparked off, there were three outstanding defenders of Welsh Non-conformity and, by implication, of the rights of Wales as a national community. One of the three, Ieuan Gwynedd, who was to die young, does not come into our story. But the other two are intimately involved in it. One was the Reverend Thomas Price of Aberdâr, and the other was Henry Richard. Price, an astonishing personality, who founded eleven Baptist Chapels in the valley, and was active in every movement for social betterment, took on the Vicar of Aberdâr, who had been among the foremost character assassins of the Welsh people, and floored him completely. The debate was of more than local significance. It was not merely the minister of Calfaria, Penpound scoring off the incumbent of Saint John's. The honour of the nation was at stake, and was successfully vindicated. But pressing social problems remained; as the century wore on, the coal-mines opened up, and the iron industry gradually declined. The 1850s saw soldiers brought into the valley to maintain order. In one ill-chronicled episode, they are reported to have thrown down their arms rather than fire on fellow-Welshmen. In 1860, the first co-operative in Wales was established at Cwm-bach, to sustain the workers in their struggles. Five years later, in 1865, the Mountain Ash district was to provide three-quarters of the first shiploads of immigrants to found a New Wales in Patagonia. But the problems of Old Wales remained. The headlong growth of industry caused Cwm Cynon to be called *'Awstralia Cymru'* and in 1867, at another important reform of Parliament, the growing importance of the area was recognized when the Merthyr Tydfil constituency was granted an additional Member of Parliament.

Then came the election of 1868. The dawn of the new age of Liberalism, when Henry Richard, the Apostle of Peace and the Member for Wales, took the stage and inaugurated the golden era of Welsh radical politics. This is an election result that everybody knows. To those of us engaged in what may sometimes seem to be a less rewarding phase of the national struggle, it will come as some consolation to learn that all was not as it seemed at the time, and to the constituency most immediately involved. Henry Richard had been a prominent national leader for over twenty years, but there was nothing easy or inevitable about his victory. Price Penpound, his one-time associate by now at the pinnacle of his immense authority in the district, did not endorse Richard's candidature, and it looked at first as if another ironmaster – another Fothergill – was to join Bruce in the House of Commons. But Bruce and Fothergill cordially detested eachother, and did not work together, and there was an element too of rivalry between the Merthyr and Aberdâr sections of the constituency, Richard being seen as the Aberdâr man. The upshot was that Fothergill and Richard went in, with Richard slightly in the lead, and Bruce had to continue his political career in another seat that Mr.Gladstone quickly found for him in Scotland.

But for all that, from now on, Wales began, after centuries of eclipse, to play a distinct and definite role in the politics of the United Kingdom, on the left wing of the vast, rather ramshackle coalition presided over by

Gladstone, which embraced the Whig aristocracy at one extreme and the first shy and nervous Labour representative at the other, all comprehended in the Liberal Party. It became apparent that there was a whole range of related questions – disestablishment of the Church, temperance, education, and land reform – on which there were distinct and different Welsh views now put forward with some vigour, the foundations being laid for the Liberal domination of the Welsh political scene which was to culminate in the dazzling career of Lloyd George.

All these Welsh demands, however reasonable, were met with stubborn opposition in Parliament and in the press and in public life generally by those elements who saw, more clearly perhaps than the champions of Wales themselves, that they contained the seeds of the ultimate and unmentionable. Home Rule as such, however, had to wait until another day before its turn was to come. Even by the end of the century, its only effective exponents had been the lonely prophet Emrys ap Iwan and the slippery opportunist Lloyd George, and both of them were well ahead of public opinion. In the mean time, there was plenty to occupy the attention of the public. After its first ineffectual beginnings, organized labour was becoming an effective force, and in the election of 1874, whilst Richard and Fothergill were returned, Halliday, challenging for Labour for the first time ever in the constituency, came a surprisingly substantial third. But the long Liberal noon was to go on for some decades. In the election of 1880, with Fothergill forced out of public life by local disputes, Richard was joined by the Merthyr caucus leader C.H.James, and in the elections of 1885 and 1886 when politics generally were in a pretty convulsive state, they were both returned unopposed. We shall meet such quiescent periods again. Even in the Valleys it is not reasonable to expect that things can be kept on the boil for ever. There were certainly more exciting days ahead, harbingered in 1888 by the resignation of C.H.James, now an old man, and the death of Henry Richard, who went to his grave with all the honour his nation could bestow. The successor to James was the rising young industrialist D.A.Thomas, who was elected without a contest. The successor to Henry Richard was Pritchard Morgan. Both men demand a closer look.

There was a time when D.A.Thomas was, after Lloyd George, the best known name in Wales, and famous far beyond her boundaries. Some would add, the best hated name. In his abilities and achievements he personified the new capitalism of what a later historian was to call American Wales, when the achievements of the previous hundred years of industrial development, mighty though they had been, seemed to be completely outshone by the almost limitless possibilities now opening up. In fact, an age rather like the present one, with coal playing the part we now assign to oil, and perhaps for that reason worth taking a closer look at than we can afford here. It is fair to say that Thomas, who bestrode this scene like a Colossus, did not earn the odium that was to overwhelm the reputation of his Cambrian Colliery Combine until after he had severed his political connection with the constituency. But from 1888 to 1909 he reigned supreme, not only politically, for he topped the poll in four successful elections, but in the economic life of the community as well. He was the most powerful single individual the Cynon Valley has ever seen, and, one must hope, ever will see.

His political career was, by his standards, something of a failure. He could never get on with Lloyd George, for two such masterful men could not be expected to defer to one another, and it was only towards the end of his life, when, as Viscount Rhondda, he organized the food supplies in the First World War, that his talents achieved due recognition. His attitude to Welsh affairs, which chiefly concerns us, was ambiguous. His family had been worshippers at Calfaria, Penpound with Thomas Price, but, says his sycophantic biographer, Mrs.Thomas was a far-sighted woman and the family transferred to the English chapel across the road; an English nurse was engaged, the young heir of Ysgubor-wen underwent the whole process of anglicization, retaining only a superficial and sentimental Welshness, which is expressed to perfection in the style of the statuary which he presented to Cardiff City Hall. One cannot say that these sculptures of national heroes are abysmally bad; some of them are quite effective, but the general effect is depressingly inadequate. At one time a member of Lloyd George's *Cymru Fydd* quasi-nationalist ginger-group inside the Liberal Party, he turned against the whole idea. Yet his could have been an honoured and remembered name in the building up of the nation. For all his talents, he is remembered today, if at all, as one of those who plundered it. It is perhaps appropriate that no adequate biography of him has been written. That may come, but it will be of purely archaeological interest.

Pritchard Morgan, whose political connection with Aberdâr began at the same time as that of D.A.Thomas, is a much slighter figure, but also more entertaining, and he is, or was until recently, far more vividly remembered, usually with intense hatred. A more unlikely successor to the saintly Apostle of Peace it is difficult to imagine. A flamboyant vulgarian, he was almost a caricature of a wicked capitalist, and was a highly embarrassing running mate to the rather austere D.A.Thomas. Yet in the by-election of 1888 he began his career by winning the miners' vote against a more conventional Liberal candidate and retained it in the two following elections of 1892 and 1895. In the latter contest Labour again fielded a candidate, a radical Cardiff lawyer of literary tastes with the rather inappropriate name of Allan Upward, for his campaign saw the Labour strength plummet downward to under seven hundred votes.

But more interesting changes were on the way, and five years after this discouraging débâcle Labour was to win one of the Merthyr seats. In the election of 1900, Keir Hardie was returned along with Thomas, and the constituency had scored another historic first. This again is one of the facts which everybody knows. And again it is worth looking at the legend a little more closely. The brutal truth is that Hardie's candidature was highly irregular, being railroaded through a delegate conference by an unrepresentative rump of ILP hard-liners after the more moderate elements had left. Even more unpalatable, perhaps, is the fact that Hardie owed much of his success to D.A.Thomas, who (with good reason) loathed the grotesque Pritchard Morgan, and quietly advised his supporters to give their support to Hardie, who, although he was a Socialist, was at least respectable. For all that, it was a creditable and significant achievement, for it was a 'Khaki Election' fought during the jingoistic atmosphere of the Boer War, and Hardie could reasonably

Keir Hardie, 1889, National Museum of Labour History

claim that he had inherited the support of the uncorrupted backers of Henry Richard. Pritchard Morgan, after a campaign of unexampled vulgarity, came bottom of the poll and was booed out of the constituency. I have talked with old men who remember the declaration of the poll – it was a pouring wet winter's day which had, perhaps fortunately, quenched much of the partisan fervour stoked up by the campaign – and Hardie quietening the crowd, so that Morgan should be allowed to make his last graceless speech. He was to turn up again, ten years later in 1910, this time suffering the additional humiliation of coming fourth and bottom, behind a gentlemanly and well-liked Conservative. But he was to have his moment of glory in the following year when a coronet of gold from one of his North Wales gold-mines was placed on the head of an English prince in a ceremony at Caernarfon. Some may consider it a fitting climax to his career.

It is almost impossible to overestimate the importance of Hardie's victory, at the end of a decade when organized Labour, after floundering about ineffectually since Robert Owen's day, sheltered for a period in the voluminous skirts of the all-embracing Liberal Party, before finally coming into its own under the inexorable pressure of world conditions. For the first time since the beginning of the Industrial Revolution, the United Kingdom no longer dominated world markets. Pressure from Germany and America exposed the weakness of the system losing its competitive effectiveness. The prophets who had preached in vain during the flood tide of Victorian imperial predominance now found their message being heeded for strictly practical economic reasons as that tide receded. As Welsh coal, one of the fundamental factors in England's maritime greatness, began to lose its price in world markets, the policy of the sliding scale, by which wages were linked to profits, and which worked well enough while they were both sliding upwards, began to lose its appeal, and the old, conciliatory unionism pioneered by Mabon had to yield to the more militant approach of which Keir Hardie was the spokesman. The bitter strike of 1898, which brought this change of emphasis, is regarded by many historians as a far more significant event in Welsh history than the emotional religious revival six years earlier. Wil John Edwards of Aberaman, one of the pioneers of Socialism in Aberdâr, in his immensely readable biography, *From the Valley I Came*, describes how his mother's Bible and *Pilgrim's Progress* were replaced on the front room table by *Das Kapital* and *The Origin of Species* and how Mr.Gladstone's picture was relegated from the front room to the kitchen, to be replaced by the likeness of Keir Hardie.

Still Liberalism had the edge on Labour, and Thomas and Hardie ran in double harness, bound by a mutual personal esteem that bridged the sharp ideological differences between them, until, at the election of 1910, Thomas left Valley politics for the more commercial atmosphere of Cardiff, and was succeeded by the less memorable figure of Edgar Jones.

The Liberals brought in the historic measures which will always by associated with the name of Lloyd George, while out on the far left the Syndicalists planned *The Miners' Next Step*, the step towards workers' control and full social responsibility in industry that was never to be taken. For in 1914 a world came to an end as the bugles blew for war and the flower of Wales, her best and bravest sons, marched to the bloody shores of Gallipoli and the slaughter of the Somme. Hardie was among the casualties, as much so as any young collier in the trenches. But his battlefield was here in Aberdâr, and his enemies did not wear Prussian field grey, but wrapped themselves in the Union Jack. In telling the story of Aberdâr we cannot omit its moment of shame, its day of black disgrace, when a jingo mob pursued Hardie through the streets, baying for his blood, at their head a man who in his day had been a militant left-wing miners' leader, Charles Butt Stanton, another strange figure who now demands our attention.

He has been described as the nearest thing British politics has ever produced to a Mussolini – a showy and theatrical figure, given to noisy bombast and flamboyant oratory, moving from extreme Socialism to violent Imperialism under the stress of war in the exact manner of his Italian counterpart. When Hardie died in 1915 of disappointment and grief, it was Stanton who inherited his seat at the hands of the Merthyr Tydfil electorate, despite a strong challenge from a more sincere Labour man, James Winstone, who is still remembered with affection. We should not think too badly of Stanton. He only did, openly and noisily, what the entire Labour leadership were to do over the next few years silently, slyly and by stealth. It is his attitudes, not those of Hardie, which have been inherited by the Labour Party as we know it today.

With the end of the war came another Khaki election, also called the Coupon Election, because the Liberal Party was now split hopelessly between Lloyd George and

Asquith, the leader whom he had replaced under the exceptional circumstances of the war. Lloyd George was bound in an uneasy and unnatural alliance with the Tories, and under these confusing circumstances candidates supporting him claimed to hold his endorsement or 'Coupon' and appealed to the electorate on the basis of his great prestige as 'the man who had won the war', and in Wales of course as *'mab enwocaf Cymru'*, the nation's greatest son.

The election of 1918 had an additional significance for Aberdâr. For now at last the old two-member constituency was split up into its natural component parts. Merthyr Tydfil pursued its own leftward course, whilst Aberdâr set about facing the problem of Stanton. He was of course an enthusiastic Lloyd George-ite. His official label seems to have been Independent Coalition National Democratic Party, though whether this party consisted of anybody besides Stanton is doubtful, and Labour were still so disorganized after the war that they had to be represented by the attractive but hardly convincing character of T.E.Nicholas (Niclas Glais), who died only recently at an immense age, loved by all who knew him, but not, in those days, the man to carry his beloved red flag to victory against Stanton and Lloyd George.

Four bitter years later it was all over. The Sankey Commission, set up to explore the deplorable condition of the mining industry, recommended a continuation of wartime controls and the establishment of outright state ownership. But Lloyd George was the prisoner of his unnatural Tory allies. He betrayed his pledge to honour the findings of the commission, sold the miners down the river, and set the stage for one of the darkest periods in our history. It could all have been so different. A man of his views and background could so easily have thrown in his lot with his own people and his own kind. He had been tempted to do so before, and would be tempted again, but by then it was too late. Blinded by the fatal glamour of Westminster, he remains one of the most tragic casualties of Welsh history, not one of its glories. But although lacking in principle, nobody can ever say that he was lacking in courage. He came to the Valleys to put his case to the miners. He came to the big stone pavilion at Mountain Ash, left over from the National Eisteddfod of 1901, and the miners came to have it out with him. There are many left today who recall how they walked to Mountain Ash from all the surrounding valleys, their anger increasing with every mile, and how the great wizard disarmed them with his eloquence, drained them of emotion and will-power with hymn-singing and, as they all say, 'did what he liked with us'.

But in 1922 the coalition was dissolved. Stanton, now standing with an honesty rare in Westminster politics quite simply as a 'Britisher', defended his seat against the check weigher from Penrhiw-ceibr, George Hall, whom he associated with Lenin, Trotsky, the Sultan of Turkey and De Valera in an impressive roll-call of assassins. But his eloquence could not prevail against the solid power of the miners' vote. Stanton, it is interesting to note, left politics after this, and made for himself a successful career as a stage and film actor, specializing in the portrayal of aristocrats and bishops. Hall was to have little effect in opposition for the next two decades. Indeed, politics once again became stagnant as the 'twenties and 'thirties dragged their weary way through the Depression. They became the politics of mere survival. In the elections of 1923, 1924 and 1925 Labour increased its impressive majority and in the elections of 1931 and 1935 Hall was returned unopposed. The valley had to all intents and purposes been written off. But it is interesting to note that Labour's election addresses of the 1920s were all fully bilingual, and that those for 1929 contained a pledge to establish Parliaments for Scotland and Wales.

For there was still something left of national sentiment in the valley, even after it had been so exploited and devalued by Lloyd George to the detriment of the entire community, and the Labour Party had to take note of it. One of the earliest branches of the national youth movement, *Urdd Gobaith Cymru,* was established at Abercynon. So too, and more significantly, was the first branch of Plaid Cymru outside Gwynedd, in January 1927 – at Abercwmboi, for many years the scene of the ill-rewarded labours of Olifer Evans, who spent himself for a pittance in the service of Wales, and who lies in an unmarked grave in Aberdâr.

It was a long haul for Plaid Cymru. Emerging from the Second World War the party was in no position locally to contest the 1945 General Election which gave Labour such a landslide majority with a sweeping mandate. Hall was opposed only by a transient Tory with the fragrant name of Captain Clover, and his election address by now contained no Welsh and no recognition of Welsh nationhood. Hall had, in fact, become Stanton. Always a man of reactionary views, and a great admirer of Winston Churchill, he was promoted by Attlee in 1946 to the House of Lords as First Lord of the Admiralty, in which capacity he is chiefly remembered as the man who sent the small gunboat HMS Amethyst up the Yangtse into the middle of the final stages of the war between the Chinese Red Army and the forces of Chiang Kai-Chek, an absurd episode only too eloquent of the decline in the quality of Labour leadership in the Valleys.

His promotion, however, had offered Plaid Cymru the chance of a by-election in 1946 , which was eagerly seized, and with encouraging results. Wynne Samuel came second with 20% of the vote, and this at a time when nobody could think of anything else but the long overdue nationalization of the coal-mines, which took place in 1947. But in the needle elections of 1950 and 1951 this good start, which had been so important for party morale at the time, was not maintained, and the party finished third behind the Tory. Hall's successor did not live long and in 1954 there was another by-election, and this time the Plaid Cymru cause was represented by Gwynfor Evans. These were the heady days of the optimistic campaign for a Parliament for Wales within five years, but although Gwynfor Evans came second with 16% of the vote the position of the party was again not to be sustained in the subsequent by-elections of 1955, 1959, 1964 and 1966. It was a long and depressing trek through the wilderness. Neither did any of the attempts to gain a seat on the Aberdâr and Mountain Ash local authorities meet with any success in those years, apart from a transient but welcome gain at Ynys-y-bŵl. In 1957 a local issue, still referred to as 'The Plan', caused consternation in the wards of Aberdâr directly affected by the monstrous scheme, but, although individual Nationalists were involved in the organized opposition to the Plan, the party as such was in no position to consolidate any political gains, and the opposition devolved on an ad hoc group called the Protectionists, which still exists.

Then came 1966 and Carmarthen, to be followed by the near misses in the neighbouring Rhondda and Caerffili constituencies. By 1970, the party was in good heart locally and Labour was now seen to be past its peak. A bridgehead had been established in local government at last, and the 1970 campaign was fought with great éclat by the party's then General Secretary, Dr.Gareth Morgan Jones. The Labour majority was halved, and Plaid Cymru obtained one vote for every two Labour votes, emerging as the pacemaker and the official opposition.

And thus our story comes almost up to date, with the two elections of 1974. The February contest was fought in the most uniquely favourable circumstances for Labour, with the miners' dispute and the three-day week as the over-riding issues in every industrial constituency. Already Plaid Cymru's showing in Aberdâr, no less than its sensational progress in neighbouring valleys, had played its part in keeping up the pressure for Wales through maintaining the Crowther-Kilbrandon report in the forefront of public controversy. The consequent internal strains in the Labour Party became very apparent when, in Aberdâr, they looked around for a candidate to replace the person who had feebly represented the constituency since 1954, and who had retained no enthusiasm for the job after the shock Plaid Cymru had administered in 1970. Their first choice withdrew on health grounds; various more distinguished names were canvassed but did not feel like taking the risk; and finally a carpet-bagging has-been was drafted in. At least his predecessors had all been native products, but now Labour in the valley was incapable of generating its own leadership. It was still capable, however, of mounting a campaign of some ferocity, and Aberdâr was treated by them as a marginal constituency, with the party's big guns seen in the area on a scale never before known, all its vast resources of patronage and pressure being deployed to the full.

Yet it was all in vain. Plaid Cymru's new-found strength abated not one jot. The Welsh vote, and the Welsh percentage of the vote, remained firm. Under the circumstances, it can only be regarded as one of Plaid Cymru's most convincing and encouraging performances anywhere.

I began by saying that in Wales politics is not only about programmes and policies, but about ideas and ideals. It is about how people see themselves and how they think of themselves and how they express their identity. The Tory openly and straightforwardly proclaims himself English; the Liberal, rather more deviously and federally, is British; the Labourite furtively and dishonestly calls himself an internationalist, remaining, in the Welsh context, more English even than the Tory. He who votes Plaid Cymru votes Welsh, and not even our opponents can pretend otherwise. After all that has happened in our history one elector in three in this constituency knows who he is, what he is and where he is, whereas only six years ago this could not be said of one out of ten. An advance on this can no longer be in doubt.

Y Saeth (1, Spring 1976)

Cheers for the Coal Exchange

THE NEWS THAT the Welsh Assembly may be set up not in the Temple of Peace but the Coal Exchange was entirely unexpected, but I hope we will all give it a big cheer. It is the sort of imaginative proposal that even the hazy prospect of partial freedom can stimulate.

To site it in the heart of dockland rather than among the barbered lawns of Cathays Park will be an act of historic restitution and it will be something more.

If we are serious in our intention of bringing power back to the people, then you couldn't possibly, in Wales, have a seat of government so near to so many of them. And very nice people too. For Butetown, to give it the official name, is a closely-knit, inner-city village, as deeply rooted as any in Wales, even if some of the roots are rather exotic.

Butetown is just as much a real community as anywhere in the Valleys or the countryside, indeed, more so than some these days. Such places often miss out, they can all too often be raped by planners and developers. And the loss in terms of social values and neighbourhood spirit is no less than when a colliery village dies or an upland valley is drowned.

And even on the purely economic level, a vast area of Cardiff south of the tracks is in limbo, while the speculators stretch their vultures' wings over the commercial core of the city. To regenerate Butetown by making it the seat of Welsh government would cause a lot of mean thinking to be revised and could cause new ideas to flourish like the daffodils in spring.

The whole Mountstuart Square area is full of magnificent Edwardian coal-boom buildings, which now look as if they have seen better days but are solid enough to claim a better future.

For the present age could never match them. Even at its infrequent best, modern architecture is skimpy and bleak in comparison. These Gothic banks and mercantile palazzos may offend the purist, but they are better than the shoe-boxes and egg-crates of the present day, and in their exuberance they are eloquent of a great period in Welsh history.

After all, some of the wealth of Wales was spent here, even if it was in the wrong hands, and these lofty and solid buildings are something of a witness to what is possible under better management.

The location of the Welsh Assembly here will bring many positive advantages. It would regenerate a whole rundown area, there would be all sorts of spin-off and new job opportunities for the local people – working people, not the hordes of bureaucrats that the enemies of self-government are always conjuring up out of their own guilty consciences. The amenities and general appearance of the area would have to be improved, and not before time.

But there are some negative advantages too. First and foremost among them, the Welsh Assembly would not be in the dreadful 'Temple of Peace'.

The building itself is tame and innocuous enough, a sort of petty-bourgeois Parthenon, a pacifist Valhalla, in itself a depressing contrast to the full-blooded baroque of the Coal Exchange, but to call an office block a temple (for I am afraid that's all it is really) has always seemed to me a bit comic.

I wonder what rites are supposed to go on there. What men and gods are these? What maidens loth? What mad pursuit? What struggles to escape? What pipes and timbrels? What wild ecstasy? Well, actually it's the headquarters of the South Glamorgan Health Authority; and its absurdly highfalutin' name, I am afraid, expresses that side of the Welsh character that is so easily seduced by empty rhetoric and vague, universal good intentions that get nowhere.

The Temple of Peace was opened just in time for the Second World War. Its pompous, tomb-like marble hall has often echoed to the bray of Mr.George Thomas. Fortunately the acoustics are appalling.

As for myself, I would rather see our Welsh Parliament building associated with coal than cant.

Welsh Nation (December 1976)

Labour and Devolution

DEVOLUTION, LIKE NECESSITY, acquainteth a man with strange bedfellows. It is a word that can mean all things to all men, and some of them are very odd and unexpected allies for anyone concerned with building Free Wales.

The whole tactic of devolution is that of the firebreak. The defenders of the status quo are chopping down a few of their own trees in order to stop the flames of nationalism spreading further. They are making minimal sacrifices of power, and marginal institutional concessions, in order to preserve as much as they can of their own area of authority. The danger is now so apparent that a consensus has emerged among all the Westminster parties. Devolution is 'on'. It has even become fashionable, mandatory, de rigueur thinking, it is the 'in' thing. The politicians preach it from their platforms, with the media following suit. You can even read about it in the *Radio Times*. Connoisseurs of political curiosities will doubtless preserve the issue of May 1976 which contains an article on devolution by a Mr.Mervyn Jones. For those unacquainted with his fame, he has been for many years a leading contributor to the *New Statesman*, the parish magazine of the Thames Valley intelligentsia, and a nauseating read for any Nationalist.

Those of us with inconveniently long Celtic memories will recall some of Mr.Jones's pronouncements about our cause over the years, and the rare occasions on which his journal deigned to notice us. In the 1960s Plaid Cymru were 'green Tories who ought to be sent back to their lecture rooms and lawyers' offices'. Come the Investiture, and what fun he had describing the dignified counter-ceremony at Cilmeri. But behold him now, waving aloft the rather frayed banner of his national identity, brandished as a symbol of a just and reasonable cause which all good men should support. What does one do? Tell him to stay in Hampstead? Or welcome him back to the fold as a strayed sheep? If we are to be all pals together, for how long and how far?

Then in the unhallowed pages of the *New Statesman* itself (I should explain at this point that I read it in the Library; it's not the sort of thing one would like to have lying about the house) there was Mr.John Morgan attempting to explain the recent Plaid Cymru advance in any terms except those of what it is all really about. Mr.Morgan is a shrewd commentator who has remained in touch with the Welsh scene, and no one would disagree with his enumeration of the causes of Labour's débâcle (corruption, incompetence, complacency, senility etc.). But his analysis does not go far enough, and stops at a vital point. The Nationalist vote is seen, by him and perhaps the majority of commentators, as reaction by the public against the deficiencies of Labour, rather than as something in its own right, something that has been patiently worked for over the years. Plaid Cymru is seen almost as the incidental, even opportunist, beneficiary of changes which it has done nothing to bring about.

But there is an element of this in all political change. What really matters is not so much the deficiencies of the system which is overthrown, or the shortcomings of the individuals who are dismissed from office, but the nature of the forces which are in a position to benefit by these weaknesses. The American Revolution, after all, was not about George III's stupidity, or even about tea! And this is what these commentators, even at their most knowledgeable or sympathetic, fail to understand, because they are inhibited from understanding (or perhaps too scared!). Their viewpoint is irredeemably anglocentric – in the expressive word devised by the agile Scottish mind of Douglas Young, a word which deserves to be more widely used. In this they reflect the attitudes of the politicians who are masterminding the big deal.

The English Labour Party in Wales (now dishonestly calling itself the Welsh Labour Party) held their 1976 Conference at Swansea, at which the subject was aired. The strains and contradictions of the present situation were vividly illustrated by the glimpse afforded to us by the television cameras of the contorted features of Mr.Michael Foot, and his equally contorted rhetoric as he stated the case for the current devolution offer. It was a sad comedown for a man of his undoubted ability. These were the overemphatic utterances of a man in a totally false position, unconvincing because the speaker himself was far from convinced. There was a last-ditch despair in the performance as he proclaimed that devolution was above all necessary to preserve the unity of the United Kingdom. Now Mr.Foot is politically something of a Puritan, almost a Roundhead, his favourite figures in the history of his own country being men who had no fondness for kingdoms, united or otherwise. When the shallower elements in the Labour Party kicked up their heels for the Ruritanian Investiture we were not surprised or disappointed, however much we may have been sickened. But Michael Foot has always been a man of integrity and ability. Now the logic of history has forced him into an indefensible position, the defender of a kingdom! When he first came to Ebbw Vale, we attacked him as the representative of an imperialist system, coming, like his brother Lord Caradon, as a colonial governor. This was new to him, and he brushed it aside as unreal, irrelevant, demonstrably false. But since then he has been angrily shouted down by the steelworkers who elected him in the first place, faced with the realities, in economic terms, of the political system he represents. Now, in a last-ditch effort to maintain the status quo, he has been enlisted (perhaps conscripted would be a better word) to promote the devolution package. Nobody with the slightest knowledge of the Labour Party in its area of strength can believe that these concessions are anything but reluctantly offered, by politicians who are profoundly anti-Welsh, traditionally hostile to the very existence of our national identity – except for its sentimental, ceremonial and convivial aspects!

The most perceptive among them have seen the way the wind is blowing, hence devolution. But the majority of them cling witlessly to the old prejudices and hatreds by which they have been conditioned, and will probably never really understand the nature of the new force that is menacing them. So their leaders, echoed by their henchmen among the pundits and commentators, are now in the undignified position of making an offer they do not believe in to a nation that is looking at it very dubiously. The Principality of Cymrutania, all foolery and feathers, is wheeled out again in the more circumspect guise of a shabby little Taffistan. Counter-productive, to say the least. The end is at hand, boys *bach*, even for those of you who are not in the nick. Only the Labour Party, proclaimed Mr.Foot, can preserve the unity of the United Kingdom. Well, he said it. What we have been saying for a long time is that it is now the sole raison d'être for the English Labour Party in Wales, the preservation of an obsolete hegemony which Nationalists seek to replace by a fraternal association of all European and other peoples.

Y Saeth (Spring 1977)

Remember Mafeking!

AT THIS LATE STAGE of the dreary Devolution proceedings, it is unlikely that anything new can be said. The claims of Wales still stand, the rights of nations cannot be abolished or any longer ignored, the welfare of our people and the health of our economy still present their urgent problems.

No amount of froth or gas can conceal the big, fundamental issues. In the second half of the twentieth century, a debate at Westminster about how much self-government the Welsh people can be trusted with is something of a non-event, a tedious formality, and a lot of the tedium has communicated itself to the public. The trail to freedom still stretches ahead, it has to be trodden inch by painful inch, and this is proving to be one of the more painful. While it is true that no new facts or arguments emerged from the pre-Christmas debate, or during current committee proceedings, we were not spared a measure of novelty in the unexampled depths of folly, filth and shame reached by the enemies of Wales. Rarely can such wildly slanderous ravings have been heard in the context of serious debate.

The evil old men of the Rotten Generation are now, most of them, in their unlamented graves, and their tenure of office in Wales is now a fading nightmare. But their successors have brought fresh access of hate into the controversy. The old scoundrels of the past, the breed that surfaced after the First World War, and continued to disgrace the scene until the 60s, were robust in their treason, bluff and four-square in their hostility. Some of them were themselves Welsh-speakers, full of phobias and complexes for which perhaps they should have been pitied rather than blamed – except that there can be no pity for that particular crime. They merely stonewalled and sneered, confident that if the question were ignored and belittled it would go away.

But small, stubborn, awkward, cantankerous nations don't give up. So the new traitors are faced with a new situation. They are faced at last with the realization that here is a question which, from their point of view, is intractable. Whatever the results of recent polls and surveys prove or disprove in detail – which is, in fact, precious little – nobody can deny that there is now a solid body of opinion in favour of constitutional change in the United Kingdom – to put it at no more than that – an opinion that has grown up very rapidly in only a short space of years and shows no sign of diminishing.

The whole ploy of devolution recognizes this fact. It is the tactic of the fire-break – chop down a few trees in order to stop the flames spreading to the rest. But this forest is well and truly on fire. The conclusion is foregone and inevitable. So the unpleasing tirades of the enemy have the venom of sheer national hatred.

The breathtaking effrontery of some of the phrases uttered in the Commons rather shocked some moderate and sober-minded people, but they should remember that there is no insolence like the insolence of the parasite. And there is always some wry amusement to be derived from the scene, the apostles of brotherhood and togetherness preaching what sounds suspiciously like naked racial hatred, the alleged successors of Keir Hardie and Lansbury and Henderson invoking imperialist standards and values with a fervour worthy of Lord Kitchener or Rudyard Kipling.

'Britain', they say, must be unitary, monolithic, centralized, ruled paternalistically from Westminster and Whitehall, otherwise all is lost, all will be chaos and corruption. Rally round the flag, chaps, Socialism hath need of you. Remember Mafeking, the pipes at Lucknow, the British square at Waterloo, Nelson's immortal signal to Lady Hamilton and all the other glories of the Raj. Your Taffies and your Jocks may be stout fellers in a scrap, and they can live off the smell of an oil-rag, but they've got to be kept in their places by the White Man, after all, and the idea that they should govern themselves is bally ludicrous, what! Karl Marx says so.

Welsh Nation (March 1977)

The Future of Wales is in Our Hands

EVERY SO OFTEN I find myself in London. Ever since Cardiff was grudgingly elevated to the status of capital of Wales I have always felt under the necessity of referring to London as 'the former capital'.

But it is still important to our affairs in many ways, and Plaid Cymru has always maintained a vigorous presence there. My recent visit was to our branch, which now has the useful task of helping our members of the English Parliament during the present period, until we are making our own laws in our own country.

It was not until I sat down to prepare some appropriate remarks that I realized that my visit, arranged well beforehand, would now fall bang in the middle of the great devolution debate, and that whatever I wrote could well be out of date by the time I got off the high-speed train (there are fewer and fewer trains in Wales of course, but a lovely one out of it!) and out of the dusty portals of Paddington.

So I held my hand, which was just as well, because the night before I arrived, the whole thing had collapsed in the shambles of the debate on the guillotine motion.

The procedural complications and technicalities which brought the measure to its knees take a bit of sorting out, even by specialists, and when I turned up at St.Stephen's Gate, to be hospitably greeted by Dafydd Wigley, nobody seemed to be sure what was going to happen next.

Waiting for him in the over-decorated Gothic Lobby of the House, which looked more than ever like the set for an elaborately-staged pantomime, I caught the eye of Saint David, gazing down with a distinctly worried expression from one of the colourful murals.

'Get me out of here', he seemed to be saying, although the artist had depicted him in the company of two well-built young ladies. (Nice goings on for a saint, and no wonder Lloyd George went off the rails.)

However, there is good news for him. For the unspeakable dishonesty of the whole shabby business of getting self-government through the English parties has now been shown up for what it is. And, indeed, so has the whole English party system. There is just one party, when it comes down to essentials, the English Party. It calls itself by different names, Conservative, Labour, Liberal, but it stands for the same thing in the end.

On the night the current devolution package was thrown out, it was the Tories who cheered most loudly and jubilantly, but I don't think any of the others were too displeased either.

They had admittedly broken promise after promise to the electors in Wales and Scotland, but they have never allowed a trifle like that to worry them. And, of course, they had the perfect get-out.

The nauseating activities and vile utterances of the openly anti-Welsh faction in the Labour Party have naturally attracted a good deal of attention in the course of the debate, and will be borne in mind by the Welsh people, but whatever was said and done by representatives from Wales and Scotland mattered not a row of beans.

It was the votes of the English Labour MPs that killed

the bill. So all the aggro inside the ranks of Labour in Wales needn't have taken place at all. They tore themselves to pieces in the vain effort to save their Welsh faces with one hand and earn their Saxon gold with the other, and they could have saved themselves the trouble. Our English friends did if for them.

The Parliament of England did, after all, the job it is there to do – to defend, first, foremost, and all the time, the interest of the people of England, and if there is anything left over, the others can scramble for the crumbs.

But later that evening, talking to the keen and active young members of Plaid Cymru who find themselves in London for the time being and can't wait to get back, a very different face of things presented itself.

'We feel so out of touch up here,' one of them said, 'so far away from where everything is happening.' Some of them had been up till quite late the previous night, for the lunatic timetable of the English parliament forces quite important decisions to be taken at impossible times when nobody can be expected to be at their most lucid (is this an explanation for a lot of recent history?).

They had witnessed the 'amazing scenes' gleefully reported in the press. They had shared in the atmosphere of electric excitement.

But to an alert Welsh person today all that is already irrelevant. Nothing much had happened at Westminster after all. It could have been predicted. Just a few more broken promises, just another stale instalment in a dragging saga of bad faith.

Their eyes were on 'where it is all happening' – here in Wales. Our future is where it always has been, in our own hands. We have not always realized this, we have been slow to understand our own strength. But with the awakening of recent years, the period of uncertainty is at an end, the new self-assurance that is walking the land expresses itself in unmistakable terms. Politically it is expressed through Plaid Cymru. The others are the English Party, whatever they like to call themselves. Plaid Cymru is what its name says – the Party of Wales.

The parasitic politics of the great cities, like the former capital and all the other fallen imperial metropolises are no longer relevant to the way the world is going, and it is time we disentangled ourselves from their grubby shadow.

The representatives of that system here in Wales have done very little to endear themselves to our people of recent years and are becoming less and less credible with every week that passes (or perhaps one should say, with every sentence that is passed).

The decision is in our own hands, and the ballot papers await our verdict.

Welsh Nation (April 1977)

The Stars of the Chamber of Horrors

WHEN TO THE sessions of sweet, silent thought I summon up remembrance of things past, I sometimes find myself recalling to mind some of the half-forgotten names that have in days gone by been blazed in the papers as heroic defenders of the sacred right of England to govern us for ever, world without end, fearless antagonists of those wicked Nationalists who had the effrontery to suggest that the Welsh people were fit to govern themselves.

They could always be guaranteed a good spread in the press for their pip-squeak pronouncements, which were invariably compounded of all the most unpleasant aspects of our national character.

The likes of them are still with us, of course, but dwindling in numbers, weakened in confidence, reactionaries of a ruined paradise.

Where now are the names that could be relied upon to strike terror into our seditious bosoms as we eagerly opened the paper to see what new shaft of scorn, what crushing, unanswerable argument, was being hurled in the general direction of Plaid Cymru?

Well, some of them are in another world by now, and it is not for us to speculate which one. Top of the bill came the good old knockabout parliamentary turn, Ness and Iori, a bit coarse for some tastes, but they packed a punch every time. The scene is poorer for their passing.

Where now are the men we can love to hate? Appealing

to a more specialized taste was Sir David Llewellyn, a waspish wit with gilded wings, last seen flying in the direction of the sacred Thames Valley, still occasionally heard from, like an echo from a bygone age.

And I believe Lord Merthyr is still around too, but he no longer harangues us from his Pembrokeshire eyrie. A near neighbour of his was Mr.J.Howard Price of Tenby, a tireless denouncer of the evils of nationalism. He, too has gone from Little England beyond Wales to the Greater England in the Skies.

And then in Cricieth, of all places, was the improbably named Mrs.Williams Doo, who preached against the cause of freedom with all the passion of Cassandra prophesying the fall of Troy. Her eldritch screeches had a particular appeal to connoisseurs of the macabre. I have an idea she might have been signed up by Hammer Films.

Then there was the gentleman who ran a small private school near Llanelli who seemed to have a divine mission to eradicate the Welsh language, of which his knowledge hardly supported the burden of his prejudice.

And of course, there was the impressive figure of Mr.Raglan Somerset, not to be confused with his kinsman, Lord Raglan, both doughty opponents, and unlike some of those we have mentioned not without a certain wry humour, as if they realized in their better moments that they were defending a lost cause.

I hope I have not left out any names that older readers will recall with tears of rapture, although I am sure there will be a few.

But this is not a catalogue of nostalgia. Who could feel nostalgia about stale offal? The point to be made is that this obscene chorus of malevolent dwarfs no longer exists.

They needed a vast apparatus of illusion, the illusion of imperial grandeur, the still-potent myth of the superiority of England, to project their antics. They needed the echo-chambers of a self-confident and strident propaganda to amplify their mouthings.

Such noises are still to be heard, of course, but they no longer command the attention of the public. One seeks them out in obscure news stories about anti-Welsh eccentrics forming fronts, movements, crusades and campaigns that get nowhere because they have nowhere to go, that don't get off the ground because they were never on it in the first place.

Wales doesn't want to know about them any more. And I have some news for them; England doesn't want to know about them either. The anti-Welsh element in Wales is one of history's write-offs. They have had a good run for their money, but now they have run into a dead end. None deadlier.

Even the most strenuous opponents of the current devolution deal are not in the same league as the old monsters of the past. Somewhere along the line, if you scrutinize the 'small print' of their utterance, they have made provision for an escape clause. They too, their fur dank and dripping, will want to scramble aboard the good ship Free Wales when the time comes. But who'll want them?

Welsh Nation (May 1977)

Tribute to a Friend

TO ANYONE COMING into it from the outside world Merthyr Tydfil in the 'fifties was a fascinating place. Perhaps it still is, but I doubt it. Too many physical and social changes have taken place for it ever to generate the atmosphere that it had in those days. It offered an experience difficult to describe, as if several layers of elapsed time were still somehow there. To speak of atmosphere and character explains nothing, would refer only to the look of the place, the group of streets that were still urban villages, each with its own identity, the impressive relics that, long before anyone was talking about industrial archaeology, were as eloquent of a mighty past as anything from medieval or Roman times: the sheer mass of the Dowlais Great Tip, the shattered and grass-grown ruins of Cyfarthfa, the former mansions of the ironmasters and the 'gwlis' where all too many of the descendants of their workers still lived. It was a place of its own, aloof, or so it claimed, from the rest of Wales, settled by a unique race of mixed origins, proud of the part it had played in great events, a fallen metropolis living on judiciously selected memories, jealous of its status as a County Borough that isolated the town (notably its rulers) from lesser breeds elsewhere. That some of its standards were wretched and that much of its undoubted past achievements had long been outstripped by others mattered little: such a statement would have been greeted with smug incredulity. There was some reason for self-satisfaction though, but it was not such as would figure in any official handbook. Merthyr was a wonderful town in which to live and enjoy oneself. If you were a man, that is, and not a teetotaller. It was emphatically a working man's town, and male chauvinist as the working man invariably is. What there was of a middle class called no audible tune, and what the women did for a social life is still a mystery. I suppose most of them stayed at home and saw that the supper was ready for the men after they came home from the pub, or found what satisfaction they could from chapel life. And that was on its last legs, too. Except for one or two vigorous causes, it certainly counted for little.

There were some pubs where women were not admitted at all. Notable among these was the Crown at the bottom of the High Street, one of the oldest inns in town, with its own history, gauntly furnished, minimally decorated and presided over by one Tom Thomas, a landlord, as they say, of the old school. Tom the Crown was never seen without his flat cap, and his collarless Welsh flannel shirt was fastened with a brass collar-stud. He was enormously respected, and ran his establishment more like a gentlemen's private club than a public house open to all-comers. The front door was kept cunningly ajar so that the casual passer-by could not be quite sure whether the place was open or not. To be fully accepted as a customer of good standing you had to be formally introduced and serve a probationary period. The arrangement was a matter of general knowledge and seemed to cause no resentment. It derived a certain sanction from the presence on the premises, every

Saturday night without fail, of our Member of Parliament, S.O.Davies, whom nobody ever called anything but S.O. To say that he held court in the back room on those nights would be an exaggeration, though there was undoubtedly a nucleus of those who saw themselves as courtiers. But that would be to do violence to the subtle societies of the place. It would be difficult to say who and what the regular clientele consisted of; there was no common denominator of occupation or even of political conviction. But they were all individuals who, in Tom's opinion, and by informal consensus of the regulars, were acceptable as good company. That S.O. was the town's most revered figure was, in this context, almost incidental. Here, he was just a nice old man who had found a pub that suited him and stuck to it, and came down every Saturday night for his couple of glasses of beer. Considering the notoriety of some of his parliamentary colleagues he was remarkably abstemious. He could never be coaxed to take more than his usual quota, and nobody could ever remember seeing him the worse for wear. He was looked after the way the regulars of an old-fashioned pub used to look after one another. If some aggrieved citizen came in and 'wanted to have it out with S.O.' (usually on some issue which was not his responsibility at all) he would be dealt with not only by Tom but by the manifest hostility of the entire membership, and if that did not discourage him, Idwal the postman would interpose his massive frame between the back-room door and the complainant in no uncertain manner.

Among ourselves we would pull S.O.'s leg about the numerous scrapes he got into with the official Labour Party because of his independent line, but there was never any serious argument, because the Crown was not the place for it, and because I think people sensed instinctively that there were no real issues at stake in the context of Westminster politics in the 'fifties. The trivial and half-forgotten business of the Nenni telegram is one that sticks out in my mind. S.O. had been one of the signatories to a message of good wishes to the wrong party in the Italian elections. Nenni's party was too left-wing for Gaitskell's party and there was an almighty row about it. I believe S.O. was suspended from the party for the umpteenth time. For weeks afterwards the mere mention, in any context, of a telegram or Italy, would set off a whole series of witticisms, whether S.O. was present or not. Among other things he was value for money.

By then, of course, the struggles of the past were behind him and he did not talk much about them. His hale old age and the serenity of his long sunset were often discussed. Partly due, of course, to a powerful frame unvitiated by excess, and to an enviable family life, it was attributed also to an equable, even sunny, temperament, which accepted every dawn as the beginning of a new day and did not spare much thought for yesterday's traumas. And, I would add, a quiet conscience. He had in his day fought the good fight for the colliers and steelworkers; he had, as a good Welshman, seen through the obvious limitations of the system in which he functioned. He was not unsympathetic to official Nationalism but felt that it had not yet gone through the fire. He was enthusiastic for the Parliament for Wales Campaign and moved a private member's bill in 1955 that was closely associated with the campaign. In this he took no notice of the views of his local Labour Party, which was passionately anti-Welsh. He was in reality what he was later to become – an independent member. He had not much time for the rest of his party, of any hue. I once heard him speak rather dismissively of "the Bevanites". But he liked Bevan personally, and spoke with him from the back of a lorry at a memorable meeting on the Waun Pound, one of the last of the old-style mass rallies. But then he liked a lot of people. It may come as a surprise, but he always spoke in the most indulgent and avuncular terms of the Queen as 'that dear girl'. And a lot of people liked him. That was proved in the dramatic circumstances of the General Election of 1970. For he had always noticeably kept at something more than arm's length from the local leaders of the party he normally represented. Of these it was difficult to speak in moderate terms. They have since been dismissed and disgraced, and may they rot. But in 1970 their satanic regime seemed unchallengeable. And by now Tom Thomas was dead and the first thing the new landlord had done was to fling the front door open wide and lay down a mat inscribed 'Welcome'! For a time the old crowd drifted uncertainly around the other hostelries – there were, after all, some dozens of them – and S.O. dubbed them 'Y Cymry ar Wasgar' [the Welsh in dispersion]. But most of them eventually settled for what had always been the next most eligible port of call: the Lamb.

In the mean time the scene had changed in other ways. Plaid Cymru had re-established itself in the town in the early 'sixties and had met with mixed fortunes. But well outside the orbit of orthodox politics, a new, feral nationalism had begun to pervade the scene. The low-ceilinged, smoke-filled, many-doored Lamb was its focus, and the Labour politicians who used to frequent it (as far as such antisocial characters were to be seen anywhere) simply decamped and left the field to a mostly young crowd who sang seditious songs. They were no loss except to certain professional careerists who had always been able to find somebody there to pour beer into and so grease the wheels of preferment. When, in 1970, S.O. was sacked by the local establishment in order to provide, as they thought, a safe seat for one of their own number, it was among this element that the campaign to re-elect S.O. took fire. Here was an old man, said to be older than he gave out, impeccably garbed in the fashion of the 'thirties at the latest: the striped trousers, the long black overcoat, the immaculate silk scarf, the venerable white hair under the broad-brimmed black felt hat. And here were his most conspicuous campaigners – a harum-scarum bunch, their leather jackets and blue jeans emblazoned with the Eagle of Snowdon, the Dragon's Tongue and the manacling, sharp-pointed Triban. It was an irresistible combination. The Old Gang did not know what had hit them. Five years later they were sent packing en masse, and Merthyr Tydfil is no longer governed from its gutters.

In the mean time, and in the course of nature, S.O. had been gathered to his fathers, and laid in the earth of Maes yr Arian, just down the road from his birthplace in the next valley. The subsequent by-election laid the foundations for Plaid Cymru's definitive advance and disclosed a fund of loyalty to Wales in an area that had seemed irredeemably alienated. It was as if S.O. were still fighting, even from the grave. The battle is not yet won, by a long way, not even in Merthyr, for it is a place of surprises and paradoxes. But there are some gains which are irreversible in their effects, and there is a new look on things, and if there is a Welsh school flourishing where it had once seemed impossible to get one started, then the march has at least begun. The old Merthyr that could arouse such uncritical affection even among its adopted children is dead; a new Merthyr demands and deserves a different attitude if it is to play its part in the forefront of those who seek to build a new nation. And when it is established, one indomitable old man will have an honoured place among the forerunners of our freedom.

Y Saeth (Autumn 1977)

BIBLIOGRAPHY

This list, far from being exhaustive, consists only of those items of Harri Webb's political journalism which were considered for inclusion in this book but which, in the end, had to be excluded for lack of space.

'Guilty Men: Judge Walter Samuel' by 'Spy' and later 'Gabriel', in *The Welsh Republican* (August 1950); this series continued in Dec.1950-Jan.1951 (Lady Megan Lloyd George); Feb.1951-March 1951 (Dr.Thomas Jones C.H.); April 1951-May 1952 (Sir J.F.Rees); June 1951-July 1951 (The Marquess of Anglesey); August 1951-Sept.1951 (Wil Ifan); Oct.1951 (Mr.Harold Watkins); Dec. 1951-Jan.1952 (Major Gwilym Lloyd George MP); April 1952-May 1952 (Major Tasker Watkins VC); Oct.1952-Nov.1952 (David Llewellyn MP); April 1953-May 1953 (Lord Lloyd); and June 1953-July 1953 (Henry Tudor).

'Mud in your Eye: Official Reports on Wales', in *The Welsh Republican* (Dec.1950-Jan.1951).

'What English Rule Means to Wales: The Alphabet of Subjection', in *The Welsh Republican* (April 1951-May 1951).

'A Letter to Mr.Jones: Wales Free-Wales Clean', in *The Welsh Republican* (June 1951-July 1951); this column also appeared in Aug.1951-Sept.1951; Oct.1951-Nov.1951; June 1952-July 1952; and Oct.-Nov.1952.

Editorial about the trades unions, in *The Welsh Republican* (June-July 1952).

'Wales and the Coal Board' by 'Our Industrial Correspondent', in *The Welsh Republican* (August 1952-Sept.1952).

Editorial: 'Standards of Living and our Right of Resistance', in *The Welsh Republican* (Oct.1952-Nov.1952).

'They Make Wales a Desert', a letter by 'Evictor' to the Rural Development Panel, in *The Welsh Republican* (Oct.1952-Nov.1952).

'Figures from the Welsh Past', a column about Welsh historical figures and events, first appeared in *The Welsh Republican* in Dec.1952-Jan.1953, and thereafter intermittently until April-May 1957; among the figures featured were Dic Penderyn, Lewis the Huntsman, Dai'r Cantwr, Ieuan Gwynedd, Dr.William Price, Lewis Humphreys, Keir Hardie, Aaron Williams, and Emrys ap Iwan; among the events were the Merthyr Rising of 1831, the Tithe War, and the Penrhyn Lock-outs.

'Welsh Workers Swindled: Miners have Higher Risks – Lower Pay', in *The Welsh Republican* (Feb.1953-March 1953).

'Welsh Trade Sabotaged: English Policy Threatens our Industries', in *The Welsh Republican* (April 1953-May 1953).

'Who's Who in Wales: Dic Shon Dafydd', in *The Welsh Republican* (April-May 1953); this column also appeared in June 1953-July 1953 (the West Anglian); Aug.1953-Sept.1953 (The Men of Harlech); Oct.1953-Nov.1953 (Dai Dismal); Dec.1953-Jan.1954 (the Walian); Feb.1954-March 1954 (Dr.Cadwgan Pengriffith DD, PhD); April 1954-May 1954 (Mr.Shadrach Sandringham-Jones); and June 1954-July 1954 (The Lamas).

'Tito's Triumph: an Inspiration for Wales', in *The Welsh Republican* (June 1953-July 1953).

Editorial about the need for Radicalism, in *The Welsh Republican* (Oct.-Nov.1953).

Editorial about the role of the police in *The Welsh Republican* (Dec.1953-Jan.1954).

'Rural Wales – Tory Betrayal', in *The Welsh Republican* (Dec.1953-Jan.1954).

Editorial about Republicanism, in *The Welsh Republican* (Feb.-March 1954).

Editorial about the scientific character of nationalism in *The Welsh Republican* (April 1954-May1954).

Editorial about nationalism and internationalism, in *The Welsh Republican* (June-July 1954).

'Wales and the Miners: a Shake-up for the Old Gang', in *The Welsh Republican* (June-July 1954).

'Empire's End: French Rule Finished', in *The Welsh Republican* (June-July 1954).

Editorial about a report on rural depolulation by the Council for Wales, in *The Welsh Republican* (August-Sept.1954).

'Welsh Pits in Danger: Home Rule Must Come to Save Industry', in *The Welsh Republican* (August-Sept.1954).

Editorial about the role of the working class, in *The Welsh Republican* (Dec.1954-Jan.1955).

'Strangled Valleys – Stricken Ports', in *The Welsh Republican* (Dec.1954-Jan.1955).

'Jim in a Jam', in *The Welsh Republican* (Dec.1954-Jan.1955).

'Welsh Statistics at Last', in *The Welsh Republican* (Dec.1954-Jan.1955).

Editorial on Labour and a Parliament for Wales, in *The Welsh Republican* (Feb. 1955-March 1955).

'Welsh Ports and Welsh Freedom: Only Independence will Bring Back the Ships', in *The Welsh Republican* (April 1955-May 1955).

Editorial about internationalism and nationalism, in *The Welsh Republican* (June-July 1955).

Editorial about the Labour Party, in *The Welsh Republican* (August-Sept.1955).

'Warning to Welsh Industry: Automation and the Future', in *The Welsh Republican* (August-Sept.1955).

Editorial about the National Coal Board, in *The Welsh Republican* (Oct.-Nov.1955).

'Welsh Ports in Peril', in *The Welsh Republican* (Oct.-Nov.1955).

Editorial about the exploitation of Wales, in *The Welsh Republican* (Dec.1955-Jan.1956).

'Wicked Extremists Confuted: Public Men Speak Out', in *The Welsh Republican* (Dec.1955-Jan.1956).

'Major Gwilym – Major Flop: the Record of the Minister for Welsh Affairs', in *The Welsh Republican* (Feb.-March 1956).

Editorial about the theory of nationalism, in *The Welsh Republican* (April-May 1956).

'A Letter to Mrs.Jones', in *The Welsh Republican* (April-May 1956).

Editorial about the Middle Ages, in *The Welsh Independent* (June-July 1956).

'An Open Letter to Jim Griffiths', in *The Welsh Republican* (June-July 1956).

'Welsh Problems – World Problems: Suez and Milford', in *The Welsh Republican* (Oct.-Nov.1956).

'A Lesson from Switzerland,' in *Welsh Nation* (24 Nov.1956).

Editorial about nationality and nationhood in *The Welsh Republican* (Feb.-March 1957).

Editorial about the Scottish TUC, in *The Welsh Republican* (April-May 1957).

'Trawsfynydd', a letter to the editor of *The Times* (12 Feb.1958).

'Ateb i Mr.David Thomas', in *Baner ac Amserau Cymru* (14 Sept.1961).

'Intellectuals and Trade Unionists?', a letter to the editor of the *Western Mail* (19 Sept.1961).

'Historic Judgement: All Honour to Gwynfor S.Evans', in *Welsh Nation* (June 1962).

'Architect of the Party Retires', in *Welsh Nation* (June 1962).

'Swansea Swindled: New Industry Goes to England', in *Welsh Nation* (June 1962).

'The Battle of Montgomeryshire', in *Welsh Nation* (June 1962).

'Plaid Fights in Twelve Towns', in *Welsh Nation* (June 1962).

'Good Evening, Mr.Jones: a Totally Imaginary Conversation', in *Welsh Nation* (June 1962).

'Wales Loses a Loveable Patriot', in *Welsh Nation* (July 1962).

'The Shadow of the Dole', in *Welsh Nation* (July 1962).

'Cerydd o'r Beibl', in *Baner ac Amersau Cymru* (22 Nov.1962).

'Plaid Cymru to Fight in Swansea East', in *Welsh Nation* (Jan.1963).

Editorial about the need for commitment, in *Welsh Nation* (Jan.1963).

Editorial on the role of Plaid Cymru, in *Welsh Nation* (April 1963).

'Labour Leads Backwards: Wilson in Cardiff', in *Welsh Nation* (April 1963).

Editorial surveying the political scene, in *Welsh Nation* (June 1963).

Editorial about events in Maentwrog and Mountain Ash, in *Welsh Nation* (Oct.1963).

'Maentwrog Stays Welsh', in *Welsh Nation* (Oct.1963).

'In the Thick of the Fight and Enjoying Every Minute', in *Welsh Nation* (Dec.1963).

Editorial looking back on 1963, in *Welsh Nation* (Jan.1964).

Column by 'Robin Clidro', in *Welsh Nation* (July 1964); this feature was continued in Sept. and Nov.1964.

'Calling the Tune', in *Welsh Nation* (Feb.-March 1965).

Editorial: 'The Faces of Wales', in *Welsh Nation* (April 1965).

'Two Cheers for Tudor', in *The London Welshman* (Sept.1966).

'Landslide Conference', in *Welsh Nation* (Sept.1967).

'Brittany on the Boil', in *Welsh Nation* (June 1968).

'One Man's Wales', in *Welsh Nation* (August 1968); this column was continued in March, April and August 1968; April 1969; Sept.1969 and June 1970.

'Lack of Organization Resulted in Celtic Subjugation', in *Welsh Nation* (Sept.1968).

'Internal Debates in Next Decade', in *Welsh Nation* (Dec.1968).

'Happy New Year to Carlo, Caio, Wales', in *Welsh Nation* (Jan.1970).

'Something has gone right somewhere,' in *Welsh Nation* (April 1970).

General Election address (Pontypool, 18 June 1970).

'Struldbugs must go! – and soon', in *Welsh Nation* (May 1970).

'Why Did Hooson Lurch to the Right?', in *Welsh Nation* (Nov.1970).

'Gas Sahibs for the Colony', in *Welsh Nation* (Dec.1970).

'The Burgos Trials', a translation of an article by Jean-Paul Sartre, in *Planet* (9, 1971).

'Heil Stan!', *Welsh Nation* (June 1972).

'It's Time for us to Learn the Basics', in *Welsh Nation* (22 Dec.1972-4 Jan.1973).

'Le Pays de Galles', in *L'Europe en Formation* (April 1973).

'Land of Pong', by 'John Spang', an occasional column about Cwmgrafft, first published in *Welsh Nation* in 1972 and intermittently thereafter until the end of 1974; a late example appeared in Feb.1977.

'Why Plaid Must Let Gwynfor Go', in *Welsh Nation* (31 Jan.1974).

'Welsh Channel', in *Welsh Nation* (1 Feb.1974).

A translation of the manifesto of *Cymdeithas yr Iaith Gymraeg,* in *Planet* (26-27, 1974).

'Some Thoughts on Mr.Hearne', in *Welsh Nation* (9-15 May 1975).

'The Jews of the Diaspora, or the vocation of a minority', a translation of an essay by Richard Marienstras, in *European Judaism* (Summer 1975).

'The Political Drought', in *Welsh Nation* (Oct.1976).

'Thoughts of an Anniversary', in *Welsh Nation* (Nov.1976).

'Andy, the Swansea Jack-in-the-box', in *Welsh Nation* (Feb.1977).

'As Wales Waits', in *Welsh Nation* (March 1977).

'Bwrw Amheuon Annheilwng', letter about the Welsh language to the editor of *Y Faner* (13 Feb.1981).

'*Faux Bonhomie* y gau-Sosialwyr', letter about 'pseudo-Socialists like Neil Kinnock' to the editor of *Y Faner* (28 Oct.1983).

A bibliography of H.W.'s literary journalism will be found in *A Militant Muse* (1997).